Kai Essig

Vision-Based Image Retrieval (VBIR)

Kai Essig

Vision-Based Image Retrieval (VBIR)

A New Eye-Tracking Based Approach to Efficient
and Intuitive Image Retrieval

VDM Verlag Dr. Müller

Imprint

Bibliographic information by the German National Library: The German National Library lists this publication at the German National Bibliography; detailed bibliographic information is available on the Internet at http://dnb.d-nb.de.

Any brand names and product names mentioned in this book are subject to trademark, brand or patent protection and are trademarks or registered trademarks of their respective holders. The use of brand names, product names, common names, trade names, product descriptions etc. even without a particular marking in this works is in no way to be construed to mean that such names may be regarded as unrestricted in respect of trademark and brand protection legislation and could thus be used by anyone.

Cover image: www.purestockx.com

Publisher:
VDM Verlag Dr. Müller Aktiengesellschaft & Co. KG, Dudweiler Landstr. 125 a, 66123 Saarbrücken, Germany,
Phone +49 681 9100-698, Fax +49 681 9100-988,
Email: info@vdm-verlag.de

Produced in USA and UK by:
Lightning Source Inc., La Vergne, Tennessee, USA
Lightning Source UK Ltd., Milton Keynes, UK
BookSurge LLC, 5341 Dorchester Road, Suite 16, North Charleston, SC 29418, USA

ISBN: 978-3-8364-9241-6

This research was conducted within the Neuroinformatics Group and the Collaborative Research Center 360 "Situated Artificial Communicators" (SFB 360, Unit B4) at Bielefeld University. I wish to acknowledge an immeasurable debt of gratitude to a few individuals who supported and encouraged me during the writing of this book:

First, I want to thank Helge Ritter for supervision and support of my work. His ideas and enthusiasm were a valuable source of inspiration for this book. Furthermore, his optimism has always been a powerful motivating force throughout my work.

Second, I am grateful to Marc Pomplun from the University of Massachusetts at Boston for his valuable feedback and for his willingness to participate in the PhD committee. He was the one, who introduced me to the fascinating research field of eye tracking.

Furthermore, I wish to express my thanks to the "Trekkies": Elena Carbone, Sonja Folker and Lorenz "Max" Sichelschmidt. You all gave me helpful comments, suggestions and advice over the last years. It is a great pleasure for me to work together with you in this interdisciplinary team. Prof. Arbee L.-P. Chen (National Hsing Hua University in HsinChu, Taiwan) and Prof. Chiou-Shann Fuh (National Taiwan University in Taipei, Taiwan) introduced me to the field of Content-Based Image Retrieval and provided me with a rich and pleasant research environment during my stay in Taiwan.

Sven Pohl's permanent willingness to help and his continuous improvement of the VDesigner were a great help in the realisation of a complex image retrieval experiment embedded in an eye-tracking environment. But more of this, Sven became a very good friend of mine during the years we worked together in the eye-tracking group. Andreas Hüwel had a hand in the SOM visualisations of the high dimensional feature vectors. Gunther Heidemann, Tim Nattkemper, Jörg Ontrop and Thies Pfeiffer gave me valuable feedback. Tanja Kämpfe, Dirk Selle, Frank Schütte and Jörg Walter supported me by proofreading this book, making it readable as well as understandable. I am also much obliged to Petra Udelhoven for her assistance in handling the manifoldness of bureaucracy. Furthermore, I thank all participants for taking part in my experiments. Moreover, I would like to express my gratitude to the staff of the child care facilities "Kita EffHa" and "Bonhöffer Tageseinrichtung der Ev. Dietrich-Bonhöffer Kirchengemeinde" in Bielefeld.

Finally, I am grateful to Li-Ying for her longstanding support, patience and confidence over the last years and to my daughter Vivienne for enriching my life.

This research was funded by grants of the "Evangelisches Studienwerk e.V. Villigst" and the Graduate and Postdoctoral Programme "Strategies & Optimisation of Behaviour".

Bielefeld, 26th March 2008   Kai Essig

Abstract

The advances in digitalisation technology demand new techniques for the retrieval of relevant images from large image databases, resulting in the foundation of a new research area called *Content-Based Image Retrieval* (CBIR) in 1992. CBIR describes a set of techniques to retrieve fast and reliably relevant images from large image repositories on the basis of *automatically* derived image features. The research on CBIR focusses on the investigation of new image features and distance functions suitable for the retrieval task at hand, and on the optimal integration of the user into the retrieval process by providing intelligent input options (*user-relevance feedback*). Recent scientific findings came to the conclusion that a retrieval system, in order to be generally accepted by the user and to be applicable to various image domains, requires not only features and distance functions that are consistent with human perception of similarity, but also sophisticated and natural human-machine interfaces that optimally integrate the user into the retrieval process.

This book documents a new approach to image retrieval, called *Vision-Based Image Retrieval* (VBIR), by using an eye tracker as a natural and elegant method for user-relevance feedback. Eye tracking denotes the process of monitoring and recording participants' gaze positions during the observation of stimuli presented on a computer screen. When humans compare images, they focus on specific image regions and check for similarities and differences. Thus, semantically important image regions receive much attention, manifested by a higher number of fixations and increasing fixation durations. The central hypothesis is that the retrieval process should be improved substantially by increasing the weights for the features of semantically important image regions. This hypothesis was investigated by comparing the performances of the new eye-tracking based image-retrieval approach (VBIR) with a classic CBIR approach. The results revealed not only higher retrieval performances for the VBIR system, but also a higher correlation of the systems' retrieval results with human measures of similarity.

Before the experiment could be performed, not only suitable colour, shape and texture features had to be found, but also an optimal weighting scheme had to be determined. The suitability of the chosen image features for the retrieval experiments in this work were evaluated with the *self-organizing map* (SOM) and the *result viewer*. The outcome shows that images with similar feature vectors are clustered together, whereby the number of outliers for the shape and texture features were higher than for the colour feature. To determine the optimal weighting scheme for the single image features, the *Shannon entropy* was calculated from the feature distance histograms. The optimal feature weight combination resulted from the highest Shannon entropy value. It was found to be 41%, 33% and 26% for colour, shape and texture, respectively. These findings are in accordance with the overall impression that colour plays a dominant role for the discrimination of flower images.

In order to test the CBIR and VBIR approaches in the experiment on a representative set of queries, the maximum number of retrieval steps for each query image was limited.

A second experiment was designed for the evaluation of the retrieval results of both approaches, especially in cases where the corresponding query was not retrieved. In this experiment, participants ranked the similarity of the retrieval results for both approaches to the corresponding query images according to their overall subjective impression. The empirical findings show significantly higher similarity values for the retrieval results of the VBIR approach. Furthermore, participants' subjective similarity estimations correspond to objectively calculated feature distances, i.e., high similarity values correlate with small feature distances.

The empirical findings then led to the development of computational models for image retrieval. Altogether five models were implemented in this book: Two of these models, CBIR and CBIR_MLP, apply the pre-calculated global image features. The main purpose behind the CBIR models is to simulate closely the human selection process of choosing the most similar image from a set of six retrieved database images. In case of CBIR, the selection of the most similar image to the query is based on the corresponding feature distances, whereas in the CBIR_MLP approach, this selection is modelled by a *multi-layer perceptron* (MLP), trained on participants' similarity estimations from the second experiment. The three VBIR models are based on pre-calculated tile-based image features. The models differ in regard to the weighting schemes for the single image tiles. The main purpose behind the VBIR models is to simulate closely the retrieval of similar images from the database. The results revealed the best overall performances for the VBIR models to find the queries of all start configurations, which are in accordance to the results of the empirical experiments. The CBIR and CBIR_MLP models on the other hand provided results which are not conform to the outcome of the retrieval experiment: Both CBIR models do not adequately simulate humans' similarity decisions.

In another model, three (bottom-up) saliency maps (i.e., colour, intensity and orientation) were calculated from the flower images. The overall saliency map resulted as a weighted combination of the different conspicuity maps. The model computes the correlation between the overall saliency map and the human fixation map, calculated from participants' eye movements recorded in the retrieval experiment, for a set of different weight combinations. The results revealed that weight combinations in the ranges of 70%-100% for colour, 10%-30% for intensity and 0%-20% for orientation resembled most closely human attention distribution.

All in all, the results of the models yield further support for the suitability of an attention-based approach to image retrieval and the adequateness of an eye tracker as a natural source for human relevance-feedback.

8

Contents

Chapter 1

Introduction

1.1 The Need for New and Intuitive Image Retrieval Techniques

With the spreading of fast computers and high speed network connections, the digital acquisition of information has become more and more widespread in recent years. Supported by the progress in digitalisation, the steady growth of computer power, declining costs for storage capacities and easier access to the Internet, the amount of available images increases every day. Compared to analog formats, digitalised information can be conveniently saved on portable storage devices or on server databases, where it can be easily downloaded, shared and distributed. Whereas the indexing and retrieval of text documents has been a research area for a long time and many sophisticated solutions have already been proposed (Baeza-Yates & Ribeiro-Neto, 1999; Salton & McGill, 1988), the automatic retrieval of images according to image content is still a challenge. The complexity of image retrieval is based mainly on two reasons: I.) It is difficult to find features suitably describing *image content*, II.) the lack of techniques in Computer Vision to understand *image semantics*. The application of text retrieval techniques for image retrieval is cumbersome, because the *manual annotation* and *indexing* of images by humans is *subjective* and very *time consuming*. Additionally, techniques successfully applied to text documents are not suitable for image retrieval. Hence, automatic image retrieval requires the design of new and more sophisticated techniques that differ from those applied to text retrieval. As a consequence, so called *Content-Based Image Retrieval Systems* (CBIRS) were developed. In CBIRS, each image is represented as a vector in a high dimensional feature space. The user mostly provides a query image and the system automatically returns those images from the database that are most similar to the query image in the feature space. CBIR techniques are useful whenever information shall be automatically retrieved from large image repositories, like medical image databases, news archives of news agencies or broadcasting stations, or digital archives in museums or education.

Whereas CBIRS use low level features (like colour, shape and texture) for image retrieval, humans interpret image contents semantically (Rui, Huang, Mehrota & Ortega, 1999). Because image semantics cannot be suitably described by primitive image features, modern CBIRS generally integrate the user into the retrieval process to provide so called *user-relevance feedback* (e.g., by ranking the retrieved images) in order to improve the system's performance and to overcome the *semantic gap* and the *subjectivity of human perception*. The former term denotes the *gap between the object in the world and the information in a (computational) description derived from a recording of that scene*, whereas the latter is the *lack of coincidence between the information that one can extract from the visual data and the meaning that the same data have for a user in a given situation* (Smeulders et al., 2000). Through relevance feedback, the system tries to narrow the search space and to retrieve images that are semantically better correlated to the users' retrieval needs. Unfortunately, the automatic mapping of those semantic descriptions to low level features is very challenging, not to say impossible for complicated images. Furthermore, different persons (or the same person under different circumstances) may perceive the same visual content differently. And finally, providing relevance feedback is quite tedious for the user, since he/she has to rate all the result images for each retrieval step. Hence, after a while, user-relevance feedback is often only provided occasionally or even not at all.

The approach to automatic retrieval systems, based on primitive image features and user-relevance feedback through keyboard or mouse input, is not a promising approach to overcome the limitations of CBIRS described above. One reason is that there are no suitable techniques to automatically relate the users' similarity ratings to the semantic content of the image. Furthermore, the feedback through mouse or keyboard does not provide a natural and intuitively to use interface between the system and the user. Thus, users are more discouraged than delighted to utilise CBIR software for long retrieval sessions. In order to provide a convenient and easy to use interface for relevance feedback, this book presents an alternative approach to image retrieval, called *Vision-Based Image Retrieval* (VBIR). This approach uses an *eye tracker* as a novel and natural source for user-relevance feedback. An eye tracker measures and records eye movements of participants looking at images. By online analysis of eye movements during image retrieval, the retrieval system can be guided to focus on important image areas (i.e., regions with a high number of fixations) so that accuracy can be improved.

In order to provide a better understanding of the link between Content-Based Image Retrieval (CBIR) and eye tracking, the two research areas are first described in more detail in this work. We start by addressing Content-Based Image Retrieval in the next section.

1.2 Content-Based Image Retrieval (CBIR)

We all know the popular saying "A picture is worth a thousand words". But in practice, a picture is worth far less than a thousand words if it cannot be found. This is where *Content-Based Image Retrieval (CBIR)* comes into play.

1.2.1 Motivation

There is a huge demand for sophisticated CBIRS because more and more visual data are digitalised as a result of the progress in digitalisation techniques. For example, museum collections need reliable indexing and retrieval techniques, whereby the number of users getting online to use those resources is steadily increasing. Broadcasting stations receive a high number of new images every day. At the British Broadcasting Corporation, for example, 750,000 hours of news material still has to be archived. Thirty employees are needed to catalogue new material so that the archive can answer the 2,000 to 3,000 requests every week (Sietmann, 2003). The advantage of the digitalised form over the traditional one is that the data cannot only be stored locally but also be conveniently distributed (for example via the Internet or on CD or DVD).

CBIR was established as a research area in 1992 with the USNSF (*US National Science Foundation*) workshop in Redwood, California. The aim of the workshop was to identify "*major research areas that should be addressed by researchers for visual information management systems that would be useful in scientific, industrial, medical, environmental, educational, entertainment, and other applications*" (Smeulders et al., 2000, p. 1). Probably Kato, Kurita, Otsu and Hirata (1992) were the first ones to use the term Content-Based Image Retrieval in order to describe their experiments on automatic retrieval of images from a database by colour and shape. From then on, the term CBIR denotes the process of retrieving desired images from a large collection based on features (mostly colour, shape and texture) that can be automatically extracted from the images. These features can be primitive or semantic. *Primitive features* are *low level features* like object perimeter, colour histogram and so on. *Semantic features* on the other hand refer to semantically-meaningful information inside an image, for example to identify a person in an image. Whereas there are already many suitable low level features, the derivation of semantic meaning from an image is still a huge challenge for existing systems. Despite all the progress made, those systems mostly lack feature extraction and retrieval techniques that match human needs closely. Even though the first long term projects have been started to analyse user behaviour for image retrieval, we still do not know enough to develop sophisticated CBIR programs that are suited to human retrieval needs (Eakins & Graham, 1999). There is also a lack of adequate visual query formulation and refinement interfaces for CBIRS (Venters, Eakins & Hartley, 1997), a barrier for effective image retrieval.

A few commercial and some research prototype systems using different features and retrieval techniques are already available, showing quite impressive retrieval results for limited application areas (Veltkamp & Tanase, 2000). Poor results of the same systems in other domains may be caused by the fact that features can describe a particular object type quite well, but show weaknesses when applied to other object classes or the same objects photographed from a different perspective or under different illumination conditions. Hence, despite all the effort, there is no *general-purpose* CBIRS available to date.

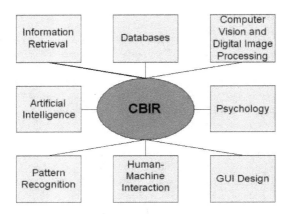

Figure 1.1: Important research fields contributing to Content-Based Image Retrieval.

Different research fields, which have evolved separately, provide valuable contributions to image retrieval. Information Retrieval, Visual Data Modelling and Representation, Image/Video Analysis and Processing, Pattern Recognition and Computer Vision, Multimedia Databases, Multidimensional Indexing, Psychological Modelling of user behaviour, Man-Machine Interaction and Data Visualisation are the most important research fields that contribute to visual information retrieval. The reason is that CBIR has to deal with a lot of challenges of various kinds, such as large image databases, semantic interpretation of image content, evaluation and presentation of retrieval results, including GUI (Graphical User Interface) Design (see Figure 1.1).

Even though there are many different CBIRS, they all show a common design and perform nearly the same basic steps to find images in large databases. In general, the user provides a query image and the system automatically retrieves those images from the image database, being most similar to the query image according to the extracted image features. This process is depicted in Figure 1.2.

The typical "components" (i.e., image database, image features, similarity measures and retrieval result presentation) and processing steps of a retrieval system will be briefly described in the following sections.

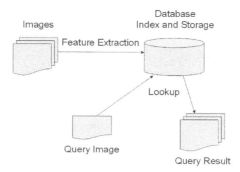

Figure 1.2: General structure of a CBIRS: The user provides a query image, the computer searches for similar images in the image repository and presents them to the user.

1.2.2   Image Database

The first step in designing a CBIRS is to build up a digital image database. The database mostly consists of different types of images (e.g., colour or greyscale), with unique or different size or resolution, selected from the same or different categories, recorded from the same or different perspectives. Examples could be landscape photos, animals, paintings or images showing parts of a scene in high resolution (for example medical images). Obviously, the image repository may be very heterogeneous. The more diverse the image database is, the more difficult it is to find features that suitably describe the content of the images. In general, CBIRS have to handle image databases usually consisting of 1,000 up to 100,000 or more images.

1.2.3   Image Features and Distance Functions

The selection of suitable features describing the image content reliably is the most important and crucial step in designing a CBIRS. The systems' retrieval performance depends on the features' robustness and their suitability to describe the content of the images from the database. During recent years many features have been suggested. A good overview can be found in Rui, Huang and Chang (1999) and Smeulders et al. (2000). Most CBIRS use a combination of different image features (mostly colour, shape and texture), because each type of feature only describes a certain aspect of the image. For example, the colour feature is crucial if the user looks for images with a red blossom, but the texture feature is more relevant if he/she is searching for leaves with a particular structure. Usually, each feature has an associated relevance weight describing its importance for the retrieval process. The selected features must be calculated for each single image of the database and additionally for the query image.

In general, features used for image retrieval are high dimensional. Hence, after feature

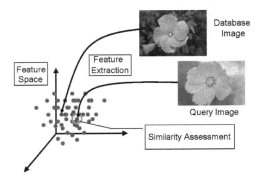

Figure 1.3: Feature space and similarity assessment.

calculation, each image is represented as a point in a high dimensional feature space, where images being located close together are assumed to be similar (see Figure 1.3). The image features are usually calculated off-line, because this process requires a lot of computational power. The resulting high dimensional feature vectors are generally stored in a database. If the user selects or provides a query image, the same feature calculation procedures are applied, so that the query image is also represented as a point in the high dimensional feature space (in the centre of the red circle in Figure 1.3). Then, a distance function is applied to find the images most similar to the query image in the feature space. The images with the shortest distances to the query image are retrieved and presented to the user in ascending order of distance values (see Figure 1.4).

Figure 1.4: Representation of the retrieval results in the SIMPLIcity system (from Wang, 2001).

Colour Features

Colour is a visual feature that is widely used in image retrieval, because it is immediately perceived when looking at images. It is relatively robust to background noise, image size and orientation but can be altered by surface texture, lighting, shading effects and viewing conditions. These colour distortions are extremely difficult to handle for computers, because they extract the colour information from an image without context information. Additionally, in different contexts, people use various levels of colour specificity. For example, an apple is generally described as being red (probably implying some type of reddish hue), whereas for a car the specific colour shade may be an important description (Smith & Chang, 1996). Colours are usually represented as points in 3D spaces. There are different colour models which can be classified as:

- Colourimetric models (like CIE) resulting from the physical measurement of spectral reflectance using calorimeters.

- Physiologically inspired models from neurophysiology (for example XYZ).

- Psychological models (describing colours on how they appear to a human observer). An example for a psychological model is HSB.

Another classification of colour models distinguish between:

- Hardware-oriented models: Define colours according to the properties of the optical devices used to reproduce the colours, e.g., TV monitor, screen, or printer. Examples for hardware-oriented models are: RGB, CMY and YIQ.

- User-oriented models: In contrast to hardware-oriented models, these models are based on human perception of colours, i.e., hue, saturation and brightness percepts. Examples for user-oriented models are: HLS, HSV, L*u*v* and L*a*b*.

Colour systems differ in their properties, such as perceptual uniformity, and their invariance to changes in viewing direction, object geometry and intensity of illumination. These differences make particular colour systems suitable for specific applications. For image retrieval it is important that the distances between two colours in the chosen colour model corresponds to human visual perception. A comprehensive discussion of various colour models and their properties can be found in Gevers (2001).

Colour Histograms

Colour histograms are commonly used to describe low-level colour properties of images. They are translation and rotation invariant and easy to calculate (Swain & Ballard, 1991). Colour histograms are mostly represented as one distribution over three primaries, obtained by discretised image colours and counting the pixels belonging to each colour. Problems that come with this description are the high dimensionality and the sensitivity to lighting changes and changes in large viewing angles. The *cumulative histogram* (Stricker & Orengo, 1995) is preferred for high dimensional and sparsely populated colour distributions. A more compact representation are the *colour moments*, proposed by Stricker and Orengo (1995). The colour distribution of an image can be interpreted as a probability distribution and can therefore be characterised by moments. Because most of the colour information is concentrated on the low-order moments, the calculation of the first three moments (mean, variance and skewness) are sufficient to describe the colour distribution.

Colour Coherence Vectors

The disadvantage of the colour features introduced above is that they do not contain spatial information, so that images with different layout can have similar histogram representations. *Colour coherence vectors* (Pass, Zabih & Miller, 1996) are used to improve histogram matching and to include spatial information. Colour coherence means that neighbouring pixels belong to a large region of similar colour. The image is discretised and for each colour the total number of coherent and incoherent pixels are calculated. The distance between two images results from the total of the differences between the number of coherent and incoherent pixels for each colour.

Colour Sets

Smith and Chang (1996) proposed *colour sets*, a compact alternative to colour histograms by binary vectors, ignoring those colours whose values in the corresponding colour histogram are below a pre-specified threshold. The basic assumption of this approach is that salient regions can be represented by a small set of colours. Images are transformed into a quantised HSV space with 166 colour bins and subsampled to approximately 196×196 pixels. Then a 5×5 median filter is applied to each HSV channel to blur the image in order to reduce noise and small details. Finally, the colour image is converted back to an indexed RGB image. Then, colour regions are extracted by systematically generating a bi-level image for each colour present in the indexed RGB image at a time, and in multiples (see Figure 1.5). Only regions with a size above 64 pixels are considered to be significant. For each significant region a colour set is calculated. Each colour of the colour set must contribute at least 20% of the region size, resulting in a maximum of five colours per region. If a region does not pass the thresholds, it will not be indexed by that colour set. If one of the colours of the colour set is not sufficiently represented, the region can still be represented by a reduced colour set. Besides colour sets, region area and location information are stored as region features. The overall distance between two images is computed as the weighted sum of distances between colour sets, spatial location, areas and spatial extent of the image regions. Further colour features used for image retrieval can be found in Del Bimbo (1999).

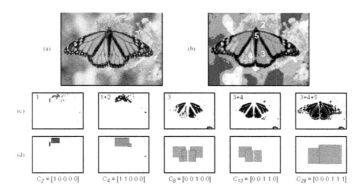

Figure 1.5: (a) Colour image of a butterfly, (b) processed colour image with 30 colours, (c) pixels from image belonging to colour set C_i, (d) minimum bounding rectangles (MBRs) for extracted regions used to index the image collection (taken from Smith & Chang, 1996).

Shape Features

Recent studies about cognition aspects of image retrieval have shown that users in most cases are more interested in retrieval by shape than by colour or texture (Schomaker, de Leau & Vuurpijl, 1999). For humans even partly occluded shapes are sufficient for identification and for the impression of a complete and real representation of the object. However, computerised retrieval by shape is still considered as one of the most difficult aspects of content-based search (Lew, 2001). Generally, shape representations can be classified into three categories: The *shape through transformation approach*, the *relational approach* and the *feature vector approach*. The choice for a particular category depends on application needs, like characteristics of objects in the utilised image domain, tolerance to occlusions and deformations, robustness against noise and so on. In the following the three categories are described in more detail and examples are given.

Shape through Transformation Approach
In the shape through transformation approach, the shape is regarded as a template, like a *snake* or a *sketch*. Active contours (or snakes) are computer-generated curves that move within images to find object boundaries. They are called snakes, because the deformable contours resemble snakes as they move. Active contours are often used in Computer Vision and Image Analysis to detect and locate objects, and to describe their shape.

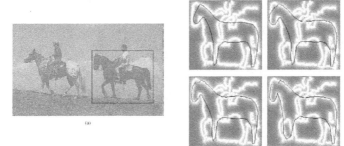

Figure 1.6: Elastic deformation of a horse-like template over an edge-image (from Del Bimbo & Pala, 1997). (a) Original image, (b) different steps of the deformation process.

Del Bimbo and Pala (1997), for example, present a technique based on elastic matching of sketched templates over the shapes in the images to evaluate similarity. The similarity between the sketch and the images in the database is evaluated according to the elastic deformation energy needed to deform the original sketch to find a reasonable fitting with the target image (see Figure 1.6). The similarity is computed through a back-propagation neural network with the following five input parameters:

(1) The degree of matching between deformed sketch and the shape in the database image (M), where 1 means that the sketch lies entirely on image areas.

(2) The quantity S, as a rough measure of how the sketch has been *stretched* by the deformation.

(3) The quantity B, as a approximate measure of the energy spent to bend the template.

(4) A qualitative measure of template deformation, measured as the correlation between the curvature of the original template and that of the deformed one.

(5) A qualitative measure of the complexity of the template, measured through the number of zeros of the shape curvature function.

Since elastic matching is computationally expensive, it can only be applied to small databases or as a refinement tool. However, the similarity ranking provided by this technique reflects very closely human perception of shape similarity.

Relational Approach

In the relational approach, mostly complex shapes are broken down into sets of salient components. The shape representation consists of the shape features for each component and the relations between them.

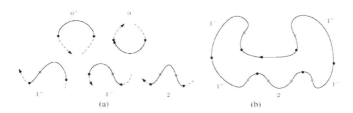

Figure 1.7: (a) Hoffmann and Richards' contour codons (a black box marks a curvature minimum, and a grey disk marks a zero curvature point). (b) Representation of a curve as a string of codons (taken from Tanase, 2005, p. 29).

An example for describing the shape of an object, using the relational approach, are the *boundary tokens*. In this approach, the boundary is divided into a set of boundary segments, called tokens. The decomposition simplifies the description process by reducing the boundary's complexity. The boundary tokens can be approximated by simpler shapes, such as polygons with vertexes at the shape's salient points (Davis, 1979). A more sophisticated representation for tokens is the *codon-based representation* (Richards & Hoffman, 1985). Codons are sets of primitive tokens, which are used as basic descriptors of a generic curve. They are parts of a curve, located between two consecutive minima of the curvature function. There are six different types of codons, differing in the location of the maximum and the number of zeros of the curvature (see Figure 1.7). The overall shape can then be described by a succession of codons.

Feature Vector Approach

Because the shape features used in the new eye-tracking based approach to image retrieval (see Section 4.5.3) are represented as numerical vectors, the feature vector approach is described more deeply in the following. This category subsumes all approaches that determine a feature vector for a given shape. It requires a mapping of the shape in the feature space and the evaluation of the difference between feature vectors using a suitable distance function, mainly the Euclidean distance.

Before shape features can be calculated, the objects in the image have to be extracted. This is mostly done by *segmentation* or *edge detection*. After region extraction, either the external boundary (*parametric external method*) or a description of the region enclosed by the boundary line (*parametric internal method*) can be used as a shape feature. Examples for the later are simple geometric attributes like region area, minimum or maximum rectangle, compactness or elongatedness (Del Bimbo, 1999). Furthermore, regions can be described by a set of seven normalised *moments*, where six of them are rotation invariant and one is skew and rotation invariant (Hu, 1962).

Prominent features to describe the external boundary of an object are the *Fourier descriptors* (Peerson & Fu, 1977). In this approach, the boundary of an object is represented

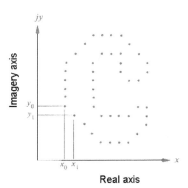

Real axis

Figure 1.8: Representation of a digital boundary as a complex sequence. The first two points of the sequence $((x_0, y_0)$ and $(x_1, y_1))$ are chosen arbitrarily (from Gonzalez & Woods, 2002, p. 499).

as a sequence of coordinates:

$$s(k) = [x(k), y(k)] \quad , k = 0, 1, 2, ..., N-1, \tag{1.1}$$

i.e., starting with the point (x_0, y_0) and traversing the boundary counterclockwise (see Figure 1.8). Moreover, the x- and y-axis can be treated as real and imaginary axes, so that the sequence of boundary pixels can be expressed as:

$$s(k) = x(k) + jy(k) \quad , k = 0, 1, 2, ..., N-1 \tag{1.2}$$

and therefore reducing the representation from 2D to 1D without changing the boundary itself. The Fourier transform of $s(k)$ is:

$$a(u) = \frac{1}{N} \sum_{k=0}^{N-1} s(k) exp\left[-\frac{j2\Pi uk}{N} \right], \tag{1.3}$$

where $a(u)$ are the *Fourier descriptors* of the boundary. The original values $s(k)$ can be restored by applying the inverse Fourier transform on the $a(u)$'s :

$$s(k) = \sum_{u=0}^{N-1} a(u) exp\left[\frac{j2\Pi uk}{N} \right] \tag{1.4}$$

for $k = 0, 1, ..., N-1$. Now the gross essence of the object boundary can be sufficiently described by using only $P << N$ Fourier coefficients, i.e., $a(u) = 0$ for $u > P-1$, resulting in the following approximation to $s(k)$:

$$\acute{s}(k) = \frac{1}{P} \sum_{u=0}^{P-1} a(u) exp\left[\frac{j2\Pi uk}{N} \right] \tag{1.5}$$

By simple transformations, Fourier descriptors can be made rotation, scale and translation invariant (Gonzalez & Woods, 2002).

There exist many more approaches in Computer Vision for shape feature calculation, such as tree pruning, generalised Hough transform or pose clustering, geometric hashing and wavelet transform. A description of important shape features used for image retrieval can be found in Mehtre, Kankanhalli and Lee (1997), Rui, Huang and Chang (1999) and Veltkamp and Hagedoorn (2001).

Texture Features

Texture is an intuitive concept which allows us to distinguish regions of the same colour. Together with colour, texture is a powerful discriminating feature, present nearly everywhere in nature. Textures can be described according to their spatial frequency or perceptual properties (e.g., periodicity, coarseness, preferred direction, or degree of complexity). In particular, textures emphasise orientation and spatial depth between overlapping objects. In contrast to colour, textures describe repeating visual patterns in homogeneous regions, i.e., texture is a region instead of a pixel property. Within a texture, there is significant variation in intensity levels between nearby pixels. A scene can contain different textures at varying scales. From a large scale, the dominant pattern in a floral cloth is the flower against the background, whereas from a finer scale it may be the weave of the cloth. In psychological experiments it was shown that different texture types can be discriminated pre-attentively, allowing texture discrimination without focussing attention (Julesz, 1981). Further research has revealed that local properties are involved in the perception of texture differences. These basic elements in early (pre-attentive) visual perception are called "textons" (Julesz, 1981). Pre-attentive texture discrimination results from a difference in texton type or some other first-order statistics of textons (e.g., density or standard deviation). Later psychophysical research did not confirm the role of textons as a plausible textural discriminating factor. Beck, Sutter and Ivry (1987) argued that the texture discrimination is primarily a function of spatial frequency analysis and not the result of a higher level symbolic grouping process. Campbell and Robson (1968) assumed that the visual system decomposes the image into filtered images of various frequencies and orientations. The application of multi-channel filtering approaches to texture analysis was motivated by the studies of De Valois, Albrecht and Thorell (1982): They found the selective response of simple cells in the visual cortex of monkeys to various frequencies and orientations.

The vague definition of the term texture leads to a variety of approaches for texture representation. Textures can be described by *statistical, structural, stochastic* and *spectral* approaches. Statistical approaches use a set of features to characterise textured images, such as contrast, correlation and entropy. Structural techniques deal with the 2D arrangement of image primitives or subpatterns, such as regular spaced parallel lines, circles, hexagons or dot patterns. Stochastic approaches model textures by stochastic processes governed by some parameters which can serve as features for texture classification and segmentation problems. Spectral techniques are based on the analysis of power spectral density functions in the frequency domain. They are used primarily to detect global periodicity in an image by identifying high-energy, narrow peaks in the spectrum. Extensive descriptions of statistical and structural approaches can be found in Levine (1985) and Haralick (1979), stochastic approaches are described in Haindl (1991), whereas spectral techniques are depicted in Lew (2001). A collection of representative texture images can be found in the classic Brodatz album (Brodatz, 1966).

Statistical Approaches

Prominent statistical approaches are the *grey level co-occurrence matrix (GLCM)* (Haralick, Shanmugam & Dinstein, 1973) and *Tamura's texture features* (Tamura, Mori & Yamawaki, 1978). They are both described in detail in Section 4.5.4. Examples for structural models, where features are extracted from non-contiguous blobs can be found in Voorhees and Poggio (1988) and in Chen, Nixon and Thomas (1995). In Voorhees and Poggio (1988) the texture is characterised by the contrast, orientation, width, length, area and area density of blobs within the texture, which correspond to dark patches in the original image. Chen, Nixon and Thomas (1995) use different intensity thresholds resulting into several binary images. Contiguous pixels in these images above or below the intensity level form bright or dark blobs, respectively. Based on the blob's average area and irregularity, calculated for each intensity threshold, granularity and elongation of the texture can be measured.

Stochastic Models

An example for stochastic models are the *gauss-markov random field* (GMRF) methods (Manjunath, Simchony & Chellappa, 1990), which model the intensity of a pixel as a stochastic function of its neighbouring pixels' intensity. The pixels' intensity in the GMRF method is modelled by using a Gaussian probability density function. The mean of the Gaussian distribution is a linear function of the neighbouring pixels' intensity, whereas its linear coefficients and variance are estimated by using a least square method.

Spectral Technics

Two popular approaches for spectral techniques are the Gabor filter and the wavelet filter banks.

Gabor Filter

Gabor filters have received considerable attention, because they have been found to be a good model for the 2D receptive fields of simple cells in the visual cortex (Jones 1985). They are widely used in Image Processing, Computer Vision, Neuroscience and Psychophysics. Gabor filters achieve optimal joint resolution in the 2D spatial- and 2D frequency-domain. Each representation alone does not provide the information needed for the rapid discrimination of differently textured regions. Image representation by impulses or pixel values does not show periodicities in the distribution of image luminance in space, whereas the analysis by global Fourier techniques alone does not reveal local distributions or combinations of image luminance. Therefore, they are inappropriate for the analysis of local features or textons (Turner, 1986). Consequently, an optimal solution is to analyse the images simultaneously in both spatial and spectral domains. Gabor filters achieve the theoretical lower limit of joint uncertainty in time and frequency and thus are well suited for texture segregation problems (Gabor, 1946):

$$g(t) = e^{-\dfrac{(t - t_0)^2}{\alpha^2}} + i\omega t \qquad (1.6)$$

Equation 1.6 describes the modulation product of a complex exponential wave with frequency ω and a Gaussian envelope of duration α occurring at time t_0.

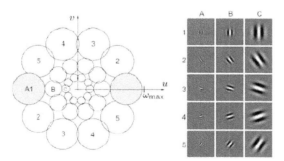

Figure 1.9: Set of Gabor functions: On the left side the daisy-like pattern of the frequency domain is seen. The corresponding receptive field of the circles in the spatial domain are depicted on the right (from Ontrup & Ritter, 1998, p. 17).

Daugman extended Gabor's work to two dimensional filters (Daugman, 1980). He showed that an extension of the joint optimisation criterion to two dimensions was satisfied by a family of functions, which can be realised as spatial filters consisting of sinusoidal plane waves within two dimensional elliptical Gaussian envelopes. The corresponding Fourier transform contains elliptical Gaussians displaced from the origin in the direction of orientation with major and minor axes inversely proportional to those of the spatial Gaussian envelopes (see Figure 1.9). This reflects the "uncertainty relation" and shows that information content in spatial- and frequency-domain are inversely related: Designing a filter for higher resolution in the spatial-domain (by decreasing the size of the Gaussian envelope along both spatial dimensions) leads to an increase of the effective area in the frequency domain, thereby decreasing its spatial frequency and orientation selectivity. A 2D Gabor function $g(x, y)$ and its Fourier transform $G(u, v)$ can be written as:

$$g(x,y) = e^{-\left(\frac{(x-x_0)^2}{\sigma_x^2} + \frac{(y-y_0)^2}{\sigma_y^2}\right)} e^{-2\pi i \omega (x - x_0)} \tag{1.7}$$

$$G(u,v) = e^{-\left(\frac{(u-\omega)^2}{\sigma_u^2} + \frac{v^2}{\sigma_v^2}\right)} e^{-2\pi i (x_0(u-\omega) + y_0 v)} \tag{1.8}$$

where (x_0, y_0) is the centre of the receptive field in the spatial domain, σ_x and σ_y are the widths of the Gaussian envelope along the x and y axes, respectively, ω is the frequency of a complex wave along the x-axis, and $\sigma_u = \frac{1}{2\pi\sigma_x}$, $\sigma_v = \frac{1}{2\pi\sigma_y}$.

Filter with a low bandwidth in the frequency space allow a fine discrimination between different textures. For the exact recognition of texture borders on the other hand, filters with a low bandwidth in the spatial domain are suitable. Mostly 2D Gabor filters are arranged in a daisy-like pattern in the frequency domain (see Figure 1.10). The ellipses indicate the half-peak contours of the Gabor filters in the frequency domain. As can be seen, there are six orientations at four different scales. The advantage of this construction scheme is that almost the whole frequency space is covered, whereas the individual filters have as little overlap as possible. Note that the filters detect orientations which are orthogonal to them.

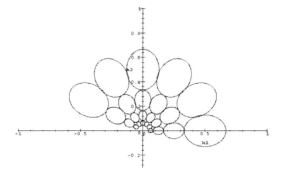

Figure 1.10: Gabor filter arrangement in a daisy like pattern (taken from Manjunath & Ma, 1996)

Two images are considered similar if they share the same distribution of filter bank results. Simple but efficient measures are the mean μ_{mn} and standard deviation σ_{mn} in each filter bank channel, resulting in a feature vector $f = [\mu_{00} \ \sigma_{00} \ \mu_{01} \ \sigma_{01} \ ... \ \mu_{53} \ \sigma_{53}]^T$ for six scales and four orientations. The distance between two images i and j, represented by the texture features f^i and f^j is defined by:

$$D_{ij}^{tex} = \sum_m \sum_n \left| \frac{\mu_{mn}^{(i)} - \mu_{mn}^{(j)}}{\sigma(\mu_{mn})} \right| + \left| \frac{\sigma_{mn}^{(i)} - \sigma_{mn}^{(j)}}{\sigma(\sigma_{mn})} \right| \qquad (1.9)$$

where $\sigma(\mu_{mn})$ and $\sigma(\sigma_{mn})$ denote the standard deviations of the respective features over the entire database, used to normalise the individual feature components. This measure has outperformed several other parametric models for measuring texture similarity (Manjunath & Ma, 1996).

Wavelet Filter Banks
Another alternative of frequency-based models for textures are the *wavelet filter banks*. The wavelet transform decomposes an image successively into scale and detail information (see Figure 1.11). As can be seen from Figure 1.11, the wavelet transformation involves filtering and subsampling. Kundu and Chen (1992) used orthogonal analysis filters of a two-band *quadrature mirror filter* (QMF) to decompose data into low-pass and high-pass frequency bands. Recursive application of the filter to the lower frequency bands produces wavelet decomposition as illustrated in Figure 1.11. Similar to the Gabor filter, the feature vectors are constructed from the mean and the variance of the energy distribution of the transform coefficients for each subband at each decomposition level.

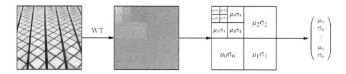

Figure 1.11: QMF-wavelet based features for texture classification (taken from Lew, 2001, p. 71). WT is the abbreviation for wavelet transform.

Gabor filter and wavelet transformations analyse textures at different scale levels. This multi-scale analysis has advantages, because the scale information of the textures in the images are not known in advance (Käster, 2005).

MPEG-7

MPEG-7 is a forthcoming description standard for multimedia information and will therefore be important for future Content-Based Image Retrieval systems. MPEG-7 is a multimedia content description standard developed by the *Moving Pictures Expert Group*. It was released in 2002. MPEG-7 was developed, because the effective identification and managing of the sheer volume of multimedia data is becoming more and more difficult with regard to storage, management and retrieval. It uses metadata, stored in a XML description scheme, for describing media contents. Neither automatic nor semi-automatic feature extraction algorithms are inside the scope of the standard. MPEG-7 just provides the format which can be used by external programs to store the extracted features. No specifications of the search engines, filter agents, or any other program that can make use of the description are within the scope of MPEG-7; competition will produce the best results. The main elements of the MPEG-7 standard are:

- *Descriptors (D)*: Standardised labels or terms for multimedia features. These descriptions are based on catalogue (e.g., creator, title), semantic (e.g., information about objects or events) or structural features (e.g., colour, texture, form, movements or noises).

- *Description Schemes (DS)*: Specify the structure and semantics of the relationships between their components that may be both Descriptors and Description Schemes.

- *Description Definition Language (DDL)*: Defines the syntax of Descriptors and Description Schemes. DDL uses the XML scheme language as the basis of its syntax. Because the XML schema language has not been designed specifically for audio-visual content description, there are certain MPEG-7 extensions which have been added.

- *System tools*: To support the binary coded representation of the DDL specifications for efficient storage and transmission (both for textual and binary formats), synchronisation of descriptions with content, and so on.

MPEG-7 is particularly useful for visual information retrieval, because Descriptors and Description Schemes are associated with the content of multimedia material, which allows fast and efficient searching. MPEG-7 allows different granularities in the descriptions for different levels of abstractions. For visual material, the lowest level is a description of features like colour, shape, texture, movements and position, whereas the highest level covers semantic information. In between, several intermediate levels of extraction may exist. Descriptions vary according to the types of data and the context of application. For retrieval, the search engine matches the query data with the MPEG-7 description. MPEG-7 addresses on- or off-line or streamed (e.g., broadcast, push models on the Internet) applications and operates in both real-time and non real-time environments. A real-time environment in this context means that the description is generated while the content is being captured. More information can be found on the MPEG home page ([2]).

1.2.4   Similarity Measures

As already mentioned above, the retrieval of images from a database requires the specification of a query, mostly by providing an example image being quite similar to the image the user is looking for. The classical approach is to extract features from the images in the database and to summarise them in a multidimensional feature vector, i.e., each database image is represented by a point in a multidimensional space. Now the query image is processed in the same way as the images in the database, resulting in a feature vector of identical dimensionality which is also projected onto the index space. To find the N most similar images from the database, the global similarities between the features of the query and each database image are calculated and those images with the highest similarity are retrieved. By providing relevance feedback, the contribution of each individual feature to the calculation of the global similarity can be optimised. The whole process is summarised in Figure 1.12.

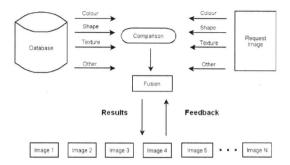

Figure 1.12: Similarity computation between the query image and the images in the database (adapted from Lew, 2001, p. 123).

Given the features and their representation associated with each image, a distance (d) is necessary to compare the features of the query image with those of each database image. The more similar the features of two images, the smaller should be their distance. A distance which satisfies the following three properties, is called a *metric* :

(1) Self-similarity: $d(I, I) = d(J, J)$

(2) Minimality: $d(I, J) \geq d(I, I)$

(3) Triangle inequality: $d(I, K) + d(K, J) \geq d(I, J)$

where I, J and K are images. Besides the features, the chosen metric is the most important component of a Content-Based Image Retrieval system. In contrast to the mathematically precisely defined metric distance measures used by the system, the similarity estimation of humans depends heavily on the individual user and the users' *point-of-view* (Tversky, 1977). Similarity experiments show that some metric properties are not conform with human perception of dissimilarity. In Figure (1.13) for example, the distance between the left and the middle and the middle and the right figure are small. On the other hand, the distance, as humans perceive it, between the left and right figure is high. In this example, the triangle inequality does not hold. Thus, instead of the three metric properties, Tversky and Gati (1982) proposed other properties, like *dominance, consistency* and *transitivity*, which are more conform to human similarity perception. Tversky (1977) also developed the *feature contrast model*, the most famous non-metric model, where the image is represented as a set of binary features.

As illustrated above, a variety of similarity theories exist that differ regarding the properties of d and the number and nature of the accepted or rejected distance axioms (Santini & Jain, 1999). In the following, different approaches for d are described. Further similarity measures can be found in Santini and Jain (1999), Rubner and Tomasi (2001) and Lew (2001).

Figure 1.13: The triangular inequality does not hold under partial matching (adapted from Lew, 2001, p. 124).

Most similarity measures in image retrieval are applied to histograms calculated for the query and database image. Two kinds of distances exist to calculate the similarity of histograms: *Bin-to-bin* and *cross-bin* similarity measures. The former can be calculated quite fast, but has the disadvantage that it only compares bins with the same index, and thus it is not illumination invariant. Furthermore, bin-to-bin similarity measures are sensitive to bin size, i.e., a coarse binning may result in insufficient discriminative power, whereas in fine binning, similar features may be placed in different bins and might not be matched. Cross-bin histogram dissimilarity measures overcome these limitations. This, on the other hand, makes them computationally more expensive. The two similarity measures are illustrated in Figure 1.14.

Bin-to-bin Dissimilarity Measures

Popular bin-to-bin dissimilarity measures used in image retrieval are the *Minkowski distance, histogram intersection, Kullback-Leibler divergence* and *Jeffrey divergence* (from information theory) and χ^2 (from statistics).

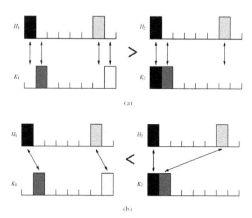

Figure 1.14: Illustrative example, where a bin-to-bin similarity measure (here classical Minkowski Distance (L_1)) is not conform with perceptual dissimilarity. (a) Assuming that histograms have unit mass, then $d_{L_1}(H_1, K_1) = 2$ and $d_{L_1}(H_2, K_2) = 1$. (b) In contrast to the classical Minkowski form distances, perceptual distances integrating cross-bin information consider the similarity of the different grey values, leading to $d_{perc}(H_1, K_1) < d_{perc}(H_2, K_2)$ (taken from Rubner & Tomasi, 2001, p. 7).

I.) Minkowski Distance

A general distance function is the *Minkowski distance*, defined as:

$$d_M(H_Q, H_D) = \left[\sum_i |H_Q(i) - H_D(i)|^p \right]^{1/p}$$ (1.10)

where H_Q and H_D are histograms of the query and database image, respectively, and i is the bin index. The L_1-distance with $p = 1$ is called *Manhattan* (or *city-block*) distance. The commonly used L_2-distance, also referred to as *Euclidean* distance, results from $p = 2$. The *Chebyshev* distance (L_∞-distance) is a special case of the Minkowski distance with $p = \infty$. Because the Minkowski metrics account only for the correspondences between bins with the same index for the distance calculation, the L_1-distance results in many false positives for image retrieval (see Figure 1.14).

II.) Kullback-Leibler Divergence

$$d_{KL}(H_Q, H_D) = \sum_i H_Q(i) \, log \frac{H_Q(i)}{H_D(i)}$$ (1.11)

The Kullback-Leibler divergence originates from information theory and measures the average inefficiency to code one histogram using the other as the code-book. Disadvantages of the Kullback-Leibler distance are its sensitivity to histogram binning and its non-symmetry.

III.) Jeffrey Divergence
The Jeffrey divergence overcomes the shortcomings of the Kullback-Leibler divergence. It is numerically stable, symmetric and robust with respect to noise and binning.

$$d_J(H_Q, H_D) = \sum_i \left(H_Q(i) \, log\frac{H_Q(i)}{m_i} + H_D(i) \, log\frac{H_D(i)}{m_i} \right) \tag{1.12}$$

with $m_i = \frac{H_Q(i) + H_D(i)}{2}$.

IV.) χ^2 Statistics

$$d_{\chi^2}(H_Q, H_D) = \sum_i \frac{(H_Q(i) - m_i)^2}{m_i} \tag{1.13}$$

with $m_i = \frac{H_Q(i) + H_D(i)}{2}$. This quantity measures how unlikely it is that one distribution was drawn from the other.

Cross-bin Dissimilarity Measures

A variety of cross-bin dissimilarity measures have been developed. The most popular ones are the *quadratic-form distance, one-dimensional match distance, Kolmogorov-Smirnov statistics* and the *Earth Movers Distance*, which will be discussed below:

I.) Quadratic-Form Distance

$$d_A(H_Q, H_D) = \sqrt{(h_Q - h_D)^T A(h_Q - h_D)} \tag{1.14}$$

where h_Q and h_D are vectors that list all single entries in H_Q and H_D. The similarity matrix $A = [a_{ij}]$ represents cross-bin information, where a_{ij} denotes the similarity between bin i in histogram H_Q and bin j in histogram H_D. The elements of A are calculated according to: $a_{ij} = 1 - d_{ij}/d_{max}$ where d_{ij} is the ground distance between the feature descriptors of bins i and j in the feature space, and $d_{max} = max_{ij} \, d_{ij}$. The disadvantage is that the quadratic-form distance compares one bin of histogram H_Q with different bins in the other histogram H_D. This is not in line with perceptual dissimilarity and therefore usually results in many false positives for image retrieval.

II.) Kolmogorov-Smirnov Statistics

$$d_{KS}(H_Q, H_D) = max_i(|\hat{h}_Q(i) - \hat{h}_D(i)|) \tag{1.15}$$

where $\hat{h}_Q(i)$ and $\hat{h}_D(i)$ are cumulative histograms. The Kolmogorov-Smirnov statistics is a common statistical measure for unbinned distributions. For consistency with the other histogram based distance measures, it is here applied to cumulative histograms.

III.) Earth Movers Distance
The *Earth Movers Distance (EMD)* computes the distance between two distributions, which are represented as *signatures* (Rubner & Tomasi, 2001). A signature, mathematically defined as $s_j = (m_j, w_j)$, represents a set of feature clusters in the feature space, where m_j denotes the mean of the cluster and w_j the fraction of pixels that belong to cluster m_j. The subscript j varies with the complexity of a particular image.

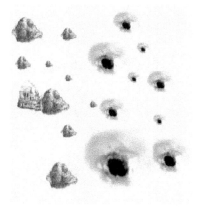

Figure 1.15: Allegory of the Earth Movers Distance (taken from Czepa, 2005, p. 5).

A colour histogram is a special case of a signature, where m_j represents the RGB values of a particular histogram bin and w_j stands for the number of pixels belonging to that bin. Imagine the colour histograms of two images described by signatures with m clusters P=$(p_1, w_{p_1}), ..., (p_m, w_{p_m})$ and Q=$(q_1, w_{q_1}), ..., (q_m, w_{q_m})$, respectively. Also a *ground distance* matrix $D = [d_{ij}]$ is given, where d_{ij} is the ground distance between clusters p_i and q_j. The ground distance can be the Euclidean, city block or any other distance metric. P can be seen as a "mass of earth" properly spread in space and Q as a collection of "holes" in the same space (see Figure 1.15).

Then the EMD measures the least amount of work needed to fill the "holes" with "earth", where a unit of work corresponds to transporting a unit of "earth" by a unit of ground distance. Mathematically this can be expressed as follows: Find a flow $F = [f_{ij}]$, where f_{ij} describes the flow between p_i and q_j that minimises the overall cost

$$WORK(P, Q, F) = \sum_{i=1}^{m} \sum_{j=1}^{n} d(p_i, q_j) f_{ij} \qquad (1.16)$$

where d is the ground distance and P and Q are the signatures of the query and database image, respectively. The calculation of Equation 1.16 is subject to the following constraints:

$$f_{ij} \geq 0, \ 1 \leq i \leq m, \ 1 \leq j \leq n, \qquad (1.17)$$

$$\sum_{j=1}^{n} f_{ij} \leq w_{pi}, \ 1 \leq i \leq m, \qquad (1.18)$$

$$\sum_{1=1}^{m} f_{ij} \leq w_{qi}, \ 1 \leq j \leq n, \qquad (1.19)$$

$$\sum_{i=1}^{m} \sum_{j=1}^{n} f_{ij} = min \left(\sum_{i=1}^{m} w_{pi}, \sum_{j=1}^{n} w_{qj} \right). \qquad (1.20)$$

Constraint 1.17 guarantees that the "earth" is only moved from P to Q and not vice versa. Constraints 1.18 and 1.19 limit the amount of "earth" that can be sent by the clusters in P or received by the clusters in Q by their weights, i.e., only as much "earth" as possible is moved. Finally, constraint 1.20 forces that the maximum amount of "earth" is moved. One advantage of the EMD is its general and flexible metric which allows partial matching. Furthermore, it can be applied to variable-length representations of distributions, it can be computed efficiently and lower bounds are readily available for it.

IV.) One-Dimensional Match Distance

$$d_M(H_Q, H_D) = \sum_i |\hat{h}_Q(i) - \hat{h}_D(i)| \qquad (1.21)$$

where $\hat{h}_Q(i)$ and $\hat{h}_D(i)$ are cumulative histograms. In case of two one-dimensional histograms, the match distance can be seen as the L_1 distance between cumulative histograms. The one-dimensional match distance cannot be extended to higher dimensions, since the relation $j \leq i$ is not a total ordering in more than one dimension. For 1D histograms with equal areas, the one-dimensional match distance becomes a special case of the Earth Movers Distance, but without being able to handle partial matches or other ground distances.

1.2.5   Categories of User Aims

The use of a large image database requires that the user has a particular search intention in mind. However, in image retrieval, users' search intention can vary from only a vague up to a quite detailed idea about the retrieval aim. In image retrieval, there are three broad search categories of user aims when using the system (Smeulders et al., 2000):

- *Search by association:* The user starts the retrieval with only a vague idea what he/she is looking for.

- *Search for a specific image:* The user is looking for a single specific image that he/she has in mind or which is similar to a provided set of images (e.g., search in catalogues).

- *Category search:* The user is looking for one or more images from general categories (e.g., trademarks).

The three categories make different demands on the particular design of CBIRS and their set of applied features. Hence, it is necessary to understand the various types of queries that can be posed in order to determine the feature vector structure suitable for queries supported by the CBIRS. In case of search by association, the system should be highly interactive (user-relevance feedback), allowing the user to browse the whole database. The search for a specific image requires a careful selection of appropriate low-level features, describing reliably the image content. Category search on the other hand requires the selection of high-level semantic features that can capture image categories, like indoor versus outdoor (Szummer & Picard, 1998) or city versus landscape (Vailaya, Jain & Zhang, 1998).

1.2.6 Query Image

The simplest way to describe the content of an image, we are looking for, is by using words. Text annotation is used in popular image search engines like Google or Yahoo, and can be directly used for keyboard-based searching, when it is available (Chang & Hsu, 1992). But text annotation is tedious, subjective, unsystematic and it is not suitable for capturing the perceptual saliency of some visual features, especially texture or the outline of a form.

If text annotation is unavailable or incomplete, three other forms of queries can be used: Query by *example image*, by *sketch* or by *iconic symbol* (Lew, 2001) (see Figure 1.16).

Probably the most intuitive way we can think of, is to draw a sketch using a painting device like a pencil or a brush. Therefore, a CBIRS can provide a drawing board and some drawing functions. But this method also has some drawbacks: I.) It is not easy to draw objects, especially with a computer mouse, II.) Different people have different drawing skills, III.) The quality of the sketch also depends on the drawing facilities provided by the system.

A variant of this technique that frees the user from drawing the image is to provide icons which can be dragged and dropped by the user on a drawing board. But the result heavily depends on the icons provided by the system: If the system only provides icons with simple objects, the result will be much poorer than for a system supporting icons depicting more complex objects. Furthermore, a system that can handle only 2D-relationships between icons is much more restricted than one being able to handle 3D-arrangements of icons.

Among the most commonly request paradigms used in CBIRS is *query by example*: The user provides a query image being quite similar to the image he/she is looking for. This image can be provided in every kind of graphical format, on the local machine or on a portable disk. This requires no drawing skills by the user. Common problems are that the provided image can be different from the desired ones with regard to recording angle,

" Find images of a cup "

Figure 1.16: Different kinds of queries: By text, sketch, icon and example image.

illumination, focus or other details. Another point is that the user mostly has much more in mind about a scene than a "one frame shot" can provide.

Some systems provide a set of starting images or a *random option* (i.e., images are retrieved randomly from the database) in order to offer the user a starting point (Wang, 2001). This approach is required for the "search by association" (see Section 1.2.5), i.e., the user has only a vague idea of what he/she is looking for or if no query image is available. Figure 1.16 illustrates the different query types for CBIRS.

1.2.7　Results and User Feedback

The process of integrating the user in the retrieval process, by evaluating the retrieval results, is called *user-relevance feedback* (see Figure 1.17). User-relevance feedback serves two main purposes: I.) To improve the retrieval performance, II.) to overcome the *semantic gap* and *subjectivity of human perception* (see Section 1.1). Because Computer Vision techniques that automatically extract semantic information from an image are not reliable enough, humans still play an indispensable part in the design of CBIRS. With this fact becomming more and more apparent, CBIRS pay more and more attention to user interaction and try to find the best images according to user input. Examples for CBIRS that integrate user-relevance feedback are *MARS*, *FourEyes*, *PicHunter* and *WEBSEEK* (Rui, Huang & Chang, 1999). Many of the existing CBIRS provide a graphical user interface for user-relevance feedback. Sliders or radio buttons allow the user to provide a graduated judgement of relevance for each single retrieved image, i.e., from highly relevant to not relevant at all. Now the query can be refined by updating the weights for different feature classes according to the user input (Rui, Huang, Mehrota & Ortega, 1998). This process repeats until the system has adapted its retrieval behaviour to user requirements and therefore retrieves the best results. The key issue here is how to incorporate the positive and negative examples provided by the user in the query and similarity refinement?

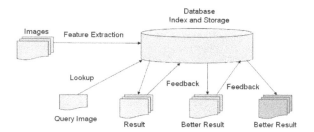

Figure 1.17: Image retrieval with user-relevance feedback.

Early techniques for relevance feedback have mainly been adopted from Text Retrieval (Salton & McGill, 1988). They can be classified into two approaches: *Query point movement (query refinement)* and *re-weighting (similarity measure refinement)*. The former method improves the estimate of the "ideal query point" by moving it towards good and away from bad example points. A prominent technique for query point movement is *Rocchio's* formula:

$$Q' = \alpha Q + \beta \left(\frac{1}{N_{R'}} \sum_{i \in D'_R} D_i \right) - \gamma \left(\frac{1}{N_{N'}} \sum_{i \in D'_N} D_i \right) \qquad (1.22)$$

where α, β and γ are parameters which have to be selectively adjusted for each application. $N_{R'}$ and $N_{I'}$ are the number of documents in D'_R (a set of relevant documents) and D'_N (a set of non-relevant documents). Q is the vector for the initial query.

For image retrieval usually high dimensional feature vectors are used. In the re-weighting method, the weights for important or unimportant feature dimensions are increased or decreased, respectively. If the variance of good examples is high along a principle axis j, then the values on this axis are relatively irrelevant to the input query and therefore receive low weights w_j. If the variance is low on the other hand, then this feature dimension receives high weights. A prominent CBIRS that uses re-weighting techniques is the *MARS* system (Rui, Huang, Mehrota & Ortega, 1998), which is described in Section 1.2.9.

Another technique uses *Bayesian learning* to incorporate user's feedback for updating the probability distribution of all images in the database. This method was implemented in the *PicHunter* system (Cox, Miller, Omohundro & Yianilos, 2000), which is also described in Section 1.2.9.

In Lee, Ma and Zhang (1998) user-relevance feedback is used to build up a semantic correlation matrix for image clusters. It has been shown that this approach does not only improve retrieval performance, but also reduces the number of iterations in the following retrieval sessions, because the system is able to learn from previous relevance feedback. User relevance and user log analysis is also used for *iFind*, a web-based image retrieval system that uses a modified form of Rocchio's formula to measure the relevance of each database image considering both semantic and low-level feature content (Lu, Hu, Zhu, Zhang & Yang, 2000). It applies a document space model that is built from the image and text content of the web pages (where irrelevant text information is removed) and a user space model, i.e., keyword vectors applied by the user to describe image content (extracted from the log files and the user-relevance feedback). By combining the document space model with the user space model, the retrieval performance can be significantly improved, because mismatches between the page author's expression and user's understanding and expectation are eliminated. Each image is linked to several keywords, whereby a weight associated with each link represents the degree of the keywords' relevance to the semantic content of the image. By user relevance, these weights can be updated and additional keywords can be learned.

Because the feedback process can be quite tedious for long retrieval sessions, users quite often provide only superficial feedback or even skip it completely, leading to a poorer performance of the system. Additionally, each type of image features only captures some aspects of image similarity and it is difficult for the user to specify which aspects he/she exactly wants or what combination of these aspects are important for defining a query.

Therefore, there is an urgent need for natural human-computer interfaces, allowing the user to intuitively provide as much feedback as possible while keeping the burden for him/her as low as possible. This is the reason why relevance feedback has become one of the most challenging topics in CBIR research.

1.2.8 Performance Evaluation of CBIRS

The performance evaluation serves as a measure for comparing the efficiency of different retrieval systems, provided with a similar set of query and database images. Performance standards defined at the annual *Text Retrieval Conference* (TREC) are commonly used in the field of Text Retrieval. It includes a standard text database of 2GB size that serves as a test set for the evaluation of new text retrieval techniques. There are two methods for defining the significance of the texts or images in the database for a particular query: The *manual labelling by humans* and the *pooling*. The former is quite tedious and the latter term denotes the process of presenting the query to all systems that should be compared, taking their respective best answers (e.g., the first 100) and finally evaluating them manually.

After defining the relevant items, the performance of retrieval systems can be evaluated as to *precision* and *recall*. These are defined as:

$$precision = \frac{\text{retrieved relevant items}}{\text{retrieved items}}$$

$$recall = \frac{\text{retrieved relevant items}}{\text{relevant items}}$$

Precision and recall are always used together and are plotted in a so called *precision versus recall graph* (see Figure 1.19). The retrieval performance is high, when the curve has a high precision with increasing recall, and plunges down at the end.

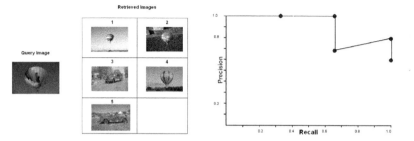

Figure 1.18: *A query image and the five best retrieval results.*

Figure 1.19: *The precision-recall graph for the results of Figure 1.18.*

Besides precision and recall, there exist also three practical methods to evaluate the retrieval performance of CBIRS:

- Providing a few examples of retrieval results and comparing them with the results of previously developed systems or methods. This evaluation allows to test directly if the new designed system performs better than existing ones. The problematic is here to find a suitable selection of example images which covers all aspects of the database.

- Systematic evaluation using a small database with only a few distinct categories (e.g., sunset, oranges or tigers). This evaluation provides a basic set of images which can be used to evaluate the performance of all retrieval systems. It can only be seen as a basic test, since it does not give any hints how good the system performs on a more complex data set.

- Systematic evaluation over several added distinct categories within a larger database. This evaluation allows a more meaningful test of the systems' performance. But again, the performance of the evaluation depends on the categories chosen for system evaluation.

Even though these evaluation methods provide some meaningful insights about whether one system is better than the other, they are not suitable to predict the systems' performance on databases of a particular application field. Furthermore, the categorisation of images is sometimes ambiguous, e.g., would an image with Iceland ponies be classified as Iceland or as horses? Smeulders et al. (2000) considered the creation of a comprehensive and publicly available reference image database, sorted by class and retrieval purposes, together with a protocol for experiment design as a standard reference against which new algorithms could be evaluated. This is in accordance to Text Retrieval where such a reference already exists ([5]). First steps towards a unique image database are proposed in a project by the University of Washington in Seattle, where a collection of freely available, categorised and annotated sets of images is available ([3]). More information regarding the performance evaluation of CBIRS can be found in Müller, Müller, Squire, Marchand-Maillet and Run (2001).

1.2.9   Examples of CBIRS

As various as the features used for image retrieval, are the CBIRS approaches. A recent survey lists 5 commercial and 29 prototype research systems (Ren, Eakins & Briggs, 2000). In the following subsections innovative CBIRS are described which set new standards for image retrieval. Comprehensive lists of available CBIRS can be found in Eakins and Graham (1999) and in Veltkamp and Tanase (2000).

QBIC

The *Query By Image Content* (QBIC) was developed at the IBM Almadan Research Center in San Jose, CA. It was the first commercially available CBIRS (Niblack et al., 1993; Faloutsos et al., 1994; Niblack et al., 1998). QBIC had a strong influence on the design of system architecture and introduced techniques taken up in later CBIRS. QBIC can be used for static images and also for videos. It supports *query by example*, but also provides a sketch interface and the selection of colour and texture patterns. For static images, the system allows query by semantic content, global colour similarity, colour-region similarity, texture similarity and query by shape and spatial relationship similarity. Colour features are histograms, calculated for the whole image or objects in different colour spaces. A weighted Euclidean distance is used to calculate the similarity between two histograms, including a weight matrix representing the extent of perceptual similarity between two histogram bins. Texture features used in QBIC are modified versions of the coarseness, contrast and directionality features proposed by Tamura, Mori and Yamawaki (1978). Shape features include shape area, circularity, eccentricity, major axis orientation and a set of algebraic moment invariants. Correspondingly, the weighted Euclidean distance is used as the distance measure for the texture and shape features.
QBIC was the first system to use multidimensional scaling techniques in order to enhance retrieval performance. The 3D colour and texture features are directly used as indices in an R^*-tree (Beckmann, Kriegel, Schneider & Seeger, 1990), whereas the high dimensional-

ity of the shape features is first reduced by using a Karhunen-Loéve-transform (Gonzalez & Woods, 2002).

The main disadvantage of QBIC is the lack of suitable relevance feedback. Only one retrieved image can serve as a seed for the next retrieval step. Hence, QBIC cannot automatically adapt its internal search parameters to user requirements.

MARS

Later systems focussed on the user-relevance feedback component. A system that set standards for relevance feedback was MARS (*Multimedia Analysis and Retrieval System*), developed at the University of Illinois at Urbana-Champaign and the University of California at Irvine (Ortega, Yong, Chakrabarti, Mehrotra & Huang, 1997; Rui, Huang, Mehrota & Ortega, 1998). Queries can be formulated either by providing an example image, on the basis of low level features (by choosing colour patterns or texture sets) or text descriptions. To calculate the colour and texture features, the image is first divided into 5×5 subimages. For each subimage a 2D colour histogram (H and S coordinates of the HSV space) is calculated. Two texture histograms (representing coarseness and directionality) and also a scalar defining contrast are additionally calculated from wavelet coefficients. Object segmentation is performed in two phases: First, a k-means clustering algorithm is applied in the colour-texture space. The resulting clusters are grouped by an attraction-based method, which is similar to the gravitation in physics, according to: $F_{ij} = M_i M_j / d_{ij}^2$, where F_{ij} is the attraction between region i and j, M_i and M_j are the sizes of regions i and j, respectively, and d_{ij} is the distance between region i and j in the spatial-colour-texture space. Finally the boundaries of the extracted objects are represented by the means of modified Fourier descriptors (Rui, She & Huang, 1998) (see Section 1.2.3). The similarity of images according to colour and texture is calculated by histogram intersection and additionally by the Euclidean distance between contrast values in case of texture features.

MARS uses the *object model* proposed in the Information Retrieval literature (Salton & McGill, 1988; Baeza-Yates & Ribeiro-Neto, 1999) and applies it to Content-Based Image Retrieval. The object model serves as a representation for images. It is defined as: $O = O(D, F, R)$, where D is the raw image data (e.g., a JPEG image), $F = f_i$ is a set of low level features associated with the image object (e.g., colour, texture, or shape) and $R = r_{ij}$ is a set of representations for a given feature f_i (e.g., colour histograms or colour moments are representations for colour features). Additionally, weights (W_i, W_{ij}, W_{ijk}) are associated with features f_i, representations r_{ij} and components r_{ijk} (see Figure 1.20). Each feature representation is associated with some similarity measure (e.g., Euclidean distance or histogram intersection). The user-relevance feedback is used to update the weights accordingly, i.e., if a representation r_{ij} reflects the users' information need, it receives more emphasis by increasing its corresponding weight vector. Hence, the aim of the relevance feedback is to adopt the weights for all applied image features and internal system parameters (e.g., similarity function and search request) to adequately model user's

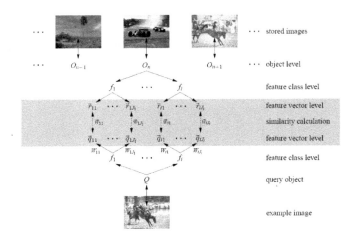

Figure 1.20: The CBIR model of MARS (taken from Kämpfe, Käster, Pfeiffer, Ritter & Sagerer, 2002).

semantic concepts.

The disadvantage of MARS is that it does not allow relevance feedback for image regions. Therefore, the user cannot indicate which image detail is particularly important for his/her retrieval needs. Furthermore, the system resets the weights for each retrieval session, so that each time the system has to relearn user's preferences.

SIMPLIcity

SIMPLIcity (*Semantics-sensitive Integrated Matching for Picture LIbraries*) is an image retrieval system which uses *high level semantics classification* and *integrated region matching* based upon image segmentation (Wang, 2001). Images are represented by a set of regions. Regions are described by colour, texture, shape and location features. The system classifies images into high level categories (such as "textured" vs. "non-textured", "graph" vs. "photograph" and "objectionable" vs. "benign") to restrict the search space and to allow semantically-adaptive searching methods. This is done by dividing the image in 4 × 4 blocks and calculating a feature vector for each block. The image is then quickly segmented into regions by using a statistical cluster algorithm (Hartigan & Wong, 1979). Finally, a classifier decides the semantic type of the image according to the segmentation result. An important progress is the *integrated region matching approach* (IRM), where each region of the query image is matched with each region in the database image, making the algorithm insensitive to poor segmentation results (see Figures 1.21 and 1.22).

This approach works as follows: The region set of the query image is described as $R_1 = \{r_1, r_2, ..., r_m\}$ and the region set of the database image as $R_2 = \{r'_1, r'_2, ..., r'_n\}$, where r_i and r'_j are the descriptors of region i in the query and region j in the database image,

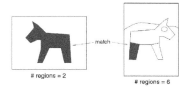

Figure 1.21: *Traditional region-based matching (taken from Wang, 2001, p. 94).*

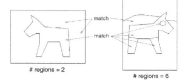

Figure 1.22: *Integrated region matching (IRM) (taken from Wang, 2001, p. 94).*

respectively. The distance between region r_i and r_j' is defined as $d(r_i, r_j')$. When comparing images, humans usually first match regions belonging to the foreground followed by those belonging to the background. For example in animal images, they would first match regions belonging to the animal and later regions belonging to background areas. It would make no sense to compare a region belonging to the animal in the first image with a background area in the second image. Furthermore, one or more regions in the query image can be compared to one or more regions in the database image. The more consistent the matching between two regions in the two images is according to human perception, the more important it should be for estimating image similarity. Thus, a *significance credit* ($s_{i,j} \geq 0$) is assigned to each matching region pair in the IRM approach, indicating the importance of the matching for determining the similarity between images. By calculating the significance credit for each matching region pair, we get a *significance matrix* (S). A set of constraints on the suitable selection of similarity measures can help in designing suitable similarity measures. Intuitively the highest significance should be assigned to the region pair with the minimum distance, which is called the *most similar highest priority* (MSHP) principle. All regions should be considered for measuring the similarity between two images. Furthermore, regions of greater size should be more important for this calculation than smaller regions. The first aspect is considered by normalisation, whereas the second aspect is taken into account by using the *area percentage scheme*: The significance of a region is calculated by dividing the area of the region by the image size. Therefore, larger regions receive higher significance values than smaller ones. Having an admissible matching between two region sets, the distance can be calculated according to:

$$d(R_1, R_2) = \sum_{i,j} s_{i,j} d(r_i, r_j')$$ (1.23)

where $s_{i,j}$ is the corresponding entry in the significance matrix (S) and $d_{i,j}$ is the distance between two regions i and j, calculated by:

$$d(r_i, r_j') = \sum_{i=1}^{n} w_i (f_{r_i} - f_{r_j'})^2$$ (1.24)

where f_{r_i} and $f_{r'_j}$ are the corresponding image features of region r_i and r'_j and n is the dimension of the feature vector. In SIMPLIcity, a nine dimensional feature vector is used (i.e., average LUV components, square roots of second order moment of wavelet coefficients in the HL, LH and HH band and the normalised inertia of order 1, 2 and 3).

PicSOM

PicSOM (Laaksonen, Koskela, Laakso & Oja, 2001), developed at the Helsinki University of Technology, uses a self-organizing map (SOM) (Kohonen, 1990; Ritter, 1993) to organise the images according to their extracted features and for the integration of relevance feedback. Each image is represented as a node on the SOM (see also Section 5.3.2), whereby similar images are mapped to neighbouring locations. Colour, shape and texture features are used, whereby for each different feature type a separate *tree structured SOM* (TS-SOM) is generated. Images with positive feedback are considered as important and images without any rating as unimportant ones. Hence, the relevance feedback leads to positive or negative impulses for the neurons on the SOM. By low-pass filtering, the regions containing many positive impulses are strengthened, whereas those with negative impulses are weakened. Images from high weighted regions, which have not been presented to the user, are relevant images. The retrieved image set results from a combination of the relevant images from all TS-SOMs.

Other CBIRS

The *NeTra* image retrieval system was developed at the Department of Electrical and Computer Engineering, University of California, CA, Santa Barbara (Ma & Manjunath, 1999). A distinguishing aspect of NeTra is its *edge flow model* for image segmentation. For each image location the directions of change in colour and texture are identified and an edge flow vector is constructed. By iteratively propagating the edge flow, an edge is detected if two corresponding neighbouring pixels have an edge flow in opposite direction. For the calculation of texture features, the system uses a set of Gabor filters at different scales and orientations (see Section 1.2.3). Beside texture features, the current implementation of NeTra utilises colour, shape and location information for region search and retrieval. Based on NeTra's feature representation, requests like "retrieve all images that have the colour of object A, texture of object B, shape of object C, and lie in the upper one-third of the image", are possible.

Another system using image segmentation is *Blobworld*, developed at the Computer Science Division, University of California, Berkeley (Carson, Thomas, Belongie, Hellerstein & Malik, 1999). It segments the image into regions coherent in colour and texture. This set of regions is called the "Blobworld" (see Figure 1.23). Image features are calculated for the single blobs and the background. During a retrieval session, the user selects one or more blobs and indicates the importance of the blob's features.

Photobook is a set of interactive tools for browsing and retrieval by image content. It was developed by the Vision and Modelling Group, MIT Media Laboratory, Cambridge,

Figure 1.23: A picture of a wolf and it's Blobworld representation (adapted from [12]).

MA (Pentland, Picard & Sclaroff, 1996). It distinguishes between three specific types of image content: Faces, shapes and textures, whereby each partition uses a category-specific approach for object description and matching. Its successor *FourEyes* is an interactive tool for segmenting and annotating images (Picard & Minka, 1997). FourEyes calculates off-line several feature extraction models, called *"society of models"*, leading to different segmentation results, depending on the set of feature models used. In case of texture, the features include among others co-occurrence matrices (see Section 4.5.4), Gabor filter and wavelets (see Section 1.2.3). The application of different feature sets is motivated by the fact that a chosen single image feature is not suitable for all kinds of labels in all kinds of imagery. Instead, FourEyes uses relevance feedback to combine those models from the "society of models" to produce a labelling that most efficiently represent positive examples provided by the user. Users select regions of interest by mouse-clicking on them or by sweeping a path through the region. Negative examples can be generated in the same way, but with another mouse button. The labels provided by the user are extrapolated to other regions of the image or the database, according to the examples provided by the user. The disadvantage of FourEyes is that all groupings have to be recalculated when a new image is added to the database. Additionally, FourEyes does not provide assistance in choosing the right set of models for the particular retrieval task at hand.

PicHunter, a system that focusses on target search, was developed at the NEC Research Institute, Princeton, NY (Cox, Miller, Omohundro & Yianilos, 2000). Its performance is measured by the average number of images viewed until the target image is found. PicHunter uses a simple instance of a general *Bayesian framework*: By applying Bayes's rules, the system can predict the target images given users' relevance feedback. In contrast to other CBIRS, PicHunter refines its answers in reply to user feedback, rather than refining any query.

Another commercial retrieval program is the *VIR Image Engine*, developed by the Virage Incorporation (Bach et al., 1996). It is an extensible framework for building CBIRS. The basic concepts are *primitives*, including feature type, computation and matching distance. The system already provides a set of general primitives, such as global and local colour, texture and shape. When defining new domain specific primitives, the user has to provide both, the algorithms for calculating the new features from the raw image data, and the distance measure. The similarity between each image pair is calculated for each primitive. The individual scores are combined in an overall score, using a set of weights, characteristic to the application. The VIR Image Engine also provides a set of GUI-tools (such as query canvas, sketch interface or keyword field) for constructing a user interface.

There are two variations of Content-Based Image Retrieval, called *Region-Based Image Retrieval* (RBIR) and *Content-Based Sub-Image Retrieval* (CBsIR), which apply user-relevance feedback to adjust the importance of image regions or image tiles. RBIR and CBsIR show communalities with the retrieval approach developed in this book.

1.3   RBIR and CBsIR

Most Content-Based Image Retrieval systems find similar images based on global features, i.e., overall image similarity. But often the user is interested in particular regions (objects) or examples from the database that contain a subimage, without restrictions on the subimage's location within the original. This led to two different approaches for image retrieval, called Region-Based Image Retrieval (RBIR) and Content-Based Sub-Image Retrieval (CBsIR), which are the subject of the following sections.

Region-Based Image Retrieval (RBIR)

In the Region-Based Image Retrieval (RBIR) approach, images are retrieved from the database according to region similarity. Thus, the performance of RBIR systems depends strongly on the quality of the segmentation preprocessing. Popular examples are the *Blob-world* project (Carson, Thomas, Belongie, Hellerstein & Malik, 1999) and the SIMPLIcity system (Wang, 2001) (see Section 1.2.9). As stated above, generally higher weights are assigned to larger regions, although region size usually does not correlate with the semantic importance.

For a better semantic region representation Jing, Zhang, Lin, Ma and Zhang (2001) developed the *Self-Learned Region Importance* (SLRI) retrieval method. In SLRI, region importance is learned via user-relevance feedback. The basic assumption is that important regions occur more often in positive than in negative examples. For each region the first three colour moments from each channel of the HSV colour space are calculated as region features. Each region is assigned an importance value depending on its similarity to the positive examples from the user-relevance feedback, i.e., the more similar the region is to a region in the positive examples and the less similar it is to those of the negative examples, the higher is its semantic importance. The similarity between two images I_a and I_b, with regions $\{R_{a,1}, R_{a,2}, ..., R_{a,n}\}$ and $\{R_{b,1}, R_{b,2}, ..., R_{b,m}\}$, is calculated according to:

$$s(I_a, I_b) = \sum_{i,j} MI_{i,j} \, s_r(R_{a,i}, R_{b,j}) \tag{1.25}$$

where $MI_{i,j}$ is the significance credit indicating the importance of the matching between region $R_{a,i}$ and $R_{b,j}$ for the estimation of the overall similarity between images I_a and I_b.

It is defined as the minimal importance of the two matched regions $R_{a,i}$ and $R_{b,j}$, because the matching of a significant with an insignificant region is meaningless. The similarity between regions $R_{a,i}$ and $R_{b,j}$ ($s_r(R_{a,i}, R_{b,j})$) is denoted by:

$$s_r(R_{a,i}, R_{b,j}) = exp\left(\frac{-d(R_{a,i}, R_{b,j})}{\sigma}\right) \tag{1.26}$$

where $d(R_{a,i}, R_{b,j})$ is the Euclidean distance between the colour feature vectors of region $R_{a,i}$ and $R_{b,j}$. σ is the standard deviation of the distances calculated over a sample of regions pairs. Analogue to the *most similar highest priority* (MSHP) principle (see Chapter 1.2.9), the algorithm tries to assign as much significance as possible to a "valid matching" with maximal similarity. For a "valid matching" of two regions $R_{a,i}$ and $R_{b,j}$, the similarity has to exceed a threshold ϵ.

During the retrieval procedure, the system adapts to the user's intention by successively adapting the importance of the regions in the query image and the positives according to:

$$RI_i(k) = \frac{\omega_i s(R_i, IS^+(k)_{R_i})}{\sum_{j=1}^{n}(\omega_j s(R_j, IS^+(k)_{R_j}))} \tag{1.27}$$

where $RI_i(k)$ is the importance of region R_i after k iterations and $\omega_i = 1 - \frac{s(R_i, IS^-(k)_{R_i})}{\sum_{j=1}^{n} s(R_j, IS^-(k)_{R_j})}$. $IS^+(k) = \{I_1^+(k), ..., I_{n_k}^+(k)\}$ and $IS^-(k) = \{I_1^-(k), ..., I_m^-(k)\}$ are the positive and negative examples, respectively. Thus, if a region R_i appears several times in the negative images ($IS_{R_i}^-$), than ω_i is close to zero and $RI_i(k)$ becomes small. If, on the other hand, region R_i appears several times in the positive images ($IS_{R_i}^+$), than ω_i is close to one and $RI_i(k)$ increases. K is the number of relevance-feedback iterations. $IS^+(k)_{R_i}$ is the similar region set of a region R_i defined on an image set $IS = \{I_1, I_2, ..., I_n\}$:

$$IS_R = \{I_i | I_i \in IS, s(R, I_i) > \epsilon\} \tag{1.28}$$

where ϵ is the similarity threshold set to 0.78. The similarity between a region R and an image set IS consisting of images $\{I_1, I_2, ..., I_n\}$ is defined as:

$$s(R, IS) = \sum_{k=1}^{n} s(R, I_k) \tag{1.29}$$

Experiments have shown that this approach is robust against poor segmentation results (because it matches all regions in the query image to all regions in the database images). Furthermore, it outperformed the IRM approach in the SIMPLIcity system (see Chapter 1.2.9) that rates region importance according to region size.

Based on the observation that information from negative examples are irrelevant, because negative images represent only a small part of all irrelevant images from the database, Jing, Li, Zhang and Zhang (2002) modified the SLRI retrieval method. In the so called *Key-Region* approach the basic assumption is that important regions should appear more often in positive images and less times in the other images of the database. This approach followed the weighting scheme, based on *term frequency* and *inverse document frequency* from Text Retrieval (Salton & McGill, 1998). Instead of the *term frequency*, which signifies the frequency of the term k in all documents, a so called region frequency (RF_i) for each image region (R_i) is calculated, reflecting the extent to which a region is similar to regions of positive examples:

$$RF_i = \sum_{j=1}^{n_i} s(R_i, I_j^+(k)) \tag{1.30}$$

where $I_1^+(k), ..., I_{n_k}^+(k)$ denote the positive images available after k feedback iterations. $s(R_i, I_j^+(k))$ is one, if the region R_i is at least similar to one region in image $I_j^+(k)$, otherwise $s(R_i, I_j^+(k))$ is zero. The larger RF_i is, the more reflects region R_i user's intention. The *inverse document frequency* from Text Retrieval, which reflects the number of documents in which term k occurs, is substituted by the *inverse image frequency* (IIF):

$$IIF_i = log\left(\frac{N}{\sum_{j=1}^{N} s(R_i, I_j)}\right) \tag{1.31}$$

Intuitively, a region becomes less important, if similar regions occur in many database images. The overall region importance (RI_i) for region i in image I can then be defined as:

$$RI_i(k) = \frac{RF_i(k) \times IIF_i}{\sum_{j=1}^{n}(RF_j(k) \times IIF_j)} \tag{1.32}$$

where k is the number of feedback iterations and n is the number of regions in image I. The importance of a region increases the more it is consistent with other regions in positive examples, but decreases if it occurs in many database images. The system learns from user-relevance feedback by adapting the region importance (RI_i) on the basis of positive examples.

Content-Based Sub-Image Retrieval (CBsIR)

Content-Based Sub-Image Retrieval comes into play, when the user is looking for images from the database that contain a query (sub)image without any restrictions on the location of the subimage. CBsIR has been defined as follows: Given a query image Q and a database S, retrieve from S those images Q' which contain Q according to some notion of similarity (Sebe, Lew & Huijsmans, 1999). The difference between CBsIR and RBIR is that in CBsIR an image is searched, which is part of another image, whereas in RBIR the aim is to search for similar regions, which result from automatic image segmentation. Hence, CBsIR does not rely on segmentation preprocessing (unlike RBIR) and is more similar to traditional CBIR, because the user has to provide a query by example.

Luo and Nascimento (2004) integrated relevance feedback in a CBsIR system by applying a tile re-weighting scheme. In this approach, each image is represented by a hierarchical tree structure of three levels: The highest level is the image itself. In the second level, the image is decomposed into 3×3 overlapping tiles, whereas on the lowest level each tile of the second level is equally divided into 4 non-overlapping sub-tiles. Two histograms of 64 quantised colours in the RGB colour space of each image tile are associated as colour features with each node of the tree, where each colour occurs in both histograms: One for the border and one for the interior pixels, allowing a more informed colour distribution abstraction that captures implicitly a notion of texture. The user submits a query (sub)-image and the system retrieves the initial-set of results from the database. This set is comprised of images containing similar tiles to the query (sub)-image. Now the user identifies positive and negative examples from the presented retrieval results. Based on this feedback, the *penalty* of each tile $TP_i(k), i = 0, ..., NT$ of all positive examples is updated according to:

$$TP_i(k) = \frac{W_i \times DTS(T_i, IS^+(k))}{\sum_{j=0}^{NT}(W_j \times DTS(T_j, IS^+(k)))} \qquad (1.33)$$

where $W_i = 1 - \frac{DTS(T_i, IS^-(k))}{\sum_{j=0}^{NT}(DTS(T_j, IS^-(k)))}$. $IS^+(k) = \{I_1^+, ..., I_p^+\}$ and $IS^-(k) = \{I_1^-, ..., I_q^-\}$ are the positive and negative examples, respectively. As can be seen, the influence of the negative examples on the calculation of the penalty is reflected by W_i. NT is the number of tiles per database image and k is the number of relevance iterations. $DTS(T, IS)$ is a measure of the distance between a tile T and an image set $IS = \{I_1, I_2, ..., I_n\}$, reflecting the extent to which the tile is consistent with other positive examples in the feature space. I.e., the smaller the value, the more important is the tile for the representation of user's intention. Then the features for each tile of the query image are recalculated according to:

$$qn_l^k[j] = \frac{\sum_{i=1}^{p}(1 - TPmin_{i_l}(k)) \times Pos_{i_l}^k[j]}{\sum_{i=1}^{p}(1 - TPmin_{i_l}(k))} \qquad (1.34)$$

where $qn_l^k[j]$ is the new feature for tile j at level l after k feedback iterations. $TPmin_{i_l}(k)$ is the minimum tile penalty for a tile at level l for the ith positive rated image after k iterations. $Pos_{i_l}^k[j]$ is the feature for tile j with minimum tile penalty at level j for the ith positive image after k iterations. P is the number of positively ranked retrieval results at iteration k. Intuitively, the features of the tiles with the minimum tile penalties within the set of positive images are used to iteratively optimise the query. Using the updated features of the query, as well as the new tile penalties, the distances between the query image and all databases images can then be recalculated according to:

$$DI_k(I, Q) = min_{i=0,...,NT}TP_i(k-1) \times DT(I_i, Q_j) \qquad (1.35)$$

where $NT + 1$ are the number of tiles in a database image. $TP_i(k-1)$ is the tile penalty for tile i of image I after $k-1$ iterations. $DT(I_i, Q_j)$ is the feature distance between tile i and j of database image I and query image Q. The results are presented to the user for relevance feedback and the steps repeat, until the user is satisfied with the retrieval results. The systems average recall rate is around 70% within the top 20 retrieved images after only 5 iterations.

1.4 Challenges for CBIRS

CBIRS have to meet a number of challenges:

- *Diversity*: Image databases are mostly diverse, i.e., the images in the database are collected from different categories, like landscapes, textures, biomedicine and so on (see Section 1.2.2). Images from different categories require different feature sets and retrieval strategies. For landscape images the overall impression is important, whereas in medical images for example, the focus could be on tumor cells in particular image regions.

- *Search Strategies*: Users want to apply different search strategies depending on the task at hand (see Section 1.2.5). For example, they would use low level features for retrieving a simple picture of a sunrise and high level features for the retrieval of complex ancient Chinese documents. Hence, before starting to think about the implementation of applied features, the indexing strategies, the system design and information about the user's retrieval needs should be figured out. At the current stage of development, computer-based image technology is not sophisticated enough to handle the needs of people in a variety of fields (Wang, 2001).

- *Maintenance*: Image archives of news broadcasting stations or biomedical image databases increase rapidly (see Section 1.2.1). Adding new images often requires a recalculation of the distances between image pairs. This can be a quite time-consuming process for large image databases.

- *Speed*: CBIRS usually work on large image domains and on remote systems. Assume that we have a database of one million images that occupies around 30 GB of disk space. An online processing of such a huge amount of images is impossible, stressing the need for off-line feature calculation or for a pre-clustering of the images. For application areas using images of high resolutions, like medicine, the situation gets even worse.

- *Performance*: Most CBIRS are designed as online retrieval systems, so that performance issues have to be taken into consideration. To use CBIRS interactively, users expect quick response times. In this context also transmission rates must be considered, and the data transfer should be as small as possible.

- *User Interface*: Venters, Eakins and Hartley (1997) have shown that the design of interfaces for query formulation and the display of results are fundamental for effective image retrieval. Knowledge from different disciplines, like Psychology, Linguistics and Computer Science can be very helpful to optimise the interface. These issues have been addressed very little in the design of CBIRS, resulting in a lack of suitable high-quality query-formulation interfaces: A longstanding barrier to effective image retrieval systems.

As discussed above, a vast majority of current CBIRS - in contrast to humans - mostly support only simple queries for image retrieval, based on primitive features, without considering the semantics of image content. The reason is that computer-based image technology is still not sophisticated enough to handle semantic concepts. Figure 1.24 illustrates a typical problem: Semantically related images may appear quite differently in visual features. The colour histogram for a white and red flower are reasonable different. Sophisticated queries require the identification of semantics primitives, like:

- Objects or roles: For example, find an image of the Golden Gate Bridge.

- Relationships between objects: For instance, find an image of a horse standing beside a barn.

- Sensations: Find colourful, bright art images.

- Images of a special style (e.g., epoch): Find artwork of the Impressionalism.

- Time, place, actions or events: Find images of a sunrise or of the Camp David meeting.

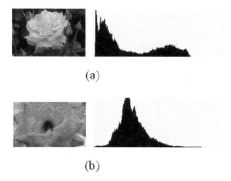

(a)

(b)

Figure 1.24: Colour histograms of a white (a) and a red (b) flower.

Solutions for the identification of semantic primitives exist, but they are usually domain-specific, e.g., for face databases (identification of eyes, nose, mouth and forehead) (Navarrete & Ruiz-del-Solar, 2002), medical databases (identification of specific pathologies), geographic information systems (Samet & Soffer, 1996) and outdoor-scene video databases for scene understanding (Campbell, Mackeown, Thomas & Troscianko, 1997).

As described above, recent retrieval systems have incorporated user-relevance feedback in order to generate perceptually and semantically more meaningful retrieval results. Most systems provide user feedback through the combination of intricate keyboard and mouse input. More recent systems provide multimodal interfaces including touch screen and natural language (Bauckhage, Käster, Pfeiffer & Sagerer, 2003). This book goes one step further and investigates, how eye tracking as an intuitive and easy to learn method for user input can improve Content-Based Image Retrieval.

1.5   A New Approach: Vision-Based Image Retrieval (VBIR)

In their endeavour to understand the mechanisms that underlie cognitive functions, researchers recently made considerable progress, in particular with regard to the human visual system. A significant contribution to this success was made by the analysis of human eye movements (for a review see Rayner, 1998). One of the most prominent experimental paradigms to investigate biological vision is visual search. Recent studies successfully employed eye-movement recording to gain a new level of insight into visual processing with regard to visual attention, object recognition, text comprehension and visual working memory (Pomplun, Sichelschmidt, Wagner, Clermont, Rickheit & Ritter, 2001). Related to this research field is the comparative visual search that has been deeply and successfully investigated using eye-tracking technology (Pomplun, 1998). In comparative visual search, humans have to find a difference in otherwise identical images. In order to solve the task, they focus on specific image regions and check for similarities and differences. This corresponds to image retrieval, where users compare important regions of the query and database images. Thus, it seems promising to combine CBIR with eye tracking. By the combination of both techniques the users' gaze positions can be used as relevance feedback. The recording of eye movements during image retrieval allows to focus the retrieval process on semantically important image regions, i.e., those regions with a high number of fixations. The adjustment of the weights for particular image regions or image tiles according to user-relevance feedback has been proved as a promising approach in RBIR and CBsIR (see Section 1.3). This results in a new approach to image retrieval, called *Vision-Based Image Retrieval* (VBIR), which is the focus of this book. By incorporating knowledge of human visual attention in the VBIR system, the new approach is able to overcome some of the challenges faced by modern CBIRS, like continuous relevance feedback, interface design and an intuitive and easy to learn handling. This brings image retrieval closer to human needs.

The next chapter discusses the processing of the visual information in the brain and the perception of colour, shape, texture and object information, which is essential for the new ideas developed in this book.

Chapter 2

Visual Information Processing

2.1 The Human Eye

The anatomy of the human eyeball is shown in Figure 2.1. When light enters the eye, it is first refracted at the anterior surface of the cornea, passes through the pupil and is refracted by the lens to project an inverted image on the retina, which is the rear part of the eye. The thickness of the lens and therefore its refractive power can be changed by contracting or relaxing the ciliary muscles. This process is called *accommodation*.

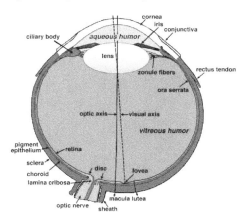

Figure 2.1: The human eye (adapted from [14]).

The human retina contains two types of photoreceptive cells, named *rods* and *cones*, which transform the incoming light into electric impulses. The rods are sensitive to low levels of illumination and give rise to *scotopic* ("dimlight") vision. Rods (around 120 million) are distributed around the fovea, which is the area of highest visual resolution in the retina (see Figure 2.1), whereas cones (around 6 million) are mostly located in the foveal and parafoveal regions. Cones, on the other side, require plenty of light to operate and are responsible for *photopic* ("bright-light") vision. They contain one of three visual pigments with spectral sensitivity peaks at 450 (blue), 525 (green) and 555 (red) nm, whereas rods are most sensitive to light at 500 nm. All other colours result from a combination of the three basic colours. The addition of red, green and blue leads to the perception of a bright or white colour. Before the electric impulses leave the retina through the *optic nerve*, they are preprocessed by different types of translucent cells, named *ganglion, amacrine, bipolar* and *horizontal cells* (see Figure 2.2). This preprocessing results in a substantial data compression which is indispensable, because the capacity of the human brain is limited and it would be extremely difficult to connect all receptors directly to the relevant brain areas. From the eyes, the information is transmitted via the optic nerv to the *lateral geniculate nucleus* (LGN).

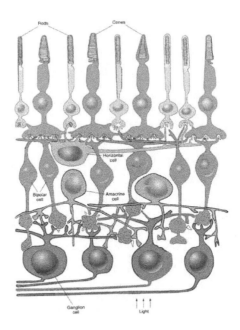

Figure 2.2: The different cell types of the retina (from [4]).

2.2 The Visual System

The visual system consists of several partly independent subsystems not only for visual perception, but also for the coordination of movements and the circadian rhythm. The emanating information from the eye in form of light impulses is not sufficient to determine the meaning of objects. Hence, visual stimuli must be coded by the brain and be included in the synchronous activity of different brain areas. Such a synchronised and spatially distributed information processing is the prerequisite for perception. In the following sections, these processes are described in more detail.

From the Eyes to the Lateral Geniculate Nucleus

The axons of the ganglion cells of each eye form the optical nerve, which represent the whole visual field of each eye. In the *optic chiasm*, axons of the nasal retina cross to the contralateral hemisphere (i.e., on the other side), whereas axons from the temporal retina project to the ipsilateral hemisphere (i.e., on the same side) (see Figure 2.3). This crossing is necessary for spatial vision because it allows the fusion of corresponding retina images of the eyes.

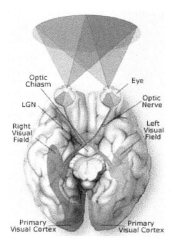

Figure 2.3: Visual pathway (adapted from [10]).

Approximately 10% of the optic nerve fibres branch to the *colliculus superior*, whereas 90% reach the *thalamus*, mostly the lateral geniculate nucleus (LGN). The LGN is a bean-shaped structure within the thalamus, divided into six layers. Each layer gets its input from one eye, i.e., layers 2, 3 and 5 from the *ipsilateral* eye, and layers 1, 4 and 6 from the *contralateral* eye. The P_{alpha} ganglion cells in the retina project to (large magnocellular or M) cells in layer 1 and 2, whereas the P_{beta} ganglion cells project to small (parvocellular or P) cells in layer 3, 4, 5 and 6 of the LGN. The interaction between the different layers of the LGN is small. P cells have relatively small receptive fields, reacting to light stimuli with long latencies (i.e., static stimuli, colour, shape, texture and depth), whereas M cells consist of cells with relatively large receptive fields with short latencies and therefore respond to rapidly alternating stimuli (i.e., movements and shape). The P and M layers show functional distinctions, for example in the wavelength and contrast sensitivity. Another cell type in the LGN is the *coniocellular* cell, which responds to colour and to the direction and orientation of stimuli. Ganglion fibres entering the LGN via the optic nerve represent only 10-20% of the incoming axons; the majority are back projections from the visual field or afferent nerves from the brain stem, which influence directly the incoming information from the retina. Synchronous stimulation of the LGN and the visual cortex can lead to a preferred selective processing of image details in the brain. Local contrast, signals from the other retina, stereopsis, eye movements and visual attention can modulate the transmission of the signals from the retina to the LGN and therefore influence cognition.

2.2.1   Visual Cortex

From the LGN the information is transmitted to the *visual cortex*, which is a part of the cerebral cortex. The visual cortex is responsible for higher level visual processing. It is probably divided into as many as thirty interconnected visual areas. The information from the LGN enters the visual cortex in layer V1, also called *striate cortex, primary visual cortex* or *area 17*, the largest and most important visual cortex area. Other areas of the visual cortex are referred to as extrastriate visual cortex, including areas V2, V3, V4 and MT (or V5). From V1 the information is transmitted via two primary pathways:

- **Ventral stream** (also called "What Pathway"): Begins with V1, goes through V2, then through area V4 and to the *inferior temporal lobe*. It is associated with form recognition, object representation and storage of long-term memory.

- **Dorsal stream** (also called "Where or How Pathway"): Starts at V1, goes through V2, V3, MT and finally to the *inferior parietal lobule*. It is associated with motion, representation of object locations, and control of eye and arm movements.

2.3   Selective Visual Attention

Although the human brain possesses a massively parallel architecture, the selection of "interesting" objects by the sensory system for further processing (e.g., planning and awareness) employs a serial computational strategy. Therefore, instead of processing the whole sensory input in parallel, a serial strategy has evolved, that achieves near real-time performance despite limited computational capacity. Attention has to be rapidly directed towards relevant objects in the visual environment to understand the whole visual scene through a combination of computationally less demanding, localised visual analysis problems. Participants selectively direct attention to relevant scene objects using both bottom-up, image-based saliency cues and top-down, task-dependent cues (Itti & Koch, 2001). Evidence for the former one results from the observation that attention can be either automatically and involuntarily directed towards salient or intrinsically conspicuous objects (e.g., flickering light). This suggests that saliency is computed in a pre-attentive manner across the entire visual field. Top-down, task-dependent processes are controlled by a selection criterion, depending on the particular task at hand (e.g., "look for a red sweatshirt"). They are controlled from higher brain areas, including the frontal lobes, connecting back into visual cortex and early visual areas.

2.4 The Indispensability of Eye Movements

As stated above, the rods and cones are not evenly distributed over the retina. The cones are most densely packed in the fovea which has a radius of approximately 1.5 degrees of visual angle (see Figure 2.1). Outside the fovea, the density of cones decrease exponentially with growing eccentricity, leading to coarse vision in the peripheral field. Because of the limited size of the fovea, only a small area of an image can be sharply analysed during each fixation. In order to explore the whole scene, the eyes have to move so that different regions fall into the foveal field. Through eye movements, humans can control the duration and the temporal and spatial order of fixations and thus, which image regions fall into the foveal field. When perceiving static objects, horizontal and vertical eye movements are smaller than one minute of arc.

2.4.1 Neural Control Mechanisms for Eye Movements

The eyes are controlled by six extraocular muscles, which act as three agonist/antagonist pairs. Each pair rotates the eye in different directions: Horizontal, vertical and torsional (i.e., around the line of sight) (see Figure 2.4).

The eye muscles are controlled by three cranial nerves. In human anatomy there are 12 pairs of cranial nerves, abbreviated by Roman numerals according to where their nuclei lie in the brain stem (see Figure 2.5). The motor (cranial) nerves controlling the eye muscles are:

(1) *Oculomotor nerve* (III): It innervates the superior and inferior recti, the medial rectus and the inferior oblique. It also controls the pupil. Therefore, its major functions are eyelid and eyeball movements.

(2) *Trochlear nerve* (IV): It only controls the superior oblique muscle, which rotates the eye away from the nose and also moves the eye downward.

(3) *Abducens nerve* (VI): It is a motor nerve that innervates the lateral rectus and therefore controls each eye's ability to abduct (i.e., move away from the nose).

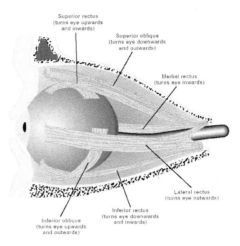

Figure 2.4: The six muscles that control eye movements (adopted from Faller, 1995).

The oculomotor and trochlear nerves originate from the midbrain, the abducens from the pons (a band of nerve fibers on the ventral surface of the brain stem).

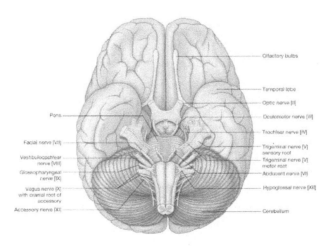

Figure 2.5: The cranial nerves (adopted from [15]).

Saccadic eye movements require to control the direction (which way to go) and the amplitude (how far to go). The amplitude is controlled by the activity of lower motor neurons within the three oculomotor nuclei. The direction of a saccade (depending on which eye muscles are activated) is controlled by the activity of premotor neurons within two separate gaze centres in the brain stem, the *paramedian pontine reticular formation* (PPRF) (horizontal gaze centre) and the *medial longitudinal fasciculus* (MLF) (vertical gaze centre) (see Figure 2.6).

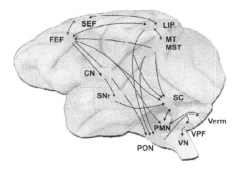

Figure 2.6: Pathways for pursuit and saccadic eye movements. FEF = frontal eye field, SC = superior colliculus, PMN = brain stem premotor nuclei (including PPRF and MLF), SNr = substantia nigra pars reticulate (from [16]).

For example, to execute a saccade to the right, the premotor neurons in the right PPRF increase the activity of the lower motor neurons in the right abducens nucleus (to turn the right eye outward), whereas the lower motor neurons in the oculomotor nucleus are innervated (to innervate the medial rectus of the left eye to move it inward). The superior colliculus, located on the roof of the midbrain, provides the motor commands to the PPRF and MLF, to move the eyes to an intended new position for the foveation of a visual stimulus. The activity of the superior colliculus on the other hand is shaped by inputs from higher *saccadic centres*, i.e., *the frontal eye fields*, the *posterior parietal cortex*, and the *substantia nigra pars reticulate* (see Figure 2.6). Recent research shows that other eye movements like smooth pursuit or vestibulo-ocular reflex eye movements (see Section 3.1), have similar functional architecture and involve many of the same brain regions (Krauzlis, 2005). Attention, fatigue, interest, or anxiety have an influence on the accuracy of the eye movements. More detailed information on the oculomotor system can be found in Purves et al. (2004).

Before describing in Chapter 3 how the eye movements can be measured, the subject of the following section are the higher visual processes for colour, shape, texture and object perception.

2.5   Colour Perception

Colour is an outstanding visual feature of objects. It is immediately perceived when looking at an image. We can distinguish about 2000000 different colours, i.e., 200 hues with
500 brightness and 20 saturation values each (Gouras, 1991). Humans are able to perceive the same colour even under changing illumination conditions (*colour constancy*).
Even though a black and white image, for example of a flower, contains all fine structures
and object boundaries, it is still very difficult to distinguish the petals from the leaves.
When colour information is added, petals and leaves can immediately be distinguished
(Gegenfurtner & Kiper, 2003). Recent psychophysical experiments have shown that colour
information helps to recognise objects faster and to remember them better (Gegenfurtner
& Rieger, 2000, Wichmann, Sharpe & Gegenfurtner, 2002). Newton discovered in 1704
that white light is split up in its spectral colours when passing a prism, showing that single
spectrum colours have different wave lengths. There are three types of cones in the human
retina: One pigment that is primarily sensitive to short wave lengths (blue). Another one
that is selective to middle wave lengths (green), and a third one that is primarily sensitive to long wave lengths (red). According to the *trichromatic theory of colour vision*,
light of different wave length leads to different activation patterns of the three cone types,
i.e., each wave length is encoded by a particular activation state of the three receptors
(Helmholtz, 1852). If light falls on an object, parts of the light are absorbed, whereas the
rest is reflected. The wave lengths of the reflected light determines the perceived colour,
e.g., yellow objects reflect light of long and medium wave lengths. Some phenomena however, cannot be explained by the trichromatic colour theory. For example that particular
colours cannot be perceived in combination, e.g., greenish-red (*colour opponency*), or that
a grey area appears yellow when it is surrounded by a blue area (*simultaneous colour
contrast*). Hering (1878) explained these phenomena with his *colour opponency theory*,
postulating three antagonistic colour pairs (black - white, red - green and blue - yellow).
This coincides with electrophysiological (Lee, Martin & Valberg, 1988) and psychophysical
(Krauskopf, Williams & Heely, 1982) experiments, showing that from the retina on, information about colour and light intensity is sorted into three "channels". These channels
consist of axon pathways from retinal ganglion cells to the brain. Two of these channels
carry colour or wavelength information, and one carries intensity information, i.e., the
degree of blackness or whiteness. Further support for the colour opponency theory results
from the detection of *concentric broadband* and *colour-opponent cells* in the retina and
the LGN. Concentric broadband cells have a concentric centre-surround receptive field
organisation (see Figure 2.7). Those cells respond to a contrast in brightness within their
receptive field but they are not involved in the perception of colour. Colour information
is transmitted by colour-opponent cells.

Concentric single-opponent cells (see Figure 2.10) have an antagonistic centre-surround
receptive field, where the antagonism in most cases is between the red and green cones.
The centre receives either input from the red or from the green cones, whereas the (antagonistic) surround receives input from the other cones. They transmit information about

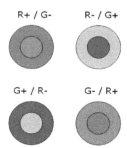

R+ / G-   R- / G+

G+ / R-   G- / R+

Figure 2.7: Concentric broadband cells (achromatic) (adapted from [6]).

both colour and brightness contrast, because the centre and surround are activated by different cone mechanisms. The signals from the blue cones are transferred to the *co-extensive single-opponent cells*, a distinct class of simple-opponent cells that have an undifferentiated receptive field (no centre-surround receptive field organisation) in which the action of blue cones is opposed to the combined action of green and red cones (see Figure 2.8).

The retinal ganglion cells involved in colour perception can either be classified as magnocellular or parvocellular, depending on which layer they project in the LGN (see Section 2.2). The concentric broad-band cells can either be of M or P type, whereas single-opponent cells are exclusively P type. Therefore, the parvocellular layers of the LGN relay colour and additionally some achromatic contrast information to the cortex, whereas the magnocellular layers transmit achromatic information.

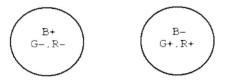

B+
G- , R-

B-
G+ , R+

Figure 2.8: Co-extensive single-opponent cells (from Kandel, Schwartz & Jessell, 1995, p. 467).

The signals from the single-opponent cells in the LGN accumulate on *concentric double-opponent cells* in the cortex, which also have an antagonistic centre-surround receptive field (see Figure 2.9). In contrast to the single-opponent cells in the retina and the LGN, each cone type operates in all parts of the receptive field but has different actions in either the centre or the surround. There are four classes of concentric double-opponent cells: Those that respond best to a red spot in a green background and vice versa, and those that respond to a blue spot in a yellow background and vice versa. The concentric double-opponent cells are mainly located in blobs of area V1 of the visual cortex (see Figure 2.12). The cells in each blob have round receptive fields (see Figure 2.9), so that they react only to colour but not to orientation, movement and shape, whereas cells in the large interblob areas (see Figure 2.12) are selective for orientation (which is in line with the parallel processing of colour and orientation). The opponent cells in the blobs are also organised in columns, i.e., in a particular column there are only blue-yellow or red-green neurons. The behaviour of the concentric double-opponent cells could be the neural basis for the psychological phenomenon of colour opponency and simultaneous colour contrast. From V1 the colour information is projected to thin stripes in the higher areas V2 and then to V4, an area with colour-selective cells.

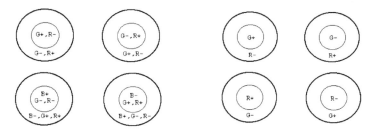

Figure 2.9: *Concentric double-opponent cells (cortex) (from Kandel, Schwartz & Jessell, 1995, p. 460-461).*

Figure 2.10: *Concentric single-opponent cells (retina and LGN) (adapted from [6]).*

Zeki (1993) discovered a neural substrate for the colour constancy in V4. This area contains many neurons responding to a particular colour of the object that is being viewed, but not to changes in the wave length composition of the illuminating light. The output of these cells is probably used by higher centres of the brain to form the colour perception of objects. A qualitative method to predict the perceived colour of objects from the receptor answers of the red, green and blue cones, is the *retinex-method* by Land (1977). The algorithm works as follows: The brightness of each object in the scene is measured for each cone. Then, for each cone type, the brightness values for each object are normalised by the brightest object in the scene. From these numbers, the colours of all objects can then be estimated. The predicted colour impressions of the retinex-method are consistent with the human colour perception. Additionally, the retinex-method correctly predicts that the perceived colour remains roughly constant as lighting conditions change, whereas the perceived colour of an object can change with appropriate changes in its background.

Colour perception is probably more complicated than illustrated by the retinex-method. Inputs from different cone types already converge at a very early stage of processing in the retina. Hence, the individual information of single cone types is not available in the cortex. Land (1977) showed that the retinex-method also works if the reactions of the three classes of opponent cells are used as a measure for the red-green, blue-yellow and black-white brightness of objects. From these values, the perceived colour of the object can be predicted. This could be an explanation of how the output signals of the different classes of double-opponent cells are processed in the cortex to determine colour information.

2.6 Shape Perception

The primary visual cortex consists of different layers (see Figure 2.12). Most M cells from the LGN, concerned with the detection of movements, project to the sublayer $IVC\alpha$. The axons of most P cells form two groups: One group terminates in layer 2 and 3, where they innervate cells of the so called blobs (see Figure 2.12). These cells are concerned with colour perception. The other group of P cells from the LGN accumulate on spiny stellate cells in sublayer $IVC\beta$ of the primary visual cortex, which have circular receptive fields (see Figure 2.11). These cells react on simple stimuli (e.g., small spots of light), whereas the other cells above and below area IVC respond to more complex stimuli, like corners and bars. Those cells are classified as simple or complex, based on their response to linear stimuli. Simple cells, which are pyramidal cells located close to input layer $IVC\beta$, are bigger than spiny stellate cells, and have an elongated and rectilinear shape. Their receptive fields are split up into excitatory and inhibitory parts (see Figure 2.11). Simple cells react most strongly on stripes of light of a particular orientation that falls only on the excitatory region and do not extend into the inhibitory region. Therefore, each simple cell reacts on stimuli in an orientation range of approximately 10°. Stepwise rotation of a stimuli up to 180° activates sequentially cells having receptive fields of slightly different orientation: Vertical, diagonal, or horizontal. Simple cells receive their input from the spiny stellate cells and converge on complex cells.

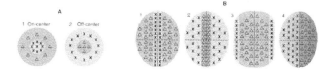

Figure 2.11: Receptive fields (x, excitatory; △, inhibitory) of concentric cells (in the retina and LGN) and stellate cells in the central cortex (A). Receptive fields of simple cells in the cortex (B) (Kandel, Schwartz & Jessell, 1995, p. 441).

Complex cells are also pyramid cells, but they are mainly located in layer II, III, V and VI (see Figure 2.12). They also have linear receptive fields of a particular orientation, but compared to the simple cells, their receptive fields are larger and they do not have clearly defined on and off zones. The exact location of the stimuli within their receptive field is not of that high importance. Complex cells react to movements in a particular direction across the receptive field. The large receptive field of complex cells and therefore their response to orientation over a range of retinal positions, may be the neural mechanism for *positional invariance*, i.e., the ability to recognise the same features within the whole visual field.

All in all, simple and complex cells do not respond to small spots, but best to linear stimuli with particular orientations. They may be important for the perception of object contours, contrast and borders, but not to the interior or background of objects.

The response of simple and complex cells are positively correlated with the length of a bar of light falling on the excitatory zone of the receptive field, until the excitatory zone is fully covered. Some simple and complex cells are *end-stopped*, i.e., their firing frequency increases only up to a certain stimulus length. From there it decreases until there is no response at all. The inhibitory regions are either at one (*single end-stopped cells*) or at both sides (*double end-stopped cells*) of the central activating region. The former ones react optimally on abruptly ending lines, extending along the orientation axis of the receptive field, whereas the later react most strongly on short lines or gradually curved borders. End-stopped cells measure the length of a line and can therefore signal corners, curvatures or sudden breaks in a line. For these cells, not only the orientation but also the length of a line are important.

The longer the distance to the retina, the more specific impulses are necessary to activate the neurons: In the retina and the LGN, only the position of the stimulus in the receptive field is important, whereas for the simple cells in the visual cortex the stimulus must have a precise position and orientation. For complex cells in the visual cortex, the orientation but not the exact position of the stimulus is important, because their receptive fields are larger. Different populations of simple and complex cells in the visual cortex also receive input from the magnocellular and parvocellular pathway, probably contributing to a first 2D estimation of the stimulus shape (primal sketch, see Section 2.8.5).

The visual cortex is modular organised into *hypercolumns* or *arrays* that represent the entire visual field (see Figure 2.12). Each array, which represents one point on the retina, consists of a right and left ocular dominance column, a complete set of orientation columns (representing 360°) and several blobs for colour information processing. Corresponding to the layered organisation of the visual cortex, the hypercolumn consists of six layers. The single arrays communicate with each other via horizontal connections between cells within a single layer, so that information over a cortex area of several milimeters can be integrated.

But how can complex shapes be identified? There are at least 32 other representations of the retina in the extrastriate regions outside of the primary visual cortex. The information processing for the shape perception takes place in the parvocellular-interblob system, extending from the parvocellular layers of the LGN, via V1 and V2 to V4. From area V4, which includes neurons that are sensitive to form and colour, the parvocellular-interblob system projects to the *inferior temporal cortex*, which is most concerned with the "what" of a visual scene. The receptive field of the cells in the inferior temporal cortex are large ($25^o \times 25^o$). They are not retinotopically organised and cover both visual hemifields.

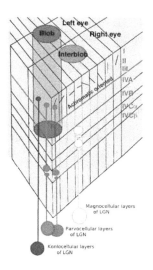

Figure 2.12: Hypercolumns of the visual cortex. Layers V and VI are not depicted (adapted from [17]).

Around 10% of these cells respond selectively on particular images, like hands or faces. Some face sensitive cells react on frontal views of faces, others more on side views, whereas still others react selectively on facial expressions. The temporal lobe also stores prototypes of different objects in order to recognise them independently from illumination, orientation and size.

2.7 Texture Perception

In natural scenes there are boundaries between different regions (e.g., sky and trees or grass). The regions differ clearly in luminance which can be detected by simple cells in the visual cortex (see Section 2.5). A change in chromaticity occurs between zebras and background (although not visible in the black and white image (see Figure 2.13)) which might be signaled by colour-opponent mechanisms. On the other hand, there is no such difference in colour or luminance between different texture regions (e.g., a pair of zebras). Humans can easily identify the borders of different texture regions. Apparently, regions are separated on the basis of local texture properties like "vertical-" and "horizontal"-ness (see Figure 2.13). Texture information can be used by the visual system during early processing stages to segment the image into separate regions for better processing in subsequent stages, and for labelling, e.g., as "looks like wood" or as "looks slippery". Hence, texture is a property of "stuff" in the images in contrast to visual features (like lines and edges), the "things" in the image (Adelson & Bergen, 1991). With the help of the region boundaries, a scene can be segmented into different 2D objects or, in case of continuous changes in texture properties, into 3D objects (Gibson, 1950).

The neurons in the cortical area V1 are selective with respect to spatial frequency and orientation and therefore serve as the first-level linear filters in texture segregation. There are also excitatory and inhibitory lateral interactions between cells in V1, which enhance responses to popout stimuli (Kastner, Nothdurft & Pigarev, 1999; Nothdurft, Gallant & Van Essen, 1999), to texture elements near texture borders (Nothdurft, Gallant & Van Essen, 2000), to orientation contrast (Sillito, Grieve, Jones, Cudeiro & Davis, 1995) and to figures (but not to ground) (Lamme, 1995). Recent research (Lennie, 1998) shows that higher areas like V2 through V4 are involved in popout and figure ground segregation, and hence, the responses in V1 are only the initial level of texture segregation. Therefore, probably not before V4, similar structures are grouped to find contours, regions and surfaces, whereas the conscious perception of texture properties are predominantly determined in even higher cortical regions. These presumptions were recently substantiated by an fMRI *(functional magnetic resonance imaging)* study by Kastner, deWeerd and Ungerleider (2000), who detected only low responses to texture borders in V1 or V2, but higher responses in V3 and V4. Altogether, higher level computations that involve texture, such as figure-ground calculations, coding of texture appearance or determination of depth and 3D shape from texture cues require more thorough analysis.

Figure 2.13: *Group of zebras (adapted from [17]).*

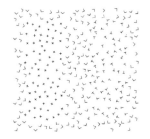

Figure 2.14: *Texture segregation (adapted from Landy & Graham, 2004).*

A typical image used to study texture perception is shown in Figure 2.14. While the X's can be easily detected as a rectangular region, standing out against the background, the T's must be checked individually. Pre-attentive segregation means segmentation of the image based on the distribution of simple properties of "texture elements" like brightness, colour, size, slope of contours or other elemental descriptors of a texture (Beck, 1972; 1973; Olson & Attneave, 1970), as well as contour terminations (Marr, 1976). Jules (1981) identified some image features to explain segregation performance. These features, named "textons", include size, orientation, line terminations and line crossings. Beck (1982) found that texture segregation does not only depend on the texture elements used, but also on their arrangement. Joseph, Chun and Nakayama (1997) found that effortless texture segregation requires selective visual attention. Alternatively, attention may only alter visual mechanisms responsible for texture segregation. Thus, texture segregation would not require selective visual attention (Yeshurun & Carrasco, 2000). However, the processing of some textures takes substantial time, showing that pre-attentive texture segregation is not always immediate and effortless (Sutter & Graham, 1995).

2.8   Object Perception

Humans can reliably classify a large number of objects just by looking at them. This classification performance is remarkable, since object representations differ with respect to perspectives, lighting conditions, distance and angle. Even though recognition may be innate to some extent (e.g., Goren, Sarty and Wu (1975) showed that human neonates' gaze follows face-like patterns), the correct classification of objects is achieved by a learning process. Although object recognition seems to be easy for humans, it is an intricate process which comprises diverse subprocesses. This becomes clear when we try to teach computers to recognise objects. Even after many years of research, computers can only recognise objects with simple contours. Object recognition is difficult because lines intersecting in a point can belong to different objects and objects can be partly occluded. A comparison between human and computer perception of objects shows that humans clearly outperform computers, even though both use the same amount of information (a 2D depiction of a scene in memory or on the retina, respectively) (Goldstein, 1996).

In the following, some models for human object recognition are shortly described. More information can be found in Barrow and Tannenbaum (1986).

2.8.1   Template Matching

Early models of object recognition focused on alphanumeric patterns. The simplest model is *template matching*: Each known numeral or letter is represented in long-term memory by a template. The perceived pattern is compared with each template and classified as the numeral or letter with the highest overlap. Slight changes in pattern size or angle can be compensated by initial standardisation and normalisation. One of the preliminaries of template matching is that single patterns are unambiguous. This makes template matching inapplicable to natural object recognition, where objects are more complicated and more variable. The comparison between the letters "O" and "Q" shows that there are some *critical* features which can be used to distinguish both letters, e.g., the position and orientation of the bar, whereas others, like the precise form of the circle, are less crucial.

A classical model using critical features for letter classification is the *Pandemonium system* (Lindsay & Norman, 1972). It consists of two classes of *demons*: *Feature demons* respond selectively to particular local configurations (e.g., vertical lines, right angles, etc.), while *cognitive demons* represent particular letters. The cognitive demon for the letter "H", for example, reacts when the feature demons for vertical (twice) and horizontal lines (once) and right angles (four times) are activated. The Pandemonium system can learn by increasing the weight for highly discriminating features. Even though the Pandemonium system seems at first glance to be consistent with the neuropsychological processes in the visual cortex, it is not consistent with human perception, since it fails to capture overall structural relationships (e.g., mirrored letters) and cannot distinguish different instances of the same object.

2.8.2   Gestalt Laws

In the late 20's of the 20th century Gestalt psychologists around Wertheimer, Koffka and Köhler proposed a general framework for object perception. The so called Gestalt laws are a set of rules which describe how we perceive objects as well-organised patterns rather than as separate component parts. The most important Gestalt laws proposed are (see Figure 2.15):

- **Law of Simplicity**: Items will be organised into simple figures according to symmetry, regularity and smoothness.

- **Law of Similarity**: Items similar in some respect tend to be grouped.

- **Law of Proximity**: Elements tend to be grouped according to their spatial contiguity.

- **Law of Closure**: Items are grouped together if they tend to complete some entity.

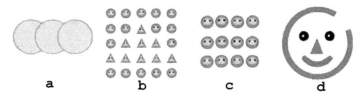

Figure 2.15: Classical illustrations for the Gestalt laws: (a) Simplicity, (b) similarity, (c) proximity, (d) closure.

Other Gestalt laws are: Law of good continuation, common fade and meaningfulness of the forms. See Boring (1942) for a list of further Gestalt laws.

Perception does not only involve organisation and grouping, but also the distinction of an object from its surrounding. Once an object is perceived, the area around that object becomes the background. Gestaltists found that symmetrical and convex areas, vertical and horizontal orientations and significant objects are more likely perceived as figures.

Even though the Gestalt laws still play a significant role for sensation and perception, they are more descriptive than predictive. They seem to work only on simple examples, and they are vaguely formulated. Hence, more recent accounts conceive of perception as a sequence of cognitive operations.

2.8.3   Object Perception as a Construction Process

Object perception as a construction process describes object perception as a multi-level process, performed by the cognitive system. The *feature integration theory* of attention, one of the most influential psychological models of human visual attention, was developed by Treisman and Gelade since the early 1980s (Treisman & Gelade, 1980). This model provides a schematic description of the different phases and steps of visual processing. In the first step of visual processing, the "pre-attentive level", several primary visual features are automatically processed in parallel and represented with separate *feature maps*. Primitive features include colour, orientation, intensity, size and distance. The single feature maps can be integrated in a *saliency map* in the second step, which can be used to direct attention to the most conspicuous areas. A 3D object is perceived in the third level. In the fourth level, the perceived object is compared with a representation stored in the memory. In case of a match, the object is identified in level five. The independent existence of primitives in the first level is consistent with the separate channels for colour, shape and movement processing and the arrangement of the hypercolumns in the visual cortex (see Section 2.6). The combination of the primitives in the second phase is in accordance with the temporal and parietal path for information processing (see also Section 2.2.1). According to Treisman (1993), attention is the "glue" which links the "where" (James, 1981) and "what" (von Helmholtz, 1925) information of both pathways. Treisman distinguished between *feature* and *conjunction search*. The former enables us to detect fast and pre-attentively target objects defined by primitive features, resulting in parallel search (see Figure 2.16). The latter on the other side requires attention to detect target objects, defined by a conjunction of primitive features, resulting in a slow sequential search (see Figure 2.17). In conjunctive search, the reaction time increases linearly with the number of elements in the image. Several years later the assumption of autonomous serial and parallel search processes, as stated by the feature integration theory, was questioned (Wolfe, Cave & Franzel, 1989). This led to the development of the *guided search model*. According to this model, image areas that are likely to contain the target object are determined by an initial parallel process. The information from the parallel process is then accessible for the following subsequent serial search process.

2.8.4   Spatial Frequency Theory

Another possible account of object perception is based on the analysis of spatial frequency in the visual system. According to this theory, the visual system divides a scene into spatial frequency constituents and reassembles them for perception. Simple cells in the cortex are sensitive to particular spatial frequencies (Maffei & Fiorentini, 1973). In a process, similar to Fourier synthesis, the different spatial frequencies are combined, resulting in a perception of the scene (Campbell & Robson, 1968). To date, it is neither clear if the spatial frequency analysis is essential for object perception, nor how information about spatial frequency is actually utilised by the visual system. Yet, the spatial frequency theory is important, because it suggests that the visual system's response to any pattern can be

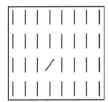

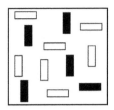

Figure 2.16: *Feature search allows parallel processing ("Pop-out effect") (adapted from [19]).*

Figure 2.17: *Conjunctive search requires serial processing (to find the horizontal black bar)(adapted from [19]).*

predicted from its response to more basic components and that the simple cells of the visual cortex perform a linear spatial integration within their receptive fields.

2.8.5 Marr's Algorithmic Approach to Object Perception

Interest in spatial frequency was further stimulated by *Marr's algorithmic approach to object perception* (Marr, 1982). Marr described vision as proceeding from a two-dimensional visual array (on the retina) to a three-dimensional description of the world. In the first phase, the visual system identifies the edges and corners of the objects by taking into account the intensity changes that occur in the real world (e.g., intensity changes that gradually or abruptly occur at the boundaries between light and shadow). It also identifies a number of primitives like blobs, contour- and edge-elements and stripes. A primal sketch is formed from the primitives and object corners. From the primal sketch a 2 1/2D sketch results by grouping the primitives according to Gestalt laws (see Section 2.8.2), thus representing the object areas and their arrangement. The 2 1/2D sketch is finally transformed into a 3D representation. Marr's system can be viewed as a computer program, which includes physical attributes in its calculation. The input are the features of the retinal images, especially the patterns of bright and dark image areas.

Marr's account is analogue to the feature integration theory (see Section 2.8.3) as far as it explains object perception as a cascaded process. The difference is that in Marr's account the resulting representation on each level is mathematically processed. Additionally, Marr's algorithmic approach deals more with naturalistic scenes, including shades and other peculiarities, making the object identification more complicated.

After describing the higher visual processes of feature and object perception, the next chapter explains how eye movements can be recorded and the eye movements occurring during scene perception.

Chapter 3

Eye Movements, Eye Tracking and Applied Software

3.1 Eye Movements

As mentioned in Section 2.4.1, the eyes can be moved in different directions (horizontal, vertical and torsional) by six extraocular muscles. These movements can reach velocities up to 600° per second (Hallett, 1986) allowing to direct the eyes precisely and systematically in a quick succession to the regions that contain objects demanding the most consideration at that point in time. These regions are important for image retrieval, because participants subsequently focus them in order to estimate the similarity between image pairs. Before it is explained in Chapter 4 how eye movements can be used to improve image retrieval, this chapter introduces the most important types of eye movements and how they can be measured and recorded.

3.1.1 Conjunctive Movements

During conjunctive movements, both eyes move in parallel and hence the angle between them remains relatively constant. They occur during the inspection of static images or when following moving objects. Let us consider the most important types of conjunctive movements in the following.

Fixations

During a fixation the eye remains directed at the same spot for a longer period (around 150-600 ms), enabling the processing of the information from the fixated region. Approximately 90% of the viewing time is spent on fixations (Irwin, 1992). Visual information can be processed only during fixations. For a clear composite view of a larger portion of the visual field, the brain combines the information from several fixations. A fixation can be disrupted at all times by the visual system.

Saccades

Because only the fovea allows clear vision, the eye has to be moved so that different parts of the scene can be processed in sequence (see Section 2.4). These movements are called *saccades*. Saccades are jerky eye movements from one fixation to another. During saccades the pupil is accelerated up to $6,000^o/s^2$, and an angle velocity of more than 300° per second is reached. Once set off (motor programming latencies up to 200 ms have been reported), saccades cannot be altered by the visual system. During a saccade no visual information is processed. A normal sighted person executes 2-3 saccades per second. The velocity and the duration (range from 10-100 ms) of saccades depends on its amplitude (Rötting, 2001). There are small and large saccades. Small saccades control the position of the eye within the central area of the retina having the highest distinction. The larger saccades show higher inaccuracies.

Smooth Pursuit Movements

Smooth pursuit eye movements occur with dynamic scenes only, when an object, moving over a static or moving background, is followed with the eyes. Their purpose is to stabilise the objects' image on the fovea, for example a tennis ball during a tennis match. The velocity of smooth pursuit movements is between $25 - 40^o/s$ (Boff & Lincoln, 1988; Young, 1971). In case of fast moving objects, often additional saccadic movements are executed, because smooth pursuit movements are not sufficient to keep the object in focus (Yamada & Fukuda, 1986).

Micro Movements of the Eyes

The photoreceptive cells of the eyes react primary to light changes. If the eyes are not moved, the activation of the photoreceptive cells decrease slowly. *Drift* and *tremor* move the image on the retina by several receptors, so that the photoreceptive cells are provided with new stimulation. *Microsaccades* compensate the displacements caused by drift and tremor, leading to a re-fixation of the focussed object (Rötting, 2001), but they can also occur at random (Thoden, 1978).

3.1.2   Disjunctive Movements

Disjunctive movements describe eye movements, where both eyes move in different directions and hence the angle between the two eyes changes. They occur during the perception of 3D-scenes and are called *vergence* movements.

Vergence Movements

When the gaze point is moved from a distant to a close object, the eyes move inward (*convergence*), whereas the eyes move outward (*divergence*), when the fixation point is shifted from a close to a distant location. It was shown in Essig, Ritter and Pomplun (2004) that convergent movements are faster than divergent movements. Vergence movements are slow $(4 - 20^o/s)$ and can be altered by the visual system during execution (Schor & Ciuffreda, 1983).

3.1.3 The Eye-Mind Hypothesis

Being familiar with the basic eye movements, a central question arises: How can our eyes serve as indicators for mental processes during scene perception? As stated above, fixations and saccades are applied to explore the content of visual scenes. If the eyes can be seen as an indicator for the brain's performance ("eyes are a window to the mind"), the *fixation duration* can be considered as a measure of the effort of information processing. The longer the visual attention is directed toward an object location, the longer it presumably takes us to deal with the information presented at that particular area of the scene. This relationship, coined the "eye-mind" hypothesis, has been strongly supported by results from reading experiments (Just & Carpenter, 1987). In these experiments, participants' fixation duration during text reading correlates with the length of the currently fixated word and it's occurrence frequency in the relevant language. The semantic and syntactic analysis of a word is performed during the fixation, because the fixation duration is *not* influenced by the previously read word. It is plausible to assume that the "eye-mind" hypothesis is valid for other stimuli as well, e.g., scenes.

Furthermore, the *number of fixations* and the *distribution of fixations* reflect the degree of cognitive processing, required for the understanding of particular scene regions. Long *fixation durations* and short *saccade lengths* signify a fine and deep processing of a particular image region, indicating that the understanding of its visual information is quite difficult. In contrast, long saccade lengths and short fixation durations indicate a fast and coarse scanning of a particular image region, signalling that the information content of that particular image region is easy to process or less important for the current task.

In summary, eye movements yield insight into the locations and temporal order of visual information processing, allowing conclusions about the underlying mental processing. A classical problem in eye tracking studies concerns the relationship between visual attention and eye movements. Humans are able to dissociate their attention from the foveal direction of gaze (Duchowski, 2003). Astronomers, for example, use parafoveal vision to detect faint stars, because that area of the retina is much more sensitive to dim stimuli. By observing the "overt" eye movements, those "covert" shifts of visual attention cannot be monitored. By a careful experimental design, the experimenter has to make sure that participants' gaze position and attention are correlated.

After discussing the different types of eye movements and the motivation and validation of their role as indicators for mental processes, the following section describes the eye movements occurring during the perception of natural scenes.

3.2 Eye Movements During the Perception of Natural Scenes

Real-world or *natural* scenes are different from the stimulus images that are normally used for experiments in visual perception. This does not only concern physical aspects, like different wave lengths, intensities and spatial frequency regularities, but also semantic and syntactic constraints resulting from objects and surfaces inherent in *real-world* scenes. The complexity of such materials makes the analysis of eye movements during scene perception much more complicated than studies with artificial images. In order to reduce the amount of information generally available to the visual system, scene perception studies use *scene depictions* (like line drawings, computer rendered images and photographs) as substitutes for real-world scenes. They allow simultaneously to capture the most important properties of real-world objects and to control factors that would be impossible to hold constant in real-world scenarios. Since scene depictions are a simplification of real-world scenes, eye movements might be different from those occurring in everyday life. The following sections will provide more insights into the main questions with regard to scene viewing: To which extend in the periphery can objects be identified (*functional field of view*)? Which factors control the location of the next fixation? At first, however, the term "scene" has to be defined.

3.2.1 Definition and Perception of a Scene

A scene is defined as a semantically coherent (and often nameable) human-scaled view of a real-world environment, comprising background elements and multiple discrete objects that are spatially organised in a meaningful way relative to each other and relative to the background elements (Henderson & Hollingworth, 1999a). Background elements are large-scale, immovable surfaces and structures, such as walls and mountains, whereas objects are smaller-scaled discrete entities which usually can move within the scene (like animals and furniture). The classification as either background or object depends on the spatial scale, which in turn depends on the actual vantage point. Humans are embedded in their environments with scenes that are specific views of this environment. The objects in a scene have to obey physical constraints, e.g., houses cannot fly (at that, sometimes a broader knowledge about objects is necessary to judge if constraints are violated or not, e.g., for transparent objects). Because of the retina's structure (see Section 2.1), single objects that need detailed analysis are focussed foveally, whereas scenes, requiring information integration over a larger spatial scale, are analysed peripherally. Therefore, different cortical recognition areas are responsible for the analysis of objects and scenes, presumably resulting in different processing systems (Levy, Hasson, Avidan, Hendler & Malach, 2001; Malach, Levy & Hasson, 2002). These considerations are supported by fMRI (*functional magnetic resonance imaging*) studies by Epstein and Kanwisher (1998), showing activation for a distinct area of the inferior temporal cortex, called *parahippocampal place area* (PPA), when viewing natural scenes including rooms, landscapes and city streets, but not when viewing objects, faces, houses or other visual patterns not requiring information integration over a larger spatial scale. Activations do not depend on familiarity with the perceived scene, motion, or changes to constituent objects in a scene, but on changes in scene viewpoint (Epstein, Graham & Downing, 2003). Taken together, the PPA is necessary for the perception of scenes, but it is not involved in the perception of objects.

Even though the content of a scene may be quite complex, the visual system can recognise the so called *gist* quite fast. Gist is a term in visual cognition literature which stands for *general semantic interpretation*, including the identity of the scene, semantic features and some basic information about the global spatial layout. There are four empirical cues that make it plausible to assume that the scene gist can be apprehended within a single fixation:

(1) Experiments by Biederman, Mezzanotte and Rabinowitz (1982) revealed that sufficient information could be perceived from brief views to decide about the presence and consistency of a target object that has been labeled before screen onset, at a position marker that appeared at screen offset. Later experiments revealed that gist is already available within 30-50 ms of scene onset.

(2) Further evidence comes from the *rapid serial presentation technique* (RSVP), where a sequence of photographs was presented to the participants who had either to detect a pre-identified target scene (detection condition) or to decide if a given scene was present in the stream (memory condition). Scenes could be detected even at the fastest presentation rates (Potter, 1976).

(3) Eye fixations are often directed towards informative scene regions after only a single initial fixation (Loftus & Mackworth, 1978). The first saccade during a visual task is directed to a particular target. This means that enough information has been detected with the first fixation to direct further eye movements appropriately. These initial eye movements are mainly guided by the visual saliency of local scene regions rather than by global scene interpretation.

(4) Photographs can be very accurately categorised after a brief presentation time of only 20 ms (Thorpe, Fize & Marlot, 1996). The fast response times suggest that categorisation performance is not based on simple colour cues (Delorme, Richard & Fabre-Thorpe, 2000), and it is not influenced by familiarity with the images. When combining the categorisation task with a simultaneous attention-demanding task, it was found that unlike other forms of visual analysis, categorisation of natural images does not require much attention (Li, VanRullen, Koch & Perona, 2002).

It is not clear if these results generalise to complex scenes, because the stimuli, presented in the experiments described above, showed objects against a relatively uniform background and therefore, the classification were likely based on object rather than on scene features. There are several possible explanations why scene recognition is so fast:

(1) The main (*diagnostic*) object is rapidly identified (or several objects are identified in parallel). Then the scene gist can either be inferred from this object (Friedman, 1979) or a few objects and their relationships (De Graef, Christiaens & d'Ydewalle, 1990). For example, the presence of a washing machine and a basin strongly suggests a washing room.

(2) Each object consists of a set of elementary components, e.g., geons. The scene gist can be identified from these elementary components without extensive processing (Biederman, 1995).

(3) Humans can use low- and high-frequency spatial information which is available in the visual periphery (Oliva & Schyns, 1997).

(4) If colour is an important feature for the classification of the scene category, a coarse distribution of colour blobs would be sufficient (Oliva & Schyns, 2000).

(5) A holistic low-dimensional scene representation (*spatial envelope*), consisting of features like naturalness, openness, roughness, ruggedness and expansion, is calculated and can be used for scene categorisation. This information can be derived from coarsely coded spectral information in a scene image, without the need for a deep analysis of scene objects (Oliva & Torralba, 2001, 2003).

All these information can be processed quite fast, during 30-50 ms after scene onset. The analysis of extrafoveal objects and of the relationships between objects in a scene requires focussed attention. During scene viewing, the eyes move on average three times per second to a new fixation position, with fixation duration varying individually or across individuals and between depicted scenes and real world images (Henderson & Hollingworth, 1998; Rayner, 1998; Land & Hayhoe, 2002). The main questions regarding eye movements during scene viewing are: *Where* are the fixations directed to, and *how long* do they typically remain there?

3.2.2   Eye Movements During Scene Viewing

The first investigation of eye movements during scene perception was conducted by Buswell (1935). Viewers' gaze and fixation directions during the observation of 55 pictures of different types of art work were recorded. Buswell found that fixations are rather clustered on informative image regions, instead of being randomly distributed over a scene. The analysis of mean fixation durations and saccade amplitudes hinted at an important relationship between eye movements and attention: "Eye movements are unconscious adjustments to the demands of attention during a visual experience" (Buswell, 1935, p. 9).

Evidence for an early analysis of visual information in the periphery is provided by Mackworth and Morandi (1967). They subdivided two colour photographs into 64 square blocks. The "informativeness" of each square block was rated by a group of participants according to how easy that portion would be to recognise on its own. The eye movements of another group of users were recorded while examining the complete pictures and judging which of the two pictures they preferred. Square blocks rated as more informative got a higher number of fixations depending on the grade of informativeness, whereas uninformative square blocks were not fixated at all (because they were rated as uninformative by participants based on the analysis of visual periphery). In the experiment, visually simple images were used, so that participants could easily find uninformative image regions in the periphery. Antes (1974) replicated the results with a set of more complicated images. A control group rated the informativeness of image regions for comprehension in relation to the whole image content. Again, the participants of a second group fixated high rated regions more frequently than low rated ones. In addition, the first saccade away from the initial fixation position was more likely directed to informative than to uninformative regions, showing that even the placement of the first fixation is controlled by the information content of local regions. In contrast to informative regions, uninformative or empty regions of a picture are typically not fixated (see Figure 3.1), except for those regions, that had previously contained interesting objects (Altmann & Kamide, 2004).

There are four different knowledge sources that influence eye movements in scenes (Henderson & Ferreira, 2004):

(1) *Short-term episodic scene knowledge*: Specific scene knowledge at a particular time (e.g., the book was recently placed on the right of the desk). It allows the refixation of previously observed, semantically interesting or informative scene areas. It can be learned over a short time in the current perceptual encounter.

(2) *Long-term episodic scene knowledge*: Specific scene knowledge stable over time (e.g., the coffee machine is beside the sink). It is learned over a long term in multiple encounters.

(3) *Scene schema knowledge*: Generic knowledge about a particular scene category (e.g., the washing machine is in the washing room) that can be used to direct attention without the viewers' awareness (Chun, 2000). It arises across multiple episodes from *semantic-semantic* knowledge (e.g., mailboxes are found on sidewalks) and *semantic-visual knowledge* (e.g., mailboxes are found on flat surfaces), as well as knowledge about relationships within (e.g., the coexistence of a fork and a knife on a dinner table) and across spatial scale (e.g., a toaster is mostly located on a counter of a kitchen). (Henderson, McClure, Pierce & Schrock, 1997; Henderson, Weeks & Hollingworth, 1999). Furthermore, it contains also information about specific image regularities and of spatial information, such as positions of particular objects (Oliva & Torralba, 2003; Oliva, Torralba, Castelhano & Henderson, 2003).

(4) *Task knowledge*: Generic knowledge about a particular task category (e.g., we know how to move our eyes during action sequences in a driving scenario, like using mirrors when crossing lanes). Gaze control varies with complex and well-learned activities, e.g., reading or driving (Henderson, 2003).

According to the scan-path theory (Norton & Stark, 1971), a picture is encoded both by the visual features as well as the eye-movement motor sequence used to encode them. When looking at the picture at a later stage, virtually the same scan path is used by the examinees. Criticism of this theory is mainly concerned with the capacity of working memory (the recording of all scan paths would require considerable storage space), the perception of the scene gist with a single fixation (see Section 3.2.1), the variation in fixation sequences over salient regions for different participants, and the little consistency in scan patterns when subjects repeatedly view the same scene (Groner, Walder & Groner, 1984; Mannan, Ruddock & Wooding, 1997). Today, the belief is widely held that long-term storage of pictorial elements occurs independently of eye-movement motor sequences, hence meaning that only fixations provide relevant information on the processing of pictures.

Even though the scan-path theory was shown to be incorrect, there may be typical sequences in which specific salient regions in a scene are fixated, resulting from the object properties or task at hand. Because objects in real world scenes normally overlap, it is quite difficult to assign fixations to the correct object regions. Another problem is the spatial resolution for the fixation location analysis: Has a cup, plate or table been fixated by the participant when viewing a typical breakfast scenario? A possible solution could be, to use the fixation information for region clustering (statistical cluster analysis) or arbitrary predefinition of regions (Groner, Walder & Groner, 1984), but none is optimal.

After pointing out that fixations are clustered on scene objects, it is interesting to know which image properties influence gaze location.

Figure 3.1: Fixations (depicted by white dots) from six participants trying to commit a natural scene to memory. Fixations are located on objects or clusters of objects (e.g., the boat and the statue) but not on empty scene regions (e.g., the water) (from Henderson & Ferreira, 2004, p. 23).

3.2.3 The Influence of Image Properties on Participants' Gaze Locations

The influence of specific image properties on the gaze location can be investigated by removing specific information from an image and comparing the eye movement patterns for the manipulated image with those from the original image. Mannan, Ruddock and Wooding (1995, 1996) filtered images, so that all mid- and high spatial frequency information was removed. They observed no differences in participants' eye movement patterns during the first 1.5 sec of viewing for the filtered and original images. Since low-pass filtering blurs the image, i.e., scene objects cannot be identified clearly, the result shows that eye movement control does not rely on object identification. This finding is consistent with the view put forward in Henderson, Weeks and Hollingworth (1999) and Henderson and Hollingworth (1998): There is no influence of the meaning of peripherally perceived objects on fixation positions unless an object has already been fixated.

A comparison between fixated and randomly chosen image regions under free viewing conditions reveals that local contrast (i.e., standard deviation of intensity in an image region) and two point correlation (i.e., the difference in the intensity between fixated and nearby points) are highly related, whereas high spatial frequency content and edge density are weakly related to fixation sites (Mannan, Ruddock & Wooding, 1997; Reinagel & Zador, 1999).

Eye movements are different during memorisation and searching tasks (Henderson, Weeks & Hollingworth, 1999); they are generally influenced by the actual task, e.g., searching for people or task-relevant information (see Figure 3.2). In experiments on natural tasks, Pelz and Canoza (2001) also reported that fixations are more related to future actions to fulfill the high-level goals of the task rather than to salient visual features of the immediate environment (*look-ahead fixations*). Furthermore, people tend to fixate an empty region if they remember that there has been an object of some sort previously (Altmann & Kamide, 2004).

To summarise, fixations are not randomly distributed during scene perception. For memorisation tasks, visual characteristics initially play a role for the selection of fixation positions. Later, the semantics of that particular region is more important. In scenarios which require a goal directed approach, like visual search, other types of contextual influences are more important, like global interpretation of a scene (Henderson, Weeks & Hollingworth, 1999; Oliva, Torralba, Castelhano & Henderson, 2003). Episodic, scene-schema and task-related knowledge act together with different cognitive processes and visual features of the scene to determine fixation locations and durations when viewing natural scenes. *Inhibition of return (IOR)* plays a central role during scene viewing. IOR is a cognitive mechanism which inhibits the return of attention to previously examined stimuli (Leek, Reppa & Tipper, 2003). It prevents the visual system from oscillating between regions of interest. IOR can be associated with the object or the location that the object occupies, or both (Christ, McCrae & Abrams, 2002).

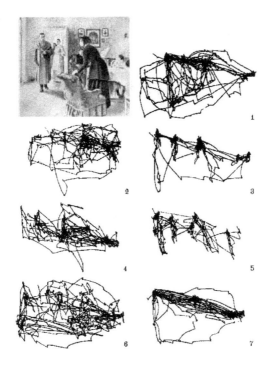

Figure 3.2: Eye movements during perception of the same scene depending on different tasks: (1) Free viewing, (2) estimate material circumstances of family, (3) ages of people, (4) what has the family done before the arrival of the "unexpected visitor", (5) remember the peoples' clothes, (6) remember positions of people and objects in the scene, (7) estimate how long the "unexpected visitor" has been away from the family (from Yarbus, 1967).

3.2.4   The Influence of Object Meaning on Participants' Gaze Locations

Are the identities and meanings of objects in the periphery typically processed to the level that they can affect fixation placement? If this is true: Why have these objects to be fixated when their meaning could already be determined before fixation? Experiments with target objects being semantically consistent or inconsistent with the overall scene (e.g., a tractor in a underwater scene) showed that inconsistent target objects are fixated earlier than consistent ones: Semantically informative scene regions attract attention. Additionally, the probability of fixating inconsistent objects immediately after the first saccade within the scene was higher. Furthermore, Loftus and Mackworth (1978) showed that participants could not only determine from peripheral information whether or not an object is semantically consistent with the scene, but also that this information has an immediate influence on gaze control. These results confirm that the gist and the relationship between the scene and specific objects in the periphery could be understood with a single fixation and this information can be used to move the gaze quickly to semantically important scene regions. But the idea of parallel processing of objects in the periphery (without an eye fixation) is inconsistent with other findings on scene perception. For example, Henderson, Weeks and Hollingworth (1999) failed to show that objects in the periphery can be processed in parallel: Performance for object identification is poor when scenes are presented in rapid succession; fixations close to an object are necessary to extract its visual properties and identities. In contrast to Loftus and Mackworth (1978), De Graf, Troy and d'Ydewalle (1990) could not confirm that inconsistent objects were fixated earlier. Furthermore, later fixations tend to be more located on consistent objects. Other anomalies like spatial inconsistencies did not influence early fixation location. In an experiment by Henderson, Weeks and Hollingworth (1999) that closely resembled that of Loftus and Mackworth (1978), target objects in a scene were fixated by viewers for the first time after an average of about 11 fixations in a scene, regardless of their consistency or inconsistency with the scene. These findings show that participants cannot recognise peripheral objects during the initial central fixation. Also, the probability of fixating consistent target objects after the first saccade in the scene was not higher than for inconsistent targets (Henderson, Weeks & Hollingworth, 1999). Furthermore, consistent targets were fixated earlier than inconsistent ones, conceivably because for consistent targets, the search could be constrained to a particular region (e.g., in a kitchen scene a blender is usually located on the countertop, whereas there is no standard location for a blender in a farmyard scene). The difference between the results of Loftus and Mackworth (1978) on the one side, and De Graf, Troy and d'Ydewalle (1990) and Henderson, Weeks and Hollingworth (1999) on the other side, can be attributed to the scenes being more complex (photographs of natural scenes) and the interpretation of peripheral objects being more difficult in the latter experiments. Obviously, in complex scenes with many objects, it is relatively difficult to acquire the information necessary to direct the gaze efficiently. At that, it shall be emphasised that the conditions in the latter experiments seem to resemble the situation in natural visual environments more closely.

The *total fixation time*, i.e., the sum of the durations of all fixations of a particular region, is longer for visually and semantically important regions. There are, however, more fine-grained measures to analyse the influence of region properties on fixations or fixation clusters: *First fixation duration* (the duration of the initial fixation in a region), *first-pass gaze duration* (the sum of all fixations from first entry to first exit in a region), *second-pass gaze duration* (the sum of all fixations from second entry to second exit in a region) and *total fixation duration* (the sum of all fixations from all entries in the region). Individual fixation durations are influenced by luminance and contrast, contour density and colour (Loftus, 1985; Loftus, Kaufman, Nishimoto & Ruthruff, 1992). Distributions of fixation durations are very similar for full-colour photographs, full-colour rendering of scenes and black- and white drawings, as well as for greyscale scenes (Henderson &

Hollingworth, 1998). The influence of visual scene properties on fixation duration can also be studied by means of *moving-window* and *change-detection* experiments. In the former, where the influence of parafoveal and peripheral information on fixation duration is eliminated, van Diepen, De Graef and d'Ydewalle (1995) found an increase in first-fixation durations in a search task for non-objects in line-drawings of real-world scenes, when the visible image area was degraded: An indication that the duration of the initial fixation is influenced by the acquisition of visual information from the fixated region. Recently, this finding was supported by experiments on natural scenes (Henderson & Ferreira, 2004).

All in all, fixation density is influenced by the amount of semantic information in a region, an effect which cannot be accounted for by approaches based on salience. Although visual information might be more important for fixation placement in the early course of scene viewing, when the viewer tries to identify objects and their relationships, fixation locations also depend on scene information perceived during the first fixation, on memory and on the task itself.

3.2.5   The Functional Field of View in Scene Perception

The *functional field of view* describes the specific size and nature of the region from which useful information can be acquired during a given eye fixation (Henderson & Ferreira, 2004). It is not easy to estimate the functional field of view in natural scenes, because the stimuli utilised in the experiments are normally not natural scenes.

Among the approaches for measuring the nature of the functional field of view in scene perception is the *moving-window* technique (van Diepen, Wampers & d'Ydewalle, 1998). The size of the functional field of view is the smallest window size, where the performance in experiments using the moving-window technique or not is equal. Results show that in scene viewing the size encompasses about half of the total scene, for scene depictions up to $14.4^o \times 18.8^o$, independent from the absolute size of the scene (Saida & Ikeda, 1979).

Whereas early studies (Loftus & Markworth, 1978) have shown that semantic object anomalies can be perceived to a large extend in the periphery (up to an eccentricity of 8° on average), newer results with more complex visual scenes found eccentricity values of $3-4^o$ (De Graef, Christiaens & d'Ydewalle, 1990; Henderson, Weeks & Hollingworth, 1999).

In an experiment by Parker (1978) with scene-like line drawings of six objects, where participants had to find differences in the actual presented scene to a previously learned one, viewers could detect changes quite fast up to 10° from the fixation point. *"The results indicate that during recognition, information is encoded from a wide area and utilized both to direct additional eye fixations and to reach response decisions"* (Parker, 1978, p. 284). Parker's findings of a quite large functional field of view are in contrast to other experiments where a relatively small field of view was found. Nelson and Loftus (1980), for example, recorded participants' eye movements while examining a set of line drawings of scenes in preparation for a difficult memory test. They found best performance, when the objects, which where tested, had been directly fixated, while performance decreased along with an increase of eccentricity ($> 2.6^o$ from the fixation). Nelson and Loftus showed that at least for memory tasks, the functional field of view is much smaller than stated by Parker (1978). Also, the results of Henderson and Hollingworth's (1999b) online change-detection tasks contradict those of Parker (1978). In these experiments, a critical object was changed online during a saccade directed toward the object, during an outgoing saccade after the object had been fixated, or during a saccade directed toward another control region. In most cases, participants' performance dropped when the before- or after-change fixation was more than 4° away from the changing object. The size of 4° for the functional field of view is also supported by experiments on the estimation of the functional field of view for object processing (Henderson, Weeks & Hollingworth, 1999). In the "flicker paradigm", participants are instructed to report scene changes across brief blank periods that alternate with two versions of the scene (Rensink, O'Regan & Clark, 1997). The results revealed that participants need some time to detect the changes, showing that only a limited amount of information can be acquired during a fixation, so that participants have to fixate the changing objects either directly or within a distance of 2° (Hollingworth, Schrock & Henderson, 2001).

The contradiction between the results by Parker (1978) and those of other studies could originate from design aspects. Parker used large objects with relatively large distances from each other. This scenario leads to inflated saccade lengths (compared to those in natural scenes) (Henderson & Hollingworth, 1999a), and the scenario allows the identification of objects quite far from the current fixation (Pollatsek, Rayner & Collins, 1984). Furthermore, the stimulus set was quite restricted and there were many repetitions in the experiments, allowing the participants to learn visual cues and therefore to detect the object differences in the periphery. Recent experiments with more complex scenes (Henderson, Williams, Castelhano & Falk, 2003) show that deletion of objects is quite difficult to notice and that the time for the correct detection of deletion was longer than for recognising object substitutions. Also, the average distance of a saccade to a changed object was 4° smaller than in Parker (1978), which is consistent with other experiments (Henderson, Weeks & Hollingworth, 1999).

Thorpe, Gegenfurtner, Fabre-Thorpe and Bülthoff (2001) demonstrated that relatively coarse information provided by the peripheral retina is sufficient for high-level visual tasks involving object vision. In the experiments, participants were shown 1400 briefly flashed (28 ms) unmasked photographs (39° high, and 26° across), located randomly at nine locations across virtually the entire extent of the horizontal visual field. Their task was to indicate by releasing a mouse if the actually presented image contains an animal. Half of the images contained animals, where the other half were distractors of different categories like landscapes, flowers and so on. During the experiments, participants were requested to fixate their eyes on a central cross of size $0.5^o \times 0.5^o$. The results revealed that the performance dropped linearly with increasing eccentricity. But even for high eccentricities the results were well above chance. The reaction time increased with increasing eccentricity. Probably there were no adjustments on image sizes for stimuli presented at higher eccentricities compensating for changes in cortical magnification. The reason for relatively good results even at high eccentricities compared to the other studies mentioned above, may be due to several reasons: a.) The choice of stimuli and task; b.) the task required only superordinate categorisation (i.e., animal or not) and no concrete classification. Even though the results show that high-level descriptions of images can be obtained without directing attention to the location of the stimulus, the finding is not in contradiction to other reports stating that direct attention is required to consciously register the information. I.e., the fast and relatively coarse processing of information in the eccentricity could be used to orientate attention for further processing of image details necessary for precise identification.

The fast comprehension of the gist of a scene shows that the functional field of view for global scene properties is relatively large. But for the perception of object details it is much smaller and depends on the complexity of the observed scene. These results are consistent with results from reading research, where the total functional field of view is much larger than that for word identities (*word span*) (Rayner, 1998). Hence, the presence of an object can be checked in the far periphery, but the identification of object details require a fixation in the near neighbourhood of the particular object.

3.2.6   Eye Movements during Image Retrieval

As stated above, human gaze is attracted to regions of a scene conveying the most important information for scene interpretation. Whereas at the beginning these regions are perceived pre-attentively, later the placement of fixations depend on participants' point of interest or experience. Furthermore, fixation density is related to the informativeness of an image region, where only few fixations are made to regions rated as uninformative (Mackworth & Morandi, 1967). For more complicated images, the participants fixated high rated regions more often than low rated ones (Antes, 1974). Uniform or empty regions are typically not fixated (Altmann & Kamide, 2004). Furthermore, fixation positions are strongly influenced by semantic informativeness, i.e., the meaning of image regions (Henderson & Hollingworth, 1999a).

In image retrieval, the user mostly starts with a vague idea about his/her retrieval aim, where the retrieval strategy can be influenced by external factors or even changed during the retrieval session. Comparing similar images requires the analysis of image details. As stated above, the functional field of view in scene perception is around 4°. This means that the user has to fixate the near neighbourhood of particular objects being important for the estimation of image similarity. If there are several regions the user has to check for image similarity, the gaze will be subsequently directed to those regions. If the differences between two images are quite small, his/her attention will be directed to regions of interest for a relatively long period of time, because it takes the user quite a long time to find the subtle differences. In the case of more dissimilar images, the attention will only be directed to those regions for a small period of time.

Since eye movements reflect attention patterns (Salojärvi, Kojo, Simola & Kaski, 2003), those image regions with the highest amount of fixations and long fixation durations are supposed to be important for estimating the similarity between an image pair. Eye movements as an indicator for cognitive processes have been deeply investigated for decades (Rayner, 1998). Salojärvi, Kojo, Simola and Kaski (2003) showed that at least to a certain degree, relevance can be deduced from eye movements.

All in all, the measuring of eye movements during image retrieval seems to be a quite promising approach to identify those image regions being important for the user for a particular retrieval task and to guide the systems' image search and retrieval strategy. These insights lead to the development of a new approach to image retrieval, called *Vision-Based Image Retrieval (VBIR)* which is described in detail in Chapter 4. After discussing the eye movements occurring during the perception of visual scenes and the implications for image retrieval in this section, the following section addresses the methodological aspects of eye-tracking research, i.e., how eye movements can be measured.

3.3   Eye Tracking

The term eye tracking denotes the process of monitoring and recording the participants' gaze positions when they look at 2D or 3D stimuli, mostly presented on a computer monitor. Researchers are interested in exact *gaze positions* measured in 2D or 3D coordinates, depending on the dimension of the stimuli and their temporal course, i.e., *spatial-temporal scan paths*.

Many researchers from different disciplines are interested in studying eye movements, because they give hints on the cognitive processes underlying information processing (see Section 3.1.3): Biologists try to find more information about the organisation and functionality of the visual system. Linguists are interested in the relations between the perception of spoken or written text and visual attention. Psychologists analyse the behaviour of participants who are looking at particular scenes in order to solve problems or to accomplish search tasks. Consumer researchers try to find out where to place the product in an advertisement so that it attracts attention from potential customers. Computer scientists are interested in the development of suitable human-computer interfaces, e.g., for artificial systems. Cultural scientists and journalists are interested in eye-tracking systems for presenting a virtual tour through a museum, or for attention tracking when reading print media or looking at images or paintings.

Recently, more and more researchers apply eye-tracking techniques, as becomes evident from the increasing number of articles published. Most of them address reading, scene perception and the analysis of human-machine interaction and cognitive processing during problem solving. The following sections describe the different eye-tracking techniques and the eye tracker used to carry out the experiments in this book.

3.3.1   Tracking of Eye Movements

The first eye-tracking experiments started already in the nineteenth century. During the experiments the experimenter stood behind the participants and observed their eye movements in a mirror (Javal, 1879). This method allowed only an observation of coarse eye movements. Later, optical methods were designed which allowed larger magnifications of the eye area or parts of the eyes. Lenses could be used for the analysis of coarser (Newhall, 1928) and microscopes for finer eye movements and fixations (Gassovskii & Nikol'skaya, 1941). Another possible method for recording eye movements was by establishing a mechanical link between the eye and a recording instrument (e.g., via an arm or a small tube). A more detailed description can be found in Ohm (1928) and Cords (1927). For highest possible precision of eye movement observation, the conditions were quite unnatural: The participants' head had to be fixed, usually by using a head-rest and a bite bar. The eyelids were fixed with adhesive tape. Surprisingly, the visualisation of the data acquired by those experiments show astonishing accordance with data recorded by modern eye trackers. Figure 3.3 shows the results of a study done by Yarbus in 1967. The fixations and the saccades of a participant during the observation of a woman's face were recorded. Yarbus fastened a tiny mirror attached to a suction-cup to the participants eyeball. The eyelids were fixed by adhesive tape stripes or held tight by the experimenter. A light source, with a slight gap, projected a light beam on the mirror. The position of the reflected light stream correlating with the perspective of the participant, could be visualised on a screen or with light sensitive material. Although this was the first time human eye movements were visualised, there was no information about their temporal course and still, the participants' head had to be fixed. Further main eye-tracking technologies are described below.

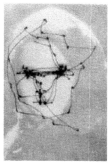

Figure 3.3: *Original image of the womans' face (left) and the corresponding gaze trajectory (right) (taken from Yarbus, 1967).*

Electrooculogram (EOG)

Eye movements can be measured electrically, because a potential difference exists between the cornea and the retina (*corneo-retinal potential*), which can be measured by electrodes attached to the facial skin around the eye. This potential difference varies with eye movements, independent of head movements, allowing to measure eye movements up to $\pm80^o$ (approximately 80% of the visual field in binocular vision) and to a high degree of spatial accuracy ($\pm1.5^o$ to 2.0^o of visual angle). Disadvantages are the decrease of the measurement accuracy in peripheral regions. Furthermore, artifacts by muscle activity around the eyes, blinks and changing light conditions can have an influence on the measurements.

Contact Lenses

The contact lens method is the most exact, but also most time-consuming method, because individually suited contact lenses have to be attached to the eyes. There are two variants of the contact lens method: (a) A mirror is attached to the contact lenses, which reflects incident light recorded by a camera or on photosensitive material; (b) minute induction coils ("search coil") are attached to the contact lenses. In the latter case, the participants' head is surrounded by an electric field which induces a low current in the coils. This induced current varies proportional with the position of the coils in the electric field, leading to a highly accurate measurement of eye positions (5 to 10 seconds of arc), but in a quite narrow field of view of only 5°. Disadvantages of both methods are the unpleasant fixation of the head, either by a bite-bar or in a electromagnetic tube, and the attachment of an artificial object to the eye.

Corneal Reflection

If a single eye is directed to fixate a small point of light, then this incident light is mirrored in a punctual spot. This cornea reflex is the first Purkinje image (see Figure 3.4), located around 3.5 mm behind the surface of the eye. For a camera located just behind the light source and directed at the eyeball of the participant, the corneal reflection will appear to be located in the centre of the pupil. As the participant moves fixation to the right, left, up or down, with respect to the light, the corneal reflect will be displaced relative to the centre of the pupil. Thus, there is a lawful (monotonic) relation between the relative position of the corneal reflection with respect to the centre of the pupil and the direction of gaze, and this relation holds for both horizontal and vertical shifts of gaze. Modern corneal reflection systems have a small error on gaze positions measurements (less than $< 0.5°$ on average) within an eye tracking range of $\pm 30°$ horizontal and $20°$ vertical.

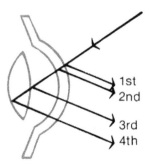

Figure 3.4: *The four corneal reflections know as Purkinje images: Front and rear surface of the cornea (1st and 2nd), front and rear surface of the lens (3rd and 4th) (taken from [24]).*

Purkinje Refraction Technique

Not only the outside surface of the cornea reflects incident light, but also the internal surface of the cornea, and the external and internal surface of the lens. These four reflections are known as Purkinje images (see Figure 3.4). These images can be used to track eye position with greater accuracy than eye trackers using the corneal-reflection method. The eye- tracker model developed by Cornsweet and Crane (1973) uses the relative motion of the first (external cornea surface) and fourth (lens internal surface) Purkinje images. These movements occur only with rotational but not with translative eye movements. The Purkinje refraction technique requires a more controlled lighting environment to be able to detect the rear surface reflections of the cornea and lens.

Advances in Eye-Tracking Technologies

The progress in eye-tracking technology came along with the development of increasing computational power and peripheral hardware. The pupils could now be continuously monitored by a camera, which sends digital images to a computer. By the use of image processing routines, the pupil position in the image could be calculated. Because mirrors were now superfluous, eye movements could be measured over a wider field of view. Furthermore, eye-movement data could now be acquired and saved digitally, allowing post-processing and visualisation of the recorded data. Moreover, the problem of imprecise data as a result of head movements could be reduced. Participants could wear a headset with head-mounted infra-red cameras to measure the movements of the pupils. The pupil is the darkest point in the infra-red image of the eye camera, so that it can be detected reliably. Another camera is placed at the front of the headset, the so called head camera. With the help of four *light emitting diodes* (LEDs), located near the corners of the monitor, on which the stimulus is presented, the system can determine the actual head position, which allows the compensation of slight head movements during the experiment. The head camera yields an infra-red image of the participants' field of view, where the four LEDs cause the only four light spots in an otherwise black image. The locations of these spots, and thus the relative position of the participants' head with respect to the screen are computed. The actual gaze-position on the screen can be calculated from the head and pupil positions by a non-linear projection, which even can be feed back into the system in case of *gaze-contingent* experiments. The parameter for this projection are gained from a calibration procedure which has to precede every experiment. During the calibration, the participant successively fixates nine fixation dots presented at nine different positions on the screen. For these points the measured eye-tracker data is correlated with the corresponding screen coordinates. The data for the other positions can then be interpolated.

The Future: Portable Eye-Tracking Techniques

Recent progress in eye-tracking technology has lead to portable devices that can be used under much less restricted conditions than the models described above (Land, Mennie & Rusted, 1999; Canosa, Pelz, Mennie & Peak, 2003). Some models use a head mounted camera to record the scene and the eyeball simultaneously on video. The portable eye trackers allow much higher freedom of head and body movements compared to the systems

Figure 3.5: SMI-EyeLink I binocular eye tracker.

described above. This allows a much more natural experiment design and tracking of eye movements even in outdoor situations (real world activities), leading to a better understanding of vision in everyday life.

3.3.2   The SMI EyeLink I Eye-Tracking System

The equipment used for the experiments in this book is a modern video based EyeLink I system developed by SensoMotoric Instruments (SMI), which allows binocular eye tracking due to the introduction of a second eye camera (see Figure 3.5). Furthermore, the system compensates small head movements without the need to re-adjust the eye tracker, allowing eye tracking under normal viewing conditions without the need to fix the head of the participant.

The SMI EyeLink I system has a high temporal resolution (it records both eye coordinates and the pupil size every 4ms) and high spatial accuracy of measurement ($< 1^o$ of visual angle). The system provides online data analysis of gaze positions, saccades, fixations and blinks and allows the experimenter to set and change recording parameters, like thresholds for the recognition of fixations. The SMI EyeLink I system consists of a light weight headset (see Figure 3.5) and two PCs, the so called Subject- and Operator-PC, depicted on the left and right hand of Figure 3.6. The Operator-PC is a Pentium 133 with a 17" ViewSonic 7 monitor running MS DOS 6.2, and the Subject-PC consists of a Pentium 4, 2.0 GHz, used to display stimuli on a 20" Trinitron monitor. Via the Operator-PC the experimenter can supervise the experiment. During eye-movement recording, the experimenter monitors participants' eye movements indicated by two moving circles. This enables the experimenter to get a first impression of the recorded eye movements and allows him/her to control the calibration and drift-correction procedures during the experiment.

Figure 3.6: *The eye-tracking laboratory of the Neuroinformatics Group.*

The image processing in real time is done on the Operator-PC. The eye-tracker data is analysed for saccades, blinks and fixations. All information is stored in a binary file, which is transmitted to the Subject-PC via an Ethernet link. With the help of the DOS-Program EDF2ASC the binary file can be transformed into an ASCII-file for further analysis.

The stimuli and the calibration procedure are presented on the monitor of the Subject-PC. The Subject-PC runs the VDesigner, a experiment control software (see Section 3.5). Participants are seated approximately 60 cm away from the monitor.

Two infra-red cameras that can be adjusted to the participants' eyes, are attached to the headset. Each camera records independently the movements of the corresponding eye. At both sides of the camera lenses, two infra-red LEDs are attached to uniformly illuminate the cameras recording field. A head camera is attached in the middle of the headset. When participants wear the eye tracker, the camera is directed towards the screen of the Subject-PC that holds four IR-LEDs for the compensation of head rotations (in a range between $\pm 15^o$ to $\pm 30^o$). Figure 3.7 shows a scheme of the whole EyeLink I system.

After introducing the hardware for recording eye movements, the next section describes the software used for the image retrieval experiments developed in this book.

3.4 Software Development in the Eye-Tracking Group

The image retrieval experiments described in this book were designed with the *VDesigner*, a visual programming environment for eye-tracking experiments and analysed with the *EyeDataAnalyser* (EDA), a visualisation and analysation tool for the recorded eye movements. Both tools were enhanced in order to carry out the studies of this book.

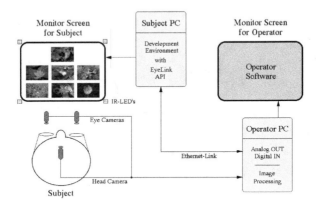

Figure 3.7: *Scheme of the SMI EyeLink I system.*

3.5 VDesigner

The design and development of eye-tracking experiments requires an in-depth knowledge of the hard- and software provided by the eye-tracker vendors. For example, the calibration and drift correction methods must be called properly, requiring extensive knowledge about the proper usage of the eye-tracker libraries and programming languages. Each experiment has a different design and therefore requires a specific order of system calls. Often experiment programmers need to start from scratch for each experiment, because programs written in control languages expose restrictions concerning usability and versatility. To free users from implementation details and draw their focus to experiment design, the visual programming language "V" and the visual programming environment "VDesigner" were developed (Clermont, 2001).

Programming languages that allow the user to specify a program with visual expressions - spatial arrangements of textual and graphical symbols - are called *visual programming languages* (VPL). Usually, the number of textual or graphical symbols provided by a VPL is small, compared to the large number of programming commands in iterative programming languages. Visual programming languages enable even unexperienced programmers to generate computer programs after a short period of practice.

The VDesigner provides objects representing certain functionalities, like "Eye-Tracker Calibration" or "Mouse-Button Press". These objects are provided on tabbed panes in the *object pool* (see Figure 3.8). The central area is the workspace (*project view*), which is used to design programs. The programming is performed by dragging and dropping the required objects from the object pool to the workspace. The objects in the workspace can be linked by using "*Connect*"-objects. The link structure corresponds to the program flow. Separated subroutines can be grouped into macros. Each macro provides a new

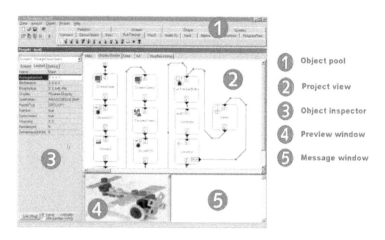

Figure 3.8: VDesigner IDE.

workplace with an input and output object. This helps the programmer to prevent placing too many objects into a single workspace. The *Object Inspector* allows the setting of object parameters, like the font and size for the *"TextOut"*-Object. Furthermore, the VDesigner provides multimedia support, such as video and sound that are often used in eye-tracking experiments.

Since Windows is not a real time operating system, its time behaviour is critical. Through the use of a PC-internal timer, an independent timing function is available which gives a highly accurate account of run-time behaviour. Extensive research and testing has proved the program's temporal behaviour to be uncritical (on average one execution cycle for one object requires $16.8\mu s$, tested under Windows'95 on a AMD Athlon Processor with 700MHz).

The object-oriented philosophy of the visual programming language V allows an easy integration of newly designed objects. Hence, the VDesigner can easily be extended with the functionality required for a particular experiment or program design. The *"Object-HelpWorkshop"* assists the programmers with the documentation of any new objects.

Altogether, the VDesigner is an extremely versatile visual programming environment, implemented in C++, which supplies unexperienced programmers with a user-friendly graphical interface for rapid program development. The VDesigner cannot only be used for the design of eye-tracking experiments, even though its "eye-tracking" class provides much functionality; it can also be used as a visual programming environment to easily develop programs for various purposes.

3.5.1   VDesigner Extensions for Vision-Based Image Retrieval

Even though the VDesigner is already a powerful tool for designing eye-tracking experiments, new objects had to be implemented in order to provide the functionalities required for the image retrieval experiments. First of all, the VDesigner had to be extended with functionality to access MySQL databases (see [20]), because the feature distances between all image pairs are stored in database tables (see Chapter 4). Therefore, VDesigner objects were implemented, which use the *MySQL-C-API* (see [20]) to communicate with the MySQL database. The communication between the VDesigner and the MySQL database is realised by SQL-commands embedded in C++-code. The MySQL-C-API allows fast access to the database, which is important for the retrieval sessions of the image retrieval experiments that require many database accesses.

Also new user interaction features were added. As described in detail in Chapter 6, in the retrieval experiments the participant has to choose the most similar image to the query image from a set of six database images (see Figure 6.1), by clicking with the mouse on it. Hence, the VDesigner was extended by an object which checks if mouse clicks occur in a particular rectangular area (here, the upper left and lower right coordinates of a database image).

The retrieval approach developed in this book require the on-line access of the exact fixation coordinates and fixation durations to calculate the fixation maps, which in turn are necessary to adjust the feature weights for the next retrieval step (see below). This was realised by extending the *"EyeTrack"*-Object of the VDesigner with *"Eyelink"*-routines providing the online access of recorded fixation data.

Fixation Maps

For the retrieval experiments, the VDesigner had to be extended with a module for the online calculation of fixation maps. Fixation maps are used to highlight image areas receiving high attention, whereas sparsely fixated areas are blurred (Pomplun, 1994; Wooding, 2002). Figure 3.9 shows a fixation map for the image retrieval experiment. Mathematically, fixation maps can be described by a two dimensional, continuous function $a : \mathbb{R} \times \mathbb{R} \to [0, 1]$, defined over the whole image, providing a normalised attention value for each image pixel. This function leads to attentional plateaus instead of attention peaks. The input for the calculation of the fixation map is provided by N fixations as recorded by the eye tracker. For each fixation point $(x_n, y_n)^T, n = 1, ..., N$, a radial, non-standardised Gaussian function is calculated for all image pixels (x, y) according to:

$$g_n(x, y) = e^{- \frac{(x-x_n)^2 + (y-y_n)^2}{2\sigma^2}} \tag{3.1}$$

leading to "hills" having the highest value at the coordinates of the corresponding fixation points and values degrading to zero with increasing distance from that point (see Figure 3.10).

The requested function, which describes the attention assigned to each image pixel, can now be obtained by summation of Equation 3.1 for each fixation point n (i.e., the

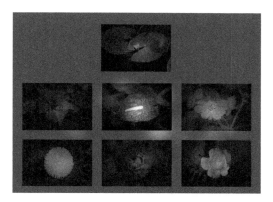

Figure 3.9: Fixation map of the experiment scenario described in Chapter 6. Extensively fixated areas are highlighted.

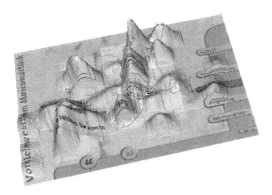

Figure 3.10: "Hills" and "plateaus" of a fixation map for a museum information system.

summation of all "hill" functions) and subsequent normalisation:

$$a(x,y) = \frac{g_{ges}(x,y) - \min_{x',y'} g_{ges}(x',y')}{\max_{x'',y''} g_{ges}(x'',y'') - \min_{x',y'} g_{ges}(x',y')} \quad with \quad g_{ges}(x,y) = \sum_{n=1}^{N} g_n(x,y)$$

(3.2)

where (x',y') and (x'',y'') are the image coordinates where $g_{ges}(x,y)$ has its minimum or maximum value, respectively. The height of the Gaussian is adjusted in proportion to the fixation duration. The shape of the requested function depends heavily on the selection of the standard deviation σ in Equation 3.1: A high value leads to a blurring of the attentional areas and therefore to an inexact representation, whereas a small value leads to many small bell-shaped curves, instead of the desired attentional plateaus. A psychological effect helps to find a suitable value for σ: If a human fixates a certain point, he cannot recognise in detail objects exceeding 1° of visual angle (Joos, Rötting & Velichkovsky, 2003). In the experiment, participants are seated in a distance of 60 cm to the screen. Therefore, the diameter of the circle of attention is set to roughly 1 cm or 28 pixels (the monitor has a resolution of 1024×768 pixels and a horizontal and vertical screen size of 36.5 and 28.0 cm, respectively). This value is used for σ in Equation 3.1. The computing time for the fixation map in the image retrieval experiments is reduced by using Equation 3.1 only for a square of size $2 * \sigma$ around the fixation points, representing 95% of the values.

3.6   EyeDataAnalyser (EDA)

The adequate visualisation and analysis of the recorded data, obtained from eye-tracking experiments, demand an in-depth knowledge of programming techniques and experiences in the analysis of experimental data. Eye-tracker vendors provide professional software for the analysis and visualisation of eye-tracking data. Those programs are specifically fitted to the specifications of the particular eye-tracker vendor and mostly do not provide the special functionality needed by researchers for their day-by-day work.

The *EyeDataAnalyser* (EDA) is a new tool to visualise and analyse eye-tracking data. It provides essentially the same functionality as professional programs, and also overcomes their above mentioned limitations (Essig, Pohl & Ritter, 2005). It is designed as an intuitive tool that is tailored to the requirements of eye-data analysis for research purposes. A distinguishing feature of the EyeDataAnalyser is its flexibility, i.e., it can not only handle data files recorded by eye trackers of different vendors, but it can also be configured to handle different user-defined messages. A message is most often text which is time stamped and written to the eye-data file during experiment recording. Message events are used for two main purposes: a.) They precisely record the time of important events (such as display changes, participant responses, and so on), b.) to record experiment specific data, such as trial conditions. Furthermore, the EDA is not only designed for professional data exploration, but also as a tool that can be used by novices having only little experience in eye-data analysis and computer programming.

The EyeDataAnalyser is programmed in Java. It is platform-independent so that it can be used under a Windows, Linux/Unix, MACOS-X or Solaris system. It also makes use of powerful Java Packages, like Java Advanced Imaging (JAI) and Java Media Framework (JMF) (see [21]).

The EyeDataAnalyser (see Figure 3.11) automatically saves the stimulus images overlayed with the corresponding fixations (depicted by circles) and saccades (depicted by lines) as JPEG images in a user specified directory. Trial related data, such as the number of fixations, the average fixation duration and so on, are stored as text files which can be easily imported into statistics software for further analysis.

The EDA allows to open the data from multiple trials or multiple participants. A comparison function allows the simultaneous display of trial data from up to four participants.

The eye movements for the right, left or both eyes can be saved as a real-time or slow-motion video that can be integrated into presentation tools, such as PowerPoint. Furthermore, the recorded eye movements can be overlayed to a video recording of the experiment. Additionally, audio data can be added to the video. The video files can be played by means of the Java Media Player (see [21]), which is integrated in the EDA.

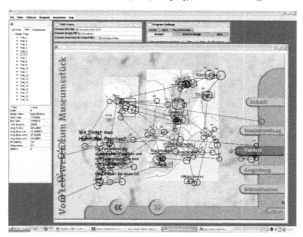

Figure 3.11: EyeDataAnalyser (Main Window).

The program uses the algorithm described above to calculate fixation maps. An example from a museum information system is depicted in Figure 3.10. The EDA also allows the selection of Regions of Interest (ROI) for further statistical analysis. The ROI can be marked by moving the mouse. In addition, the program allows the specification of a fixation threshold in order to eliminate extremely short fixations and the specification and analysis of partial trajectories. EDA's functionality is documented in an integrated online-help system. In the future, a XML-Interface is planned that stores data in a more convenient form (e.g., to export it into a text file, which can be imported into statistical software like SPSS) and to provide a communication platform with the VDesigner (see Section 3.5).

The visualisations of the scan paths in the following chapters are all created with the EyeDataAnalyser.

All in all, the VDesigner and the EyeDataAnalyser are powerful programs that can be easily extended, making them quite suitable for further research assignments.

The next chapter explains how both, the basic concepts behind Content-Based Image Retrieval and the measurement of eye movements can be combined to create a new type of image retrieval system that shows better retrieval performances and provides a more intuitive and natural human-computer interface.

Chapter 4

Vision-Based Image Retrieval (VBIR)

4.1 Motivation

The estimation of image similarity is very subjective and depends on the intention of the user: It may be defined by objects, configuration, illumination, camera position or zoom, by semantic aspects, or any combinations of them (Neumann & Gegenfurtner, 2006). The consideration of all these aspects would require a computer system which is able to use representations similar to the ones implemented in the primary visual cortex. Even though there has been a tremendous progress in image feature extraction in recent years (Rui, Huang & Chang, 1999), common CBIRS usually operate on (globally calculated) low-level features and their performance is rated by the experimenters or designers of the feature extraction algorithms (Neumann & Gegenfurtner, 2006). These judgements are highly dependent on the strictness of the similarity criteria used by the observers, the homogeneity of the image database and the number of displayed images (Cox, Miller, Omohundro & Yianilos, 2000). Furthermore, low level features are often similar for images from different categories (Oliva & Torralba, 2001) (see also Figure 1.24) and cannot capture human vision, cognition, emotions or subjective views.

As stated in Section 3.5.1, the fovea, the region of highest acuity in the retina, comprises around 2° of the visual field. Visual resolution decreases towards the periphery of the retina. Therefore, to explore a scene, eye movements (called saccades) (see Section 3.1.1) have to be executed to orientate the fovea towards different parts of the image (see Figure 4.1). During saccades the perception of the environment is suppressed. The visual system compensates these effects so that we neither perceive a temporal gap in the perception of visual space. When observing the environment, human gaze is successively attracted to regions of a scene conveying the most important information for scene interpretation. Only few fixations are made to regions rated as uninformative (Mackworth & Morandi, 1967).

The functional field of view in scene perception is around 4° (see Section 3.2.5). Thus, fixations in the near neighbourhood of particular objects are necessary to perceive their details. When comparing quite similar images, the user has to focus on image details, i.e., the user has to check several regions for image similarity. The user's gaze will be subsequently directed to those regions for a longer period of time. On the other hand, in case of more dissimilar images, attention will only be directed shortly to regions of interest, because the differences can be perceived quickly.

Figure 4.1: Exploration of the visual environment. Only a small area of the scene that falls on the fovea can be perceived sharply, whereas the rest is blurred. Eye movements are applied to bring the focus on different parts of the image. In the example, two saccades (indicated by the arrows) are successively executed to bring the focus on the mouth, eyes and ear of the gorilla. Humans always perceive a sharp environment, even though most of the visual field is blurred (from Awater, 2002, p. 2).

The experiments of Jaimes, Pelz, Grabowski, Babcock and Chang (2001) on peoples' gaze pattern when viewing images from different semantic categories, revealed similar viewing patterns for different users on various images from the same semantic category. This suggests that different participants should execute similar eye movements when searching for images from the same category presented on a computer screen. Thus, eye gaze pattern should be suitable for determining important regions for image retrieval.

These findings about eye movements occurring during scene perception predestines an eye tracker as an input media for image retrieval. Relevant parts or similar regions are supposed to receive the highest amount of attention when participants compare the query image with the database images. Since eye movements reflect attention patterns (Salojärvi, Kojo, Simola & Kaski, 2003), those image regions with the highest amount of fixations and long fixation durations are supposed to be important for estimating the similarity between an image pair. By focussing on these important image regions, the system's retrieval strategy can be guided to improve its accuracy. Here, the eye tracker serves as a natural and intuitive source for relevance feedback. These techniques are the basis of the new attention-based image retrieval system, called *Vision-Based Image Retrieval* (VBIR) system. The implementation of the VBIR system as well as its' evaluation are the central aspects of this book.

Before describing in detail how these techniques can be implemented adequately, first the reasons for the utilisation of an eye tracker as a suitable input medium for user relevance are explained.

4.2 Eye Tracker as an Input Medium

The technical progress over the recent years led to the development of modern eye-tracking systems which are completely non-intrusive and almost transparent to the user in terms of operation, while assuring precise gaze position measurement even at high temporal resolutions (see Section 3.3.1). Motivated by the relationship between attention and eye-movement patterns, research on the application of eye-tracking techniques in gaze-controlled interfaces is recently increasing (Duchowski, 2002). Eye-tracking techniques rather replace or extend existing interface mechanisms instead of creating new forms of interaction. In studies regarding the evaluation of different input media for retrieval tasks, Oyekoya and Stentiford (2005) compared participants' response times when searching for a target image in a series of displays under varying conditions using either the computer mouse or the eye. Participants had to locate a target image from a series of 50 grid displays of 25 stimuli (one target image and 24 distractors) either by a mouse click or by fixating on it for longer than 40 ms. Four different sequences (alternating between mouse and eye interface) of the 50 grid displays were presented to each participant, where half of them started with the mouse and the other half with the eye interface. The time needed to find the target image was recorded. The results showed significantly faster mean response times for the eye interface (2.08 s) compared to the mouse input (2.43 s). Additionally, the response time was faster with the eye interface than with the mouse, when the mouse was first used but not vice versa. Thus, users benefit in visual tasks from the experiences they gained from the mouse interface if they subsequently used the eye interface.

The results of Oyekoya and Stentiford (2005) are in accordance with Ohno (1998), who found that eye gaze is faster than a mouse for the operation of menu based interfaces. Furthermore, Ware and Mikaelian (1987) have shown the suitability of an eye tracker as an input device for different selection methods (like button press, fixation dwell time and screen select button), providing the target size is not too small. An evaluation of adjustment techniques by eye and mouse during operations in GUI environments was conducted by Yamato, Monden, Matsumoto, Inoue and Torii (2000). They observed that gross adjustment movements for the cursor by eye, followed by final fine adjustments with the mouse on the desired GUI button, performed best. Sibert and Jacob (2000) demonstrated the feasibility of natural eye gaze as a source of computer input. They performed two experiments to compare their self-developed interaction technique for object selection based on where a person is looking, with the common selection method using the mouse. In the first and second experiment the participants had to select a highlighted circle in a set of circles, or a letter vocalised over an audio speaker from a grid of letters, respectively. It was found that the eye gaze interaction technique performed faster than the selection by mouse (338 ms in case of letters, 428 ms in case of circles).

4.3   Feedback through Eye Movements

As discussed in Section 1.2.7, the performance of retrieval systems has been significantly improved through relevance feedback. As stated in Section 3.2.2, fixations are clustered on informative image regions, instead of being randomly distributed over the scene (Buswell 1935), i.e., the eye is attracted to the regions that convey the most important information for scene interpretation. This motivates the application of eye-tracking techniques as a natural source of relevance feedback. Modern eye trackers record the position of both eyes every 4 ms (or even more frequently), so that they provide a huge amount of data on participants' eye movements during scene perception (see Section 3.2.2). There are documented cases, where eye movements have been used as a source of relevance feedback for text and image retrieval. These approaches are described in more detail in the following.

Feedback through Eye Movements in Text Retrieval

The use of eye-tracking information as a source of relevance feedback in text retrieval is a relatively new concept. Salojärvi, Puolamäki and Kaski (2003) were the first, who used eye movements in text retrieval tasks. In an experiment, participants' eye movements were recorded while they had to choose the correct answer to a question from a list of 10 pre-classified sentences. Based on the eye-tracking data, a subset of 22 commonly used features from psychological literature were calculated for each word. After a training with the calculated eye-tracking features, different *Hidden Markov Models* (HMM) that take the sequential nature of eye movements into account, were able to predict the relevance of a sentence by analysing the recorded eye movements. The authors used cross-validation to compare the performance of the different HMMs among each other and additionally to a dump method and a linear discriminant analysis method that did not consider the sequential nature of eye-tracking data. The results revealed that the HMM clearly outperformed the other two models. The discriminate HMM showed the best performance.

In a more recent work on *proactive* information retrieval, eye-tracking data had been used to refine the accuracy of relevance predictions (Puolamäki, Salojärvi, Savia, Simola & Kaski, 2005). Proactive image retrieval means that the system tries to anticipate users' preferences from implicit feedback (i.e., users' eye movements). In these experiments, the task was to find interesting scientific articles by browsing. Participants were instructed to successively choose the two most interesting titles of scientific articles from 80 lists, each consisting of six article titles. Again, Hidden Markov Models were used to predict the articles' relevance from the eye-movement data. Additionally, *collaborative filtering*, a technique for predicting the relevance of a document to a given user, based on a database of explicit or implicit relevance ratings from a large population of users, was used as a complementary source of relevance feedback. Proactive information retrieval and the combination of many sources of relevance feedback turned out to be feasible for document retrieval and improved the system's retrieval performance.

Some recent approaches used eye-tracking data for image retrieval. These approaches were developed for different purposes. They will be described in more detail in the following.

Feedback through Eye Movements in Image Retrieval

Grecu, Cudalbu and Buzuloiu (2005) propose a retrieval approach that learns online from eye-movement data. The system starts by using a saliency measure to automatically detect important image locations. Each salient image location is associated with a so called "virtual fixation", which in turn is associated with a set of virtual content descriptors, stored in a database. For each retrieved image, eye movements are concomitantly gathered during a normal user-relevance feedback process, consisting of assigning an acceptance or rejection tag. From the relevance feedback, the system learns to differentiate between relevant and irrelevant fixations for the current retrieval task. The actual fixations are determined from the recorded eye movements and their corresponding visual descriptors are calculated applying exactly the same techniques as for the visual features. A supervised classifier is trained with the actual fixation pattern to learn the relevance of the actual and virtual fixations. Based on these relevance scores an overall feature distance between the images can be calculated. The top ranked images are then presented to the user for further retrieval loops. This approach is not available as a fully integrated system. However, in an offline simulation the standard relevance feedback process was compared with the eye-gaze enhanced approach (both using the same learning algorithm on a simplified colour orientation image representation) and provided better results by exploiting the user's attention.

The overall goal of *EyeVisionBot* (Scherffig & Diebner, 2005) is to optimise image retrieval from databases and the Internet by using eye tracking and adaptive algorithms. A prototype is installed at the *Center for Art and Media* in Karlsruhe (Germany). Depending on the monitor size, the system presents the user 9 to 25 images, randomly chosen from the work of art database (see Figure 4.2). The time, participants' gaze dwells on the individual images, is measured by an eye tracker. Based on the analysis of the image features as well as on metadata generated from the previous search behaviour for the images with the highest viewing times, an intelligent algorithm estimates the desired image category and retrieves new images. The metadata used by the system is taken from the MediaArtNet database ("MedienKunstNetz-Datenbank"), created by artists. The relationship between the images and the experts' classification is hidden from the participants, because the metadata is not shown. Additionally, structural comparisons of the retrieved images with the so far longest viewed images are performed. The retrieval steps repeat until the user is satisfied with the retrieval results. Displaying randomly retrieved images prevents the system from narrowing the search space. The multi-threaded architecture of EyeVisionBot allows to start a new retrieval process while images are still shown and zoomed. The viewing times for all images as well as the retrieval results are stored in a database.

Figure 4.2: The EyeVisionBot retrieval system (from [13]). The system presents the user 9 to 25 images randomly chosen from the art database.

Oyekoya and Stentiford (2004a) investigated the correspondence between fixation locations and regions of high visual attention values, as predicted by their *visual attention* (VA) model (Bamidele, Stentiford & Morphett, 2004). The model is based on the theory of surround suppression in primate V1 (Nothdurft, Gallant & Van Essen, 1999): High values of visual attention are assigned to pixels when randomly selected neighbouring pixel configurations do not match identical positional configurations at other randomly selected neighbourhoods in the image (see Section 7.2.3). Thus, regions with common or salient features receive low or high visual attention values, respectively.

Eye movements of four participants viewing a series of six images for five seconds were recorded, each separated by a blank screen followed by a central black dot on a white background. Participants were not given specific tasks when viewing the images. The analysis of the eye-tracking data revealed the correspondence of regions with high visual attention in the VA-model with eye gaze patterns. There was also a considerable variation in the gaze patterns of the four participants, but all looked at regions of high visual importance during the first two seconds of exposure. For images with a clear region of interest, there were more continuous gaze shifts from important regions to background areas than for the images with no clear regions of interest. These observations are consistent with findings of rapid visual comparisons between anomalous material and material with a relatively predictable background. For a more reliable statistical analysis of the results, more participants need to take part in the experiment and they should be given a specific task when viewing the images.

Oyekoya (2007) used an eye-tracking interface for the retrieval of eight query images (four easy-to-find and four hard-to-find ones) in a database of 1000 images from different domains. The query and 19 database images were shown on the screen and participants' eye movements were recorded during the retrieval session. If the cumulative fixation duration on one image was above 400 ms, its 19 neighbours from the database were retrieved according to the pre-computed similarity measures based on the visual attention values (see above). These images were then shown on the screen and the process started anew. The results revealed a significantly better retrieval performance for the eye-tracking interface than for a random selection strategy using the same similarity information. There was no effect on gaze performance when including one randomly-retrieved image in the retrieved set. Further experiments revealed that rapid pre-attentive vision plays a significant part in visual search, because participants were also able to find target images with a 200ms cumulative fixation threshold.

Jaimes, Pelz, Grabowski, Babcock and Chang (2001) investigated how people gaze at images from different semantic categories and how this information could be applied to improve automatic image classifiers. Participants' eye movements were recorded while observing 50 colour images from each of five different semantic categories: Handshake (two people shaking hands), crowd (e.g., many people), landscape (no people), main objects in uncluttered background (e.g., an airplane flying) and miscellaneous (people and still lifes). Participants were instructed to observe the images, without being aware of the number of the different categories and the goal of the experiment. The 250 images were shown in random order with each image presented for four seconds. The recorded eye movement data were analysed according to: (1.) *Within image variations* (similar or dissimilar viewing patterns for an image across several participants); (2.) *across image variations* (participants' viewing patterns depend strongly on the image); (3.) *within or across image category variations* (similar or dissimilar patterns for images in the same category, across several participants). Regarding (1.), the recorded eye-tracking data revealed similar viewing patterns for different participants on the same image (see Figure 4.3), with some idiosyncratic behaviour. However, there was also a wide variation between the eye movements for different participants on the same image. This was true for images of the categories landscape, crowd and miscellaneous. The results for (2.) showed a strong image-dependency of viewing patterns. Regarding (3), the recorded eye movements of the participants were different for images across different categories.

All in all, the eye tracker as an input medium for image retrieval is a promising approach to identify those image regions being important for the user in a particular retrieval task and to guide the system's image search and retrieval strategy. This led to a new approach to image retrieval that learns online from eye-tracking data. This approach is described in detail in the following sections.

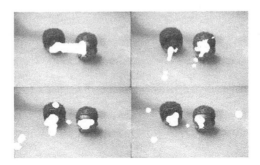

Figure 4.3: Fixation mask overlay for four different participants (from Jaimes, Pelz, Grabowski, Babcock & Chang, 2001).

4.4   The Vision-Based Image Retrieval (VBIR) Approach

So far we discussed the main aspects of image retrieval: In Content-Based Image Retrieval (CBIR) global features are calculated from the whole image information. During image retrieval a distance metric is used to calculate the distances between the global features of each image pair. Those images having the smallest distance to the query image are supposed to be the most similar ones. Some systems allow the user to comment the retrieval results (user-relevance feedback) in order to direct the retrieval process in the desired direction, by providing rather simple user interfaces like a slider or by clicking on the result images which are most similar to the query. Ideally, CBIRS should be modelled with respect to the user and retrieve images in accordance to human similarity perception. However, CBIRS mostly rely on global features which fail to capture sufficiently the properties of individual objects the user is looking for. The user usually cannot mark specific image regions as relevant and the relevance input via sliders and mouse clicking is neither elegant nor natural and tires the user. Thus, during long lasting retrieval sessions, user-relevance feedback is seldom provided or even completely ignored. Approaches to overcome these limitations are Region-Based Image Retrieval (RBIR) and Content-Based Sub-Image Retrieval (CBsIR), using user-relevance feedback to adjust the importance of single image regions or image tiles (see Section 1.3). Venters, Eakins and Hartley (1997) have shown that the design of high-quality interfaces for query formulation and display of results are fundamental for effective image retrieval. These issues have been addressed very little in the design of CBIRS, resulting in a lack of suitable high-quality query formulation interfaces: A longstanding barrier to effective image retrieval systems.

In order to overcome the limitations of CBIRS, a new approach to image retrieval was developed in this book. This new, intuitive and more natural approach to image retrieval based on eye-tracking techniques is called **V**ision-**B**ased **I**mage **R**etrieval (*VBIR*) (Essig

& Ritter, 2005). The aims of VBIR can be summarised as follows:

- To provide a natural and easy to use interface for user-relevance feedback.

- Making the retrieval faster and more robust by using the information provided by eye tracking.

- To analyse online the importance of image regions or features for a particular search task.

- Providing a natural and elegant navigation method for huge image databases.

4.4.1 Principles behind VBIR

In the VBIR approach, the image (size: 288×200 pixels) is divided into 16 non-overlapping, equally sized tiles (see Figure 4.5). Thus, each tile has a size of 72×50 pixels. Colour, shape and texture features (see Section 4.5) are successively calculated for each tile and separately stored in a database. Afterwards, the distances for each image feature are separately calculated between the corresponding tiles of each image pair. For each image in the database, a table is created that stores all the feature distances (for each tile) between this image and all the other images from the database. Because of the high computational complexity, all feature and distance calculations are performed off-line.

In the VBIR approach, an eye tracker is used to record user's eye movements during a retrieval session. A typical eye-gaze pattern for a retrieval task is shown in Figure 4.4. The user provided relevance feedback by selecting the most similar image to the query (depicted on top of Figure 4.4) with a mouse click and by his eye movements. For the selected image, the gaze pattern is analysed (see Figure 4.6). On the basis of the fixation distribution, a fixation map (see Section 3.5) is calculated. The result of this calculation is a value for each image pixel between zero and one, representing the assigned attention. A value of one means that this pixel is assigned high attention, whereas a value of zero means that the pixel is assigned no attention at all. Then, the average attention values for each tile are calculated by a summation of the single attention values for each pixel belonging to that tile, divided by the number of pixels in the tile. Image tiles receiving a high number of fixations are supposed to be important for the actual retrieval task (see Figures 4.6 and 4.7). Their average attention values are significantly higher than those of tiles receiving only a low number of fixations. In this way, the weights of the feature values for the highly fixated image tiles are increased. This means that in the next retrieval step, those images are retrieved preferably that have similar features in those tiles receiving a high amount of attention. These regions are either very important for the retrieval task at hand or included features that are quite similar to the features in the corresponding tiles of the query. This approach is similar to the techniques described in Luo and Nascimento (2004), where traditional user-relevance techniques, instead of eye movements, were used to adopt the importance of tiles (tile penalty) for image retrieval (see also Section 1.3). By increasing the weights of the features for image tiles receiving the highest number of fixations (i.e., for important subareas), the retrieval process should be improved substantially.

Figure 4.4: Visualisation of fixations and saccades during the retrieval task. For a given query image (top) the user selects the most similar image by mouse click.

The subdivision of an image and the extraction of the image features for each tile make the calculated features rotation and translation variant. Since all images in the VBIR approach were equally subdivided into 16 non-overlapping tiles, i.e., all tiles have the same positions, and the task was to retrieve the identical image from the database, this drawback was not relevant for the experiments in this book.

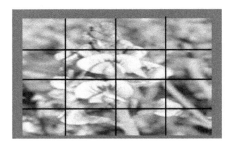

Figure 4.5: Image divided into 16 non-overlapping, equally sized tiles.

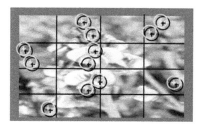

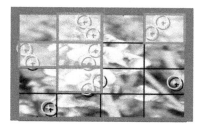

Figure 4.6: *Fixation distribution depicted for all 16 tiles.*

Figure 4.7: *The five tiles with the highest number of fixations are selected (marked by red rectangles).*

4.4.2　Evaluation of the New Approach to Image Retrieval

In order to test the suitability of the new eye-tracking based approach to image retrieval (*VBIR*), it was compared with a system based on the traditional relevance feedback by mouse clicks, herein after referred to as *CBIR*. For a reliable comparison, two retrieval systems had to be implemented where both approaches operated on the same database, used the same colour, shape and texture features as well as the corresponding distance functions. The only difference between the two systems was that in the CBIR approach similar images were retrieved based on the image selected by the user with a mouse click, whereas in the VBIR approach not only the mouse click but also the users' eye movements on the clicked image were considered. In the CBIR approach the feature calculation was performed on the whole image (global features), because the mouse click did not provide any functionality to emphasise the importance of particular image regions. In the VBIR approach on the other hand, the image features were successively calculated for each out of 16 non-overlapping image tiles. The VBIR approach allowed the user to focus on particular image regions that were relevant for the actual retrieval process at hand. Based on the user's fixation distributions on the selected image the tile re-weighting was computed.

The technical implementation of both retrieval approaches are described in the following.

4.5　Implementation of the Retrieval Systems (CBIR and VBIR)

As stated in Section 1.2, retrieval systems consist of typical "components" (i.e., image database, image features, similarity measures and retrieval result presentation). The following sections describe the components of the CBIR and VBIR retrieval approaches applied in this book. Additionally, the slight differences in the feature and distance calculations between both retrieval approaches are illustrated. The description of the typical "components" starts with an outline of the image database.

4.5.1   Image Database: Flower Images

The database consisted of 2,000 flower images from the Art Explosion ([7]) and the "Schmeil-Fitschen" ([8]) image collection. All images had a size of 288 × 200 pixels, so that they could be divided into 16 non-overlapping, equally sized tiles (see Figure 4.5). Each tile had a size of 72 × 50 pixels. The image format was JPEG. The image database consisted of a collection of various sized flowers with differently shaped blossoms, petals and leaves. Examples consisted of roses, water lilies, tulips, cactuses and so on. The flowers were photographed in front of different backgrounds, like sky, leaves, grass, water, cars, etc. Some flowers were also depicted against a monochrome background, mostly black or blue. Furthermore, the background structure was of high variance: Large-area monochromatic colours, fine structured ground or walls, big or small sized petals and trees with different textures and different colour shades. The flowers were mainly photographed in the image centre and the images had landscape format. However, there were also a lot of images, where the flowers were not centered. The majority of the images contained one blossom. All in all, the flower database was quite heterogeneous and representative. Because of its high variety, the chosen image set demanded high quality feature vectors that reflect reliably the properties of the flower images.

4.5.2   Colour Feature: Colour Histogram

Prior to any histogram calculation being performed on the colour images, a uniform colour quantisation was used to reduce the number of colours in the image. A full-colour image in the RGB model may have a gamut of 16,777,216 (256 × 256 × 256) colours. Both, the processing and storing of such a large colour set is non-trivial. For humans, differences between two adjacent colours in such large colour sets become negligible. Furthermore, histograms calculated from the total set of colours are sparsely populated and therefore they are inappropriate as colour features. Thus, a colour quantisation was applied first to reduce the colour set to a small representative number of 216 colours. For image comparison and retrieval, it was important to use the same standard colour palette for all images in the database.

Colour Quantisation

The colour quantisation started with the design of a 216 colour palette. From the whole RGB colour space, 216 colours were selected forming a 6 × 6 × 6 homogeneous grid. This palette was used to quantise the original, fully-coloured flower images: Each of the original colours was mapped to the colour in the palette with the smallest Euclidean distance to the original RGB values. An example of an image before and after the quantisation can be seen in Figures 4.8 and 4.9, respectively.

Figure 4.8: *Original image.*   **Figure 4.9:** *Quantised image.*

Histogram Calculation

After the image had been quantised to 216 colours, the colour histogram was calculated. Since two different retrieval approaches were evaluated in this book, the histograms were calculated in two different ways: Either for the whole image (CBIR) or for each of the 16 image tiles (VBIR). Since a 216 colour standard palette was used for image quantisation, the resulting histograms consisted of 216 bins. The histograms were created by sequentially extracting the pixels' RGB values from the quantised images and incrementing the corresponding bins of the colour histogram. All histograms were stored in the database. Each histogram was represented as a feature vector of the form $(Pix_1, Pix_2, ..., Pix_{216})$, where Pix_n is the number of pixels with RGB values (r_n, g_n, b_n) in either the whole image or the image tile ($n = 1, .., 216$). It was not necessary to store the corresponding red, green and blue values $((r_n, g_n, b_n))$, because they were the same for each histogram. For the calculation of the distances between colour histograms, the histogram intersection was used.

Colour Histogram Distance: Histogram Intersection

Histogram intersection was introduced by Swain and Ballard (1991) for colour matching and indexing in large image databases. It is defined as:

$$D_H(I_Q, I_D) = \frac{\sum_{j=1}^n min(H(I_Q, j), H(I_D, j))}{\sum_{j=1}^n H(I_D, j)} \qquad (4.1)$$

where $H(I_Q, j)$ and $H(I_D, j)$ are the j-th histogram bins of the query and database image, respectively. Colours not present in the query image do not contribute to the intersection distance.

The histogram intersection measures the similarity of two histograms, i.e., the higher the value, the more similar are the histograms (see Figure 4.10). For image retrieval the dissimilarity $(1.0 - D_H(I_Q, I_D))$ between two histograms is more important.

For very large databases and high dimensional histograms, Swain and Ballard (1991) proposed a faster variant of the histogram intersection, called *incremental intersection*. In contrast to histogram intersection, a partial histogram intersection is calculated by using

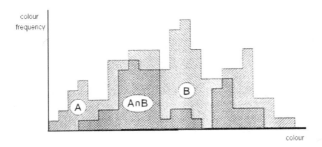

Figure 4.10: Histogram Intersection between two histograms (labelled A and B) (from Del Bimbo, 1999, p. 101). If two images are a perfect match (i.e., matching with itself), the histogram intersection returns a value of one ($D_H = 1$). The more different the histograms, the closer is D_H to zero.

only the largest bins of the histograms. Bins are sorted by size. With at least 10 bins, incremental intersection achieves good results (Del Bimbo, 1999).

4.5.3 Shape Features: Eccentricity, Solidity, Compactness and Bounding Box

Before the shape features could be calculated, the images had to be segmented into foreground (e.g., blossoms and petals) and background (e.g., ground, walls and sky).

Segmentation

The automatic segmentation of natural images is still an unsolved problem in Computer Vision. Currently there is no non-stereo image segmentation algorithm that can perform at the level of the *human visual system* (HVS) (Wang, 2001). Most of the flower images were photographed in a portrait or landscape formatted shot with the object in the image centre. Thus, for the majority of the flower images, the blossom was located in the image centre.

A simple solution for the segmentation problem was to take the average colour value of a rectangular region in the image centre as a reference colour vector for the blossom. The rectangular region was selected by "roping a lasso" with the mouse (see Figure 4.14). A reference vector for the background colour could be calculated by taking the colour values of all pixels in a five pixel wide outer frame. Each image pixel was assigned as fore- or background depending on its colour distance to the respective reference vectors. Even though this procedure is extremely simple, the segmentation results for many flower images were quite appealing (see Figure 4.11). Particularly for large-sized blossoms in the image centre, the reference colour vector calculated from the selected rectangular regions was quite representative, because of the blossoms' homogeneous colour gradient. The background of those images consisted mostly of dark colours (e.g., ground, leaves or branches) with RGB values being quite different from those pixels belonging to the blossom. These differences in the RGB values between the foreground and background pixels facilitated the segmentation.

Figure 4.11: Selected results of the simple segmentation process for three flower images.

Better Segmentation Results through Vector Quantisation

Although the results of the simple segmentation procedure were promising, the shape features chosen for the retrieval approaches in this book were quite sensitive to inexact segmentation results, because the shape feature calculation depended on the region area and perimeter. Additionally, there were also many flower images in the database with small blossoms, which were not located in central parts of the image. Hence, the simple segmentation procedure described above was not sufficient in all cases. Taking the average colour of all the pixels of a rectangular central image area and refer to it as the reference colour for the blossom was a quite coarse approach. The rectangular area might contain pixels belonging to the background, which had a strong influence on the computation of the reference colour vector. Furthermore, colour shades in the blossom could not be represented by a single average colour vector.

Thus, a better approach was to apply *vector quantisation* to map the pixels of the rectangularly marked areas to a finite set of reference vectors $R = r_i : i = 1, ..., N$ in the 3D RGB colour space. Each vector r_i is called a *code vector*. The set of all code vectors is denoted as *codebook*. With each code vector, a nearest neighbour region, called *Voronoi cell*, is associated which is defined by:

$$V_i = \{x \in [0, 255]^3 : \|x - r_i\| \leq \|x - r_j\|, \quad \forall j \neq i\} \tag{4.2}$$

Thus, the entire RGB colour space was divided into a set of Voronoi cells, such that:

$$\bigcup_{i=1}^{N} V_i = [0, 255]^3 \tag{4.3}$$

$$\bigcap_{i=1}^{N} V_i = \phi \quad \forall j \neq i \tag{4.4}$$

Figure 4.12 shows a tessalation of a 2D space into different Voronoi cells. In this book, the vector quantisation was realised by applying the *lazy-pairwise nearest neighbour algorithm* (Lazy-PNN).

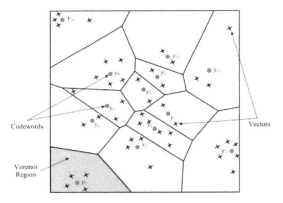

Figure 4.12: Voronoi tessalation of a 2D space. Input vectors (T_i) are denoted by x. Codebook vectors (C_i) are marked by red dots (from [11]).

Lazy-Pairwise Nearest Neighbour Algorithm

A well-known method for data clustering and codebook construction is the *pairwise nearest neighbour algorithm* (PNN), described by Equitz (1989). A drawback of the PNN is its computational complexity for large data sets, because each time a pair of vectors is merged, all pairwise distances between all input vectors have to be recalculated. Hence, in this book, the *Lazy-PNN*, a variant of the *pairwise nearest neighbour algorithm* (PNN) was used (Kaukoranta, Fränti & Nevalainen, 1999), which preserves the exactness of the PNN, but speeds it up by postponing a number of distance calculations.

The Lazy-PNN algorithm starts by creating an initial codebook where each training vector (T) (i.e., every pixel), with $T = \{T_1, T_2, ..., T_N\}$, is considered as a code vector (or cluster). The algorithm starts by initialising each training vector T_i as its own cluster S_i. For each cluster S_i, the distances to all the other clusters S_j $(i \neq j)$ are calculated as the

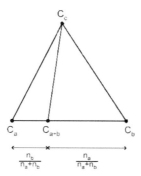

Figure 4.13: Clustering in a 2D space. C_a and C_b are the centroids of the two clusters to be merged. C_c is the centroid of a third cluster. C_{a+b} is the centroid of the merged cluster (from Kaukoranta, Fränti & Nevalainen, 1999).

squared Euclidean distance between the code vectors, weighted by the number of vectors in the two clusters:

$$d(S_i, S_j) = \frac{n_i n_j}{n_i + n_j} \|C_i - C_j\|^2 \quad , for \ i, j = 1, ..., N \tag{4.5}$$

where S_i and S_j are clusters of the input vector set T and C_i and C_j are the corresponding code vectors. The size of cluster S_i is denoted by n_i. The nearest neighbour to cluster S_i, called NN_i, is the cluster, for which Equation 4.5 is minimal. The nearest neighbour distances d_i for all clusters, together with the corresponding nearest neighbour pointers (NN_i) and an additional flag (R_i), which indicates whether the distance value is up-to-date, are inserted on a minimum heap, with the smallest distance value at the top and the largest one at the bottom. Now, the cluster S_a with the smallest distance value (see Equation 4.5) is deleted from the heap and merged with its nearest neighbour S_b ($b = NN_a$). After merging, the size of the combined cluster S_{a+b} is $n_{a+b} = n_a + n_b$, and the new code vector C_{a+b} for cluster S_{a+b} is calculated as the weighted average of the code vector C_a for cluster S_a and C_b for cluster S_b (see Figure 4.13):

$$C_{a+b} = \frac{n_a C_a + n_b C_b}{n_a + n_b} \tag{4.6}$$

The nearest neighbour of S_{a+b} is now determined and inserted into the heap according to its distance value. The cluster information for S_{a+b} is stored in the place of S_a on the heap, and cluster S_b is removed. In successive steps, the two clusters with the smallest distance are merged until the final codebook size is reached.

Whereas in the original PNN algorithm the distances between all cluster pairs are recalculated after each merging step, a recalculation of the distance between a cluster pair in the Lazy-PNN algorithm is only performed if an out-dated pair is on top of the heap. The distance calculations can be delayed until an old cost function value becomes a candidate for being the smallest distance. The delay is justified by the *monotony property* of the nearest neighbour distances: The merge cost between a merged cluster and a third cluster $d(S_{a+b}, S_c)$ is never smaller than the merge cost between the single clusters $(min\{d(S_a, S_b), d(S_b, S_c)\})$, since the potential decrease of the Euclidean distance is compensated by the large size of the merged cluster (see Figure 4.13). The cost function is therefore monotonically increasing with time. For more details see Kaukoranta, Fränti and Nevalainen (1999).

The Lazy-PNN algorithm is on average about 35% faster than the original PNN, because it remarkably reduces the number of expensive distance calculations.

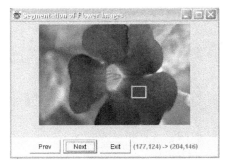

Figure 4.14: Semiautomatic segmentation: The user selects a typical blossom area by "roping a lasso" with the mouse.

For the segmentation of the flower images in this book, a semiautomatic procedure was used. The user "roped" the blossom in the image with the mouse (see Figure 4.14) to ensure that the correct image areas were used to extract the code vectors for the foreground object. Furthermore, the pixels belonging to the outer frame of the image, with a width of five pixels, were used for vector quantisation of the background pixels. The Lazy-PNN algorithm was applied to the pixels of the selected foreground and the outer frame area (background). The final number of code vectors could be specified in the Lazy-PNN algorithm and was set to 10. A further improvement of the algorithm was to skip the reference vectors of the clusters, representing less than 10% of the selected image area, because they were assumed to be outliers. Furthermore, some flower images had blossoms touching the edges of the images. With the above mentioned approach, their values would have been assigned to the background codebook, although they belonged to the foreground. Hence, after the vector quantisation was performed for the foreground- and background areas and the outliers were skipped, the Euclidean distances between the codebook vectors for the fore- and background were calculated in a further step. Reference vectors for background colours were skipped, if their Euclidean distance to a code vector of the foreground was below a pre-specified threshold. Thus, colour vectors of blossoms touching the image edges were not regarded as background pixels.

The application of the Lazy-PNN algorithm on a flower image resulted in two codebooks: One for the foreground and the other for the background. Each codebook consisted of code vectors, represented as RGB-tripel.

The image segmentation could now be calculated on the basis of the codebooks. For each RGB value of the original flower image, the Euclidean distance to each of the 20 code vectors from both codebooks was calculated. The pixel was assigned as a foreground pixel, if it had a minimum colour distance to one of the code vectors from the codebook for the foreground pixels. Otherwise, it was classified as a background pixel. Foreground pixels were set to black, whereas those belonging to the background were set to white. Hence, the result of the vector quantisation was a bilevel image, where blossoms were depicted as black objects in front of a white background. An example of an original flower image and its segmentation result is depicted in Figure 4.15 and 4.16, respectively. Before the shape features could be calculated from the bilevel images, some postprocessing of the segmented images was necessary in order to overcome the limitations of the segmentation algorithm.

Figure 4.15: *Original image.*   **Figure 4.16:** *Segmentation result for the flower depicted in Figure 4.15.*

Postprocessing of the Segmented Images

The segmentation algorithm described above had limitations if the flower centre contained colours that also occured in the background. For example, the petals of the flower in Figure 4.15 are blue and the flower centre is yellow. During the segmentation procedure, a section of the petals was selected as foreground (see Figure 4.14). In the segmented image, the flower centre was classified as background and appeared as a white hole in the flower centre (see Figure 4.16).

The segmented images were postprocessed to eliminate those segmentation artefacts. Image processing routines from $MATLAB^©$ were used for the postprocessing. The binary image was first inverted, i.e., the flower became white, whereas the background changed to black (see Figure 4.17 (a)). Then, the outside frame (5 pixels wide) was filled with black colour (see Figure 4.17 (b)). $MATLAB^©$'s *flood-fill* operation on background pixels was used to fill the holes of the binary input image with the foreground colour (white).

A hole is defined by $MATLAB^{©}$ as a set of background pixels that cannot be reached by filling in the background from the edge of the image. The result of the flood-filling algorithm on the example image can be seen in Figure 4.17 (c). The hole in the centre of the blossom is eliminated. Then the image was inverted again so that foreground and background pixels became black and white, respectively. Now, all segmentation artefacts were eliminated and the shape features could be calculated from the segmented regions.

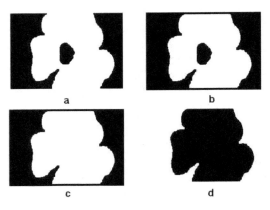

Figure 4.17: (a) Segmented image (inverted) (see Figure 4.16), (b) filling the outer frame of the inverted image, (c) the segmented image after filling the holes, (d) reinverted image.

Shape Features Calculated from the Segmented Images

For the calculation of the shape features, the postprocessed binary image was first inverted. Then a 3×3 median filter (Gonzalez & Woods, 2002) was applied to the image to reduce noise. Figure 4.18 (a) and 4.18 (b) show the original and segmented image, respectively. The inverted image is depicted in Figure 4.18 (c). The result of the median filter applied to the inverted image is shown in Figure 4.18 (d).

Then morphological operations (precisely an *erosion* followed by a *dilation*) were applied to the inverted image (see Figure 4.18(e)). In general, dilation expands a region, whereas erosion shrinks it (Gonzalez & Woods, 2002). The structuring element was a 5×5 array of ones. It controls how many pixels were removed (in case of erosion) or added (in case of dilation). An erosion followed by a dilation is called *opening*. This morphological operation generally smoothes the contour of a region, breaks narrow isthmuses, and eliminates thin protrusions and small areas. A dilation followed by an erosion is called *closing*. Closing also smoothes regions, but, as opposed to opening, it generally fuses narrow breaks and long thin gulfs, eliminates small holes and fills gaps.

After the region contours had been smoothed by the morphological operators, the

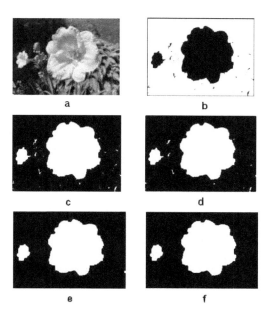

Figure 4.18: (a) Original image, (b) segmented image, (c) inverted segmented image, (d) median filter applied to the inverted image, (e) image after erosion and dilation, (f) "regionproped" image.

image was labelled and the region properties were calculated by using $MATLAB^{©}$'s *regionprops* function. These properties include regional descriptors for each image region, like area, bounding box, axes length and so on. Regions with a size smaller than 0.75% of the original image size were eliminated (see Figure 4.18 (e)) and the image was labelled again. Then, the region properties were recalculated for the remaining regions. From the region properties, the following shape features were calculated for each region of the segmented image:

- Eccentricity, defined as:

$$E = \frac{I_{min}}{I_{max}} = \frac{u_{20} + u_{02} - \sqrt{(u_{20} - u_{02})^2 + 4u_{11}^2}}{u_{20} + u_{02} + \sqrt{(u_{20} - u_{02})^2 + 4u_{11}^2}} \tag{4.7}$$

where $u_{p,q} = \sum_x \sum_y (x - \overline{x})^p (y - \overline{y})^q$ is the (p, q) order central moment of the shape and $(\overline{x}, \overline{y})$ is the centre of the shape. Hence, eccentricity is the ratio of the short axis length (I_{min}) to the long axis length (I_{max}) of the best fitting ellipse. An ellipse with an eccentricity value of 0 is a circle, while an ellipse with an eccentricity value of 1 is a line segment.

- Solidity is defined as:

$$S = \frac{A}{H} \tag{4.8}$$

where A is the area of the region and H is the convex hull area of the polygon. The polygon is a closed chain of points obtained by tracing along the region's border. Solidity describes the extent to which the shape is convex or concave, where the solidity of a convex contour is 1.

- Compactness is defined as:

$$C = \frac{4\pi A}{P^2} \tag{4.9}$$

where P is the perimeter and A is the area of the region. Compactness expresses the extent to which a shape is a circle, where the compactness for a circle is 1 and for a long bar close to 0.

- Proportion is defined as the ratio between the short and long side of the bounding box.

In case of the CBIR scenario, for each flower image the shape features for all segmented regions were calculated and stored in the corresponding table in the database.

The calculation of the shape features in the VBIR scenario was realised in the same way as in the CBIR scenario. However, the tiling of the flower images had to be considered: For each tile, the shape features of each region (i.e., each blossom), which completely or partly overlaps the tile, and the corresponding percentage of pixels that fall within the coordinates of the tile were stored in the database (see Figure 4.19). These percentages were considered as tile-specific weights for the corresponding shape features. They are used for the calculation of the shape distances between the single image tiles in the VBIR approach (see below).

Shape Feature Distance

For the overall shape distance, the Euclidean distances between the four single shape features were calculated and added up:

$$D_{Shape} = \frac{1}{4}d_E + \frac{1}{4}d_S + \frac{1}{4}d_C + \frac{1}{4}d_P \tag{4.10}$$

where d_E, d_S, d_C and d_P are the Euclidean distances between the eccentricity, solidity, compactness and proportion features of the query and database image, respectively. For the calculation of the shape feature distances, three different cases were distinguished, depending on the number of regions in each image or tile:

(1) Both images contained no regions: The shape distance was set to the maximum value, which was one. In that case, both images did not contain any blossoms and therefore they were not important for the retrieval task.

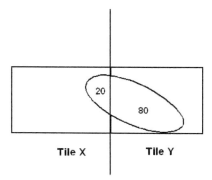

Figure 4.19: The shape feature calculation in the VBIR approach. The blossom (indicated by the ellipse) covers $tileX$ and $tileY$. The blossom covers 20 pixels in $tileX$ and 80 pixels in $tileY$, respectively. Thus, the calculated eccentricity, solidity, compactness and proportion features of the blossom were stored as shape features of $tileX$ and also of $tileY$. Additionally, the percentage of pixels belonging to the blossom that were located within $tileX$ is $w_{tileX} = \frac{20}{3600}$ and $w_{tileY} = \frac{80}{3600}$ in case of $tileY$. The size of the tiles was 72×50 pixels (see Section 4.5.1).

(2) One image had one or more than one region, whereas the other image had no regions: The distance was set to the maximum value, because there was no reason to compare an image with no blossoms to one with one or more segmented regions.

(3) Both images or tiles contained at least one or more regions: Two lists were created, each containing the regions for one image. The distances between the shape features of all region pairs were calculated and the pair with the smallest distance was chosen. The distance between this region pair was additionally weighted by the difference between the number of pixels belonging to the selected regions. The region pair was deleted from the lists and the matching procedure was repeated for the remaining regions, until all regions in one image were matched with the regions in the other image. Finally, the resulting distance was divided by the number of matches to determine the average distance value. This distance value was stored in the database.

This procedure allowed the matching of blossom subsets. For example, assume one image with two and another one with four blossoms, where two of them had nearly the same shape. The algorithm stopped, when the two regions of the first image were matched with the two most similar regions of the second image. The distance between these two images was small, even though one image had two additional blossoms with a shape completely different to the regions in the first image.

In case of the VBIR scenario, the distance calculation was implemented in the same way, except that it was done separately for each image tile.

$$D_{Shape}^{VBIR} = cDiff + (\frac{1}{4}d_E + \frac{1}{4}d_S + \frac{1}{4}d_C + \frac{1}{4}d_P) \tag{4.11}$$

where d_E, d_S, d_C and d_P were the Euclidean distances between the eccentricity, solidity, compactness and proportion features, respectively. $CDiff$ was defined as the absolute difference between the percentages of pixels belonging to the blossoms in the corresponding image tiles of the query and database image, for which the distance was calculated.

4.5.4 Texture Features: Grey Level Co-Occurrence Matrix (GLCM)

A prominent statistical texture measure is the *grey level co-occurrence matrix (GLCM)* (Haralick, Shanmugam & Dinstein, 1973). This texture feature provides information about the repetitive nature of the texture. For fine or coarse textures, grey level values change rapidly or slowly with distance, respectively. The grey level co-occurrence matrix ($P[i,j]$) is a tabulation of how often pixels, separated by distance d, occur in the image, where one has grey level i and the other j. These matrices are symmetric. Normally, also the orientation (horizontal, vertical and the two diagonals) is of concern, resulting in four separate GLCMs for each direction of interest. Figure 4.20 shows an example of a GLCM for $d = 1$ in horizontal direction. Instead of using the whole information of the (or even several) co-occurrence matrices directly as texture features, a set of numerical (low dimensional) descriptors are calculated from them. For the image retrieval approaches in this book, a set of four texture descriptors, i.e., entropy, contrast, correlation and homogeneity, were used:

- Entropy:

$$E = -\sum_i \sum_j P[i,j] log P[i,j] \tag{4.12}$$

  measures the information content of a co-occurrence matrix P. Large empty (featureless) spaces have little information content, whereas cluttered areas have a large information content.

- Contrast:

$$C(k,n) = \sum_i \sum_j |i - j|^k P[i,j]^n \tag{4.13}$$

  amounts to the expected value of the difference between two pixels.

- Correlation:

$$Cor = \sum_{i,j} \frac{(i - \mu)(j - \mu)P_{ij}}{\sigma^2} \tag{4.14}$$

  where $\mu = \sum_{i,j} i P_{ij}$. It measures the linear dependency of grey levels on those of neighbouring pixels.

- Homogeneity, calculated by

$$H = \sum_i \sum_j \frac{P[i,j]}{1 + |i - j|} \tag{4.15}$$

where a small value of H indicate that the large values of P are located close to the principle diagonal.

GLCMs are easy to compute. They provided a correct classification rate around 82% (Haralick & Bosley, 1973) on a set of aerial imagery and terrain classes (i.e., old and new residential, lake, swamp, marsh, urban, railroad yard, scrub or wooded). Gotlieb and Kreyszig (1990) found that contrast, inverse difference moment and entropy had the highest discriminatory power. The spatial interrelationships of the grey levels in a textural pattern, characterised by the grey level co-occurrence approach, is invariant to monotonic grey level transformations. GLCM do not capture the shape aspects of the grey level primitives, so that they are not suited to work on textures composed of large patches (Haralick & Shapiro, 1992).

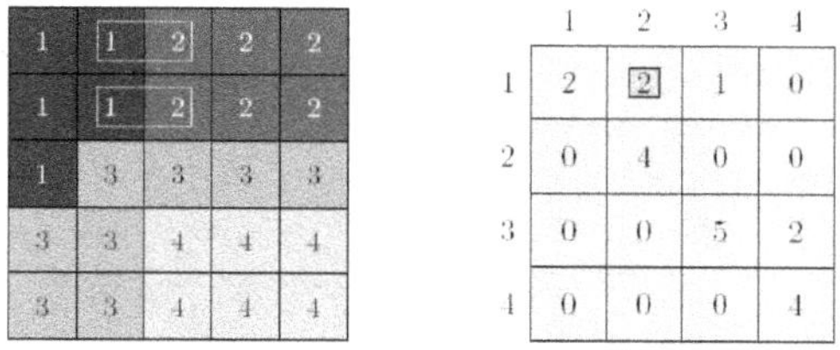

Figure 4.20: Computation of a grey level co-occurrence matrix (GLCM): Image quantised to four intensity levels (left). Corresponding GLCM matrix computed with the offset $(d_x, d_y) = (1, 0)$ (from Sebe & Lew, 2001, p. 63). The framed cells in the right figure means that the combination of the grey values 1 and 2, with an horizontal offset of one, occurs two times in the left figure.

Texture Feature Distance

For the distance calculation the texture features were first normalised. Then, the distances for entropy, contrast, correlation and homogeneity were separately calculated, using the Euclidean distance:

$$d_E = \sqrt{(E_{qi} - E_{db})^2} \tag{4.16}$$

$$d_C = \sqrt{(C_{qi} - C_{db})^2} \tag{4.17}$$

$$d_H = \sqrt{(H_{qi} - H_{db})^2} \tag{4.18}$$

$$d_{Cor} = \sqrt{(Cor_{qi} - Cor_{db})^2} \tag{4.19}$$

where E_{qi}, C_{qi}, H_{qi} and Cor_{qi} and E_{db}, C_{db}, H_{db} and Cor_{db} are the entropy, contrast, homogeneity and correlation descriptors for the query and database image, respectively. The total distance between the texture features of an image pair resulted from:

$$d_{total} = \frac{1}{4}d_E + \frac{1}{4}d_C + \frac{1}{4}d_H + \frac{1}{4}d_{Cor} \qquad (4.20)$$

The total distance was stored in the database. In case of VBIR, the total distances between the GLMC features for all corresponding tiles of all image pairs were calculated and stored in the database.

After describing the applied colour, shape and texture features as well as their distance functions, the optimal feature weights have to be determined. The technique for the estimation of the optimal feature weights is described in the next section. The weighting is a central aspect in this work: The optimal weights are not only used for the experiments (see Chapter 6), but also for the different image retrieval models (see Chapter 7).

4.6 Optimal Feature Weight Estimation

The performance of CBIRS usually depends on the quality of the selected image features (i.e., how reliable they describe the image content) as well as on the optimal feature weights. The correspondence of the colour, shape and texture features and their distances, used for the retrieval approaches in this book, with human measures of similarity is subject of Chapter 5. This chapter discusses the determination of the optimal weights for each image feature. The adequate adjustment of the single feature weights significantly improves the retrieval performance of CBIRS. Usually, there are two widespread methods: The single weights for the colour, shape and texture features are either set by the system designers or they are adjusted according to positive and negative examples from user-relevance feedback. In Müller, Müller, Squire, Marchand-Maillet and Pun (2000), for example, information from user log files is applied to adjust the feature weights. Features occurring in positively ranked images received higher weights than features present mainly in negative examples. The subjective estimation of feature weights by system designers leads to weightings that do not necessarily reflect the importance of each single feature. In case of user-relevance feedback, the single feature weights usually have to be re-calculated for each retrieval session, and various input data from different users must be considered.

In order to develop a method, which renders user input and re-calculation unnecessary, the optimal weight combination for the chosen colour, shape and texture features in this book is calculated from distance histograms by using the *Shannon entropy*.

4.6.1 Optimal Feature Weight Estimation through Shannon Entropy

The term *entropy* originates from thermodynamics where it has two meanings: For one, the amount of energy in a physical system that cannot be used for work. For another, a measure for the disorder present in a system. Shannon (1948) introduced the term into information theory as a measure of the average number of binary symbols needed to encode a string of symbols (Sayood, 2000). Additionally, the Shannon entropy can be used to describe the distribution of histograms.

Consider a probability density function $p(i)$ for a single random variable i. The density function is conveniently depicted by a histogram with n bins plotted on the x-axis (see Figure 4.21). Then the Shannon entropy for the histogram is defined as:

$$S = -\sum_{i=1}^{n} p_i \ln p_i \qquad (4.21)$$

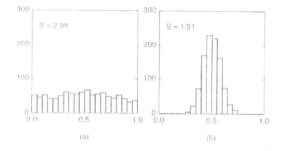

(a) (b)

Figure 4.21: Examples of two histograms together with their Shannon entropy values (after Bishop, 1995, p. 241). The more "peaked" the histogram distribution, the lower is the entropy value. The interval between zero and one is equally divided into 20 intervals.

Obviously, sharply "peaked" distributions have low entropy values (see Figure 4.21 (b)), whereas spreaded distributions have high ones (see Figure 4.21 (a)). The lowest value for the entropy (S=0) results, when all values are located in one bin, i.e., one of the p_i is one and all the others are zero. The highest value for the entropy on the other hand results if the values are evenly distributed over all bins (Bishop, 1995, p. 241).

The Shannon entropy can be used to evaluate the variability and with it the suitability of the image features for image retrieval. This is the reason, why the Shannon entropy plays such a central role for the adjustment of the optimal feature weights. Features with a small variation are not suitable for image retrieval. In that case, all feature distances are located in a few bins and the variation in the distances between all image pairs is quite small. Thus, distances between similar flowers are not much different from those for dissimilar ones. Obviously, this is not conform with human measures of similarity. Additionally, the performance of a retrieval system based on features with "peaked" distributions is quite error-prone: The difference in the feature distances between all image pairs is quite small, so that minimal changes in the system's parameters, e.g., the weighting scheme, can distort its retrieval performance significantly.

Image features with spreaded distance histograms on the other hand are much more suitable for image retrieval. Distances between similar flowers are significantly smaller than those for dissimilar ones. This clearly reflects human measures of similarity. Because of the high variation in the feature distances between all image pairs, the system is much less error-prone. Suboptimal settings in the system's parameters, e.g., the weighting scheme, can be compensated by the large differences in the feature distances, without a significant distortion of the system's retrieval performance.

Hence, image features with a high Shannon entropy value have a high variability and are therefore suitable for image retrieval. Image features with a low entropy value on the other side, have a low variability and should therefore not be used for image retrieval.

But how exactly can the optimal weights for the colour, shape and texture features be determined by the Shannon entropy? Consider a database containing pre-calculated normalised colour, shape and texture distances for all image pairs. From these values, a distance histogram can be calculated by dividing the x-axis into equally sized bins and counting the number of image pairs with distances within the corresponding interval. The distance range (from 0 to 1) is divided into 20 equal distance intervals, i.e., [[0.0,0.05[,[0.05,0.1[,...,[0.95,1.0]]]. Now, the pre-calculated feature distances for all image pairs are retrieved from the database and the corresponding bins are incremented. This is separately done for the colour, shape and texture distances, resulting in three different distance histograms (see Figures 4.22- 4.24). For the calculation of the optimal weighting scheme in this book, the distances between the global features are used (see Section 4.5).

For each feature distance histogram, the Shannon entropy is calculated according to the following steps: First, the number of histogram entries is determined according to:

$$N = \sum_{i=1}^{n} B_i \tag{4.22}$$

where n is the number of bins (here 20), and B_i is the number of image pairs with feature distances within the i-th bin of the corresponding distance histogram. The probability corresponding to the i-th bin is defined as: $p_i = \frac{B_i}{N}$. Then, the entropy results from:

$$E_{feature} = - \sum_{i=1}^{n} p_i \, ln \, p_i \tag{4.23}$$

where $E_{feature}$ is the resulting entropy value for the features' distance histogram. The entropy values calculated from the colour, shape and texture distance histograms of the chosen image features in this book (see Chapter 4.5) are $E_{colour} = 2.4028$, $E_{shape} = 1.9315$ and $E_{texture} = 1.5437$, respectively. The *total entropy* (E_{total}) results as the sum of the single entropy values for colour, shape and texture:

$$E_{total} = E_{colour} + E_{shape} + E_{texture} = 5.878 \tag{4.24}$$

Finally, the optimal weight for each single image feature is determined according to its contribution to the total entropy. The higher the entropy value of its distance histogram, the more suitable is the feature for the image retrieval task, and therefore the higher its importance should be for the image retrieval task. Thus, the optimal weight for the colour feature is calculated according to:

$$W_{colour} = \frac{E_{colour}}{E_{total}} = 40.88\% \tag{4.25}$$

where W_{colour} is the optimal weight for the colour feature.

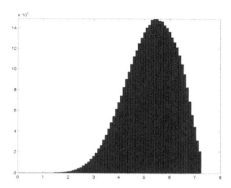

Figure 4.22: Distance histogram for the colour feature ($S = 2.4028$).

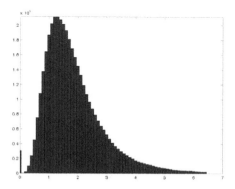

Figure 4.23: Distance histogram for the shape feature ($S = 1.9315$).

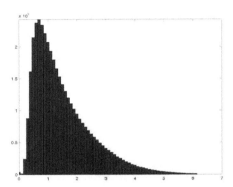

Figure 4.24: Distance histogram for the texture feature ($S = 1.5437$).

The optimal weights for the shape and texture features are calculated in the same way, resulting in $W_{shape} = 32.86\%$ and $W_{texture} = 26.26\%$, respectively. Rounding leads to $W_{colour} = 41\%$, $W_{shape} = 33\%$, and $W_{texture} = 26\%$. This result substantiates the prominent role of the colour feature for the retrieval of flower images, which is in accordance with the findings of Gegenfurtner and Rieger (2000). They investigated the dominant role of the colour feature for the early stages of visual information processing and found that colour improves the recognition and commemoration of objects and therefore improves image retrieval.

All in all, a feature and its corresponding distance function, leading to a widely distributed distance histogram, is quite suitable for an image retrieval task. The distance distribution of an image feature can be reliably described by the Shannon entropy. The entropy values for features with widely distributed distance values are higher than for those with a "peaked" distribution. Therefore, those features should receive higher weights to increase their contribution for the total distance calculation between image pairs. On the other hand, features with a "peaked" distance distribution do not reliably reflect image similarity and therefore should receive only small weights.

This chapter explained the Vision-Based Image Retrieval (VBIR) approach and described in detail the applied colour, shape and texture features and their associated distance functions for both retrieval approaches (CBIR and VBIR) as well as their computation. Additionally, it was shown, how the optimal feature weights can be calculated by using the Shannon entropy. In the next chapter, the quality of the chosen features and applied distance functions are evaluated in order to determine if they are conform with human measures of similarity.

Chapter 5

Feature Evaluation

5.1 Motivation

The previous chapter described the underlying concepts of the Vision-Based Image Retrieval (VBIR) approach as well as the image features and distance functions used for the retrieval experiments in this book (see Chapter 6). The image features are represented as vectors in a high dimensional space. This high dimensionality makes it quite difficult for humans to evaluate how reliably the chosen image features represent image content, because the environment and the objects we perceive and manipulate are rather three-dimensional. Higher dimensions cannot be perceived by humans. Hence, before visualisation, the dimensionality of the presented data should be reduced. Furthermore, there should be sufficient agreement between the calculated feature representations and their distances with human measures of similarity. In case of representative image features, the feature vectors for similar images should be clustered, whereas those for dissimilar images should be scattered throughout the feature space.

This chapter presents two techniques developed in this book for the visualisation of the shape and the evaluation of the colour and texture features calculated for both retrieval approaches: The *result viewer* and the *self-organizing map* (SOM). Before these two techniques are described in more detail, the next section outlines two proven methods for the analysis of high-dimensional data.

5.2 Methods for the Analysis of High-Dimensional Feature Vectors

In order to estimate the similarity between the high-dimensional feature vectors, they first have to be transformed into lower dimensional representations that can be adequately visualised. This section focusses on the *principal components analysis* (PCA) and *multidimensional scaling* (MDS).

5.2.1   Principal Components Analysis (PCA)

One of the oldest and most widely used multivariate technique is the *principal components analysis* (PCA), also known as the Eigen-XY analysis or Karhunen-Loève expansion. The basic idea behind PCA is to describe the variation of a set of multivariate data in terms of a (small) set of uncorrelated variables, called *principal components*, each of which is a particular linear combination of the original variables. The first variable (first principal component) accounts for as much as possible of the variation of the original data, and each succeeding component accounts for as much as possible of the remaining variability. The principal components are orientated orthogonal to each other. For many purposes, the first few components are sufficient to describe the original data: The others are discarded. This reduction in the dimensionality of the original data simplifies later visualisation and analysis.

Squire and Pun (1997) found that the partition of a set of 100 colour images into eight subsets using the *normalised principal components analysis* (NPCA) showed the highest agreement with human measures of image similarity. In the study, NPCA was compared with a variety of machine clustering techniques, such as *ascendent hierarchical classification* (ACH), *correspondence analysis* (CA) and *principal components analysis* (PCA).

5.2.2   Multidimensional Scaling (MDS)

Multidimensional scaling (MDS) provides a visual representation of the pattern of commonalities (i.e., similarities or distances) among a set of objects. The goal of MDS is to find a suitable representation of proximity relations of N objects in a low dimensional space L (usually Euclidean), where the pairwise distances $d_{ij} = d(x_i, x_j)$ between two objects x_i and x_j match the given dissimilarity $\delta_{ij} \in I\!\!R_0^+$ as closely as possible $\forall_{i \neq j} \, \delta_{ij} \approx d_{ij}$. Kruskal's formulation of this problem requires minimising the following quantity (Kruskal, 1964):

$$STRESS(x_1, ..., x_N) = \frac{\sqrt{\sum_{i=1}^{N} \sum_{j>i} (d_{ij} - \delta_{ij})^2}}{\sqrt{\sum_{i=1}^{N} \sum_{j>i} \delta_{ij}^2}} \tag{5.1}$$

where $x_1, ..., x_N$ are the desired coordinates in the low-dimensional target space L (with $L = 2$ or 3). Equation 5.1 is primarily the sum over all pairwise distance distortions with a normalisation constant in the denominator. $STRESS$ is a non-negative number that reflects how well the given dissimilarities (δ_{ij}) are preserved in the low dimensional space. A successful embedding has a $STRESS$ value below 0.2 (Rubner & Tomasi, 2001).

A MDS display of the 20 best matches when the user was looking for flowers in a dataset of 20,000 images is depicted in Figure 5.1. The red and violet flowers are clustered together, respectively. Thus, the user can see immediately the commonalities of the retrieved images and what cluster is most relevant for his/her retrieval needs. Methods for browsing and navigation in a two- or three-dimensional MDS space containing thumbnails of retrieved images are described in Rubner and Tomasi (2001).

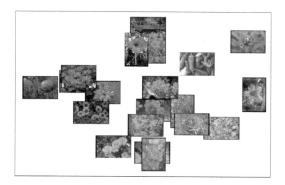

Figure 5.1: *MDS display of a query result where the user was looking for flower images from an image set of 20,000 images (from Rubner & Tomasi, 2001, p. 83). The images are arranged from pink to red flowers on one axis and according to the shades of green on the other axis.*

5.3 Evaluation of the Global and Tile-Based Image Features

Although PCA and MDS are two proven methods for reducing multidimensional datasets to lower dimensions for visualisation and analysis, they are not suitable for the evaluation of the chosen image features for the retrieval approaches developed in this book. As stated above, the PCA concentrates on the components with the "greatest variance" in the original data, whereas those with "less variance" are discarded. Depending on the application, these remaining dimensions are not necessarily the most important ones. Some dimensions of the feature vectors are discarded anyway. Furthermore, the results of the PCA have to be adequately visualised in a separate step. Whereas PCA uses data points, MDS starts from a distance matrix (see Section 5.2.2). The data points are arranged in a low-dimensional space such that the Euclidean distances between the data points are as close as possible to the elements of the given distance matrix.

For the visualisation and evaluation of the chosen features for the CBIR and VBIR retrieval approaches, I have used two other techniques that consider all feature dimensions and do not rely on pre-calculated distances: For one, the *self-organizing map* (SOM), where images with similar feature vectors are mapped to neighbouring locations on a 2D grid. The SOM is used for the evaluation of the global and tile-based colour and texture features (see Section 4.5). For another, the *result viewer*, a *Java* program which displays images from the flower database according to increasing distance to the query image. The result viewer serves for the visualisation of the global shape feature distances (see Section 4.5.3). The shape features cannot be used as input vectors for the SOM, because they have various dimensions for the different images. Both techniques are described in more detail in the following sections, starting with the result viewer.

5.3.1 The Result Viewer

The purpose of the result viewer (see Figure 5.2) is to provide a simple visualisation of the retrieval results in order to evaluate the quality of the applied global image features and their distance functions. If many similar images to the query appear within the best matches, then the corresponding features and their distance functions are suitable for the retrieval of flower images, because they describe reliably the image content and the similarity between image pairs. Additionally, the result viewer allows to validate whether the image features reflect human measures of similarity. In this book the result viewer is used for the visualisation of the global shape feature distances (see Section 4.5.3).

The program displays flower images ordered by increasing feature distances (i.e., colour, shape or texture) to the query image (located at the top) in a rectangular matrix. This form of the presentation of retrieved images follows the usual way in common Content-Based Image Retrieval systems (see Figure 1.4). The result viewer depicts the best 24 matches from the database (see Section 4.5.1) according to the selected image feature. The number inside the brackets below each thumbnail shows the image number (in the range from 1 to 2,000) and the corresponding feature distance to the query image, respectively. As described in Chapter 4, the single feature distances were pre-calculated and stored in the database. Figure 5.2 shows the retrieval results for an orange flower according to the shape distances. All four similar images from the database appear on the first row. Additionally, yellow, violet and bright orange flowers with similarly shaped blossoms are within the best 24 matches. Some outliers in the list, for example image 683 (position 7 in Figure 5.2), are due to poor segmentation results (see Section 4.5.3).

The first step to use the program is to select the feature that should be evaluated, i.e., colour, shape or texture. By clicking the *"LoadImage"*-button, a *"FileOpen"*-dialog appears through which one image from the database of 2,000 flower images can be selected as a query. By pressing the *"Retrieve"*-button, the best 24 nearest neighbours are shown - those that have the smallest distances to the query image in terms of the selected image feature. These steps can be repeated for as many images as desired.

The result viewer presents the 24 best retrieval results as a rectangular matrix of thumbnails, ordered by their ranks in the search result. Although this arrangement is straightforward and allows a quick estimation of the features' suitability for image retrieval, it does not convey information about the similarities between the retrieval results, for example which images are clustered together. As stated above, multidimensional scaling (MDS) provides a visual representation of the commonalities among a set of images. Unfortunately, in the 2D MDS-display the space for the presentation of information is restricted. Furthermore, the display lacks an natural way of zooming and focussing. The *hyperbolic multidimensional scaling* (HMDS) method overcomes these limitations. Additionally, HMDS provides an effective human-computer interaction, where the user can navigate in the images by moving his/her "focus" via the mouse. The HMDS technique

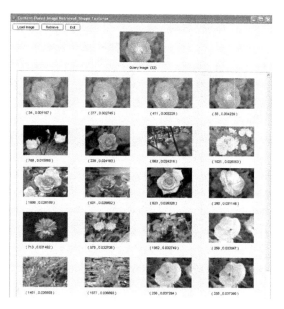

Figure 5.2: Result Viewer: Visualisation of retrieval results with the smallest distance from the query (depicted at the top) according to the selected feature (here shape). The entries below each image are the image number and the corresponding feature distance to the query image.

is described in more detail in the following.

Hyperbolic Multidimensional Scaling (HMDS)

In the *hyperbolic multidimensional scaling* (HMDS) method (Walter & Ritter, 2002), the concept of MDS (see Section 5.2.2) is transferred to the hyperbolic geometry. The hyperbolic space ($I\!H^2$) is a non-Euclidean space with negative curvature (see Figure 5.3). On most available 2D display devices - like screens or paper - the neighbourhood around a point is restricted and therefore only a limited number of information can be depicted. In the hyperbolic space on the other hand, the neighbourhood around a point increases exponentially with increasing radius and provides more options to layout objects compared to the Euclidean space. A further advantage is the availability for a suitable mapping of the objects on the hyperbolic space allowing interactive browsing and navigation.

Because of the curvature mismatch, the hyperbolic space cannot be perfectly projected into a 2D space (Walter, 2004). Among the possible compromise solutions, the *Poincaré Disk model* (see Figure 5.4) is one of the most prominent, because:

- The infinitely large area of the hyperbolic space can be mapped entirely into a fixed circle area (called Poincaré Disk, PD).

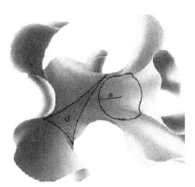

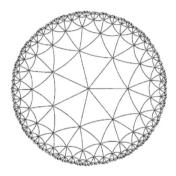

Figure 5.3: *Projection of a small patch of the hyperbolic space embedded in $\mathbf{R}^3$. With increasing radius R of the circle, more and more wrinkling structures of the hyperbolic space are included, leading to an exponential growth of its area and outline (from Walter, 2004, p. 164).*

Figure 5.4: *Tessalation grid on a Poincaré disk model, where eight triangles meet at each vertex. Lines appear as circle segments. Although the triangles in the centre appear bigger than those near the rim, they are all of equal size, because the magnification shrinks with increasing distance from the centre (from Walter, 2004, p. 183).*

- Remote points are close to the rim, without touching it.

- The focus can be moved to each location on the Poincaré Disk.

- Fovea-like focus and context: Just as in the human retina, less spatial representation in the current display is assigned to areas with increasing distance from the focus centre (see Figure 5.4).

The concepts of MDS can be transferred to the hyperbolic geometry by replacing the usual Euclidean metric $d_{ij} = ||x_i - x_j||$ with $x_i \in \mathbf{R}^L$, $i, j \in \{1, 2, ..., N\}$ in the target space by an appropriate distance metric for the Poincaré model:

$$d_{ij} = 2\, arctanh(\frac{|x_i - x_j|}{|1 - x_i \bar{x}_j|}), \quad x_i, x_j \in PD \tag{5.2}$$

where $\bar{x}_j$ is the mean of the objects x_j. The spatial representation x_i of each object i on the Poincaré Disk model can be found iteratively by minimising Sammon's cost function:

$$E(\{x_i\}) = \frac{4}{N(N-1)} \sum_{i=1}^{N} \sum_{j>i} (\frac{d_{ij} - \delta_{ij}}{\delta_{ij}})^2 \tag{5.3}$$

where N is the number of objects and $\delta_{ij} \in \mathbf{R}_0^+$ is the given dissimilarity between objects i and j. The gradients $\partial d_{ij,q}/\partial x_{i,q}$, with $q \in 1, .., L$, where L is the dimension of the target space, required for the gradient descent, become complex for Equation 5.2. More details can be found in Walter (2004).

In the *hyperbolic image viewer prototype* (Walter, 2004; Walter, Weßling, Essig & Ritter, 2006), the colour distances, calculated for an image database (consisting of 100 colour images) by means of the *Earth-Movers Distance* metric (see Section 1.2.4), are projected on the $I\!H^2$ (see Figure 5.5). The clustering of the images with similar colours and content is clearly visible: Images with similar colour features are projected onto neighbouring positions on the Poincaré Disk. Users can interact with the hyperbolic image viewer. For example, they can navigate in the images by moving the "focus" via the mouse to each desired location on the $I\!H^2$.

Figure 5.5: Images on the hyperbolic image viewer prototype arranged by colour distances calculated with the Earth Movers Distance (EMD) (from Walter, 2004, p. 215).

All in all, the result viewer allows a fast visualisation of the retrieval results and a coarse estimation of the suitability of the chosen colour, shape and texture features for image retrieval. However, only one query image can be evaluated at a time and only its best 24 matches are shown. While the presentation of the images in the result viewer is straightforward, no information on the structure of the image subset can be deduced (for example, about the clustering of the retrieved images and their distances to the other images in the database). Furthermore, it is not possible to deduce general statements about the whole database from the image subset. Here, MDS is a better technique to visualise the communalities in the calculated features between the images of the database. However, the limited 2D space in a MDS display does not supply enough space for pictorial representations. Furthermore, the MDS display lacks of suitable browsing and navigation facilities. For a better visualisation and navigation in the data set, the HMDS can be used. The exponential growth of the neighbourhood in the $I\!H^2$ facilitates a suitable representation of thumbnail images. The fovea-like focus and context enables a natural navigation in the images via the mouse. Furthermore, the HMDS allows the interactive modulation of the distance metric while observing the resulting rearrangement of the images in the $I\!H^2$.

However, the described techniques are not suitable for a convincing evaluation of the feature distances between all image pairs of the flower database. For these purposes, a 2D representation of the similarities between the feature vectors for the single images of the whole database is helpful. Such a representation is provided by the self-organizing map (SOM).

5.3.2 Self-Organizing Map (SOM)

The *self-organizing map* (SOM) (Kohonen, 1990; Ritter, Martinetz & Schulten, 1991) is used as a more sophisticated technique for feature evaluation in this book. The biological motivation behind SOMs is the organisation of the human brain in a topologically ordered manner: For example, signals from neighbouring skin regions are mapped on neighbouring neurons of the cerebral cortex. Figure 5.6 shows the organisation of the self-organizing map as a lattice A of neurons. Each neuron a in the lattice A is linked to a reference vector w_a, which projects on the input space X (see Figure 5.6). All neurons on the lattice are fully connected to all source nodes in the input layer. The principle goal of the SOM is to transform input vectors of arbitrary dimensionality into a usually one or two dimensional discrete lattice, where adjacent neurons are specialised on similar statistical features contained in the input patterns, for example RGB coordinates.

The SOM-algorithm starts by initialising the synaptic weights in the network. For each input vector $\vec{x}$, the neurons of the network compete among each other (*competitive learning*), with the result, that only one neuron (*winner-takes-all neuron*) is activated at any one time. By the learning rule, the reference vector of the winning neuron (including its neighbours) is moved toward the input vector. In course of the learning process with the training data and synaptic weight adaptation, a *topographic map* of the input patterns is created over the lattice (Kohonen, 1990). Thus, input samples with identical or nearly identical features are assigned to the same winner neuron or to neurons in its near neighbourhood. Input samples with different features are assigned to neurons that are far away from each other (*principle of topographic map formation*). In the self-organizing map, used to evaluate the image features in this book, the neurons were placed on nodes of a 2D lattice.

An m-dimensional input vector for the SOM is denoted by $\vec{x} = [\vec{x}_1, \vec{x}_2, ..., \vec{x}_m]^T$. The reference vector for each neuron a in the lattice is denoted by $\vec{w}_a = [\vec{w}_{a1}, \vec{w}_{a2}, ..., \vec{w}_{am}]^T$ for $a = 1, ..., k$, where k is the total number of neurons in the lattice. The neuron that best matches the input vector $\vec{x}$, is determined according to:

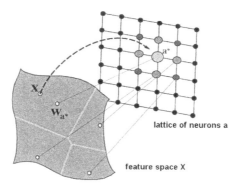

Figure 5.6: The SOM consists of processing neurons placed on a lattice A. Each neuron a of lattice A has a dedicated reference vector $\vec{w}_a$, embedded in the continuous input space X. A new input vector $\vec{x} \in X$ is mapped to the neuron with the closest reference vector $\vec{w}_a$. This competitive mechanism divides the input space into discrete sections, called *Voronoi cells* (from Walter, 2004, p. 137).

$$a^* = \arg\min_{\forall a' \in A} \|\vec{w}_{a'} - \vec{x}\| \qquad (5.4)$$

i.e., the neuron a^* for which the Euclidean distance between its reference vector $\vec{w}_a$ and the input vector $\vec{x}$ is the minimum. Thus, Equation 5.4 expresses the competition process between the neurons of the SOM.

The adaptive process of the SOM uses a short-range excitatory mechanism as well as a long-range inhibitory mechanism. This is in accordance with neurobiological evidence for *lateral interaction*, i.e., the winner neuron excites the neurons in its neighbourhood more than neurons farther away from it. The uniform decrease of excitation in the topological neighbourhood of the winner neuron is modelled by the following Gaussian function:

$$h_{\vec{a},\vec{a}^*} = exp - \frac{\|\vec{a} - \vec{a}^*\|^2}{\sigma^2} \qquad (5.5)$$

where σ is the "effective width" of the topological neighbourhood. The exponential function decays rapidly with distance from the winner neuron (expressed by $|\vec{a} - \vec{a}^*|$), so that only neurons in its close neighbourhood are excited.

The learning rule for the adjustment of the reference vector of the winning neuron (including its excited neighbours) in relation to the input data is expressed by:

$$\Delta\vec{w}_a = \epsilon\, h_{\vec{a},\vec{a}^*}\, (\vec{x} - \vec{w}_a) \qquad (5.6)$$

where ϵ is the *learning-rate parameter* of the algorithm. By adjustment of the reference vectors according to Equation 5.6, the response of the winning neuron to recurrent patterns is increased. The neighbourhood function ($h_{\vec{a},\vec{a}^*}$) in Equation 5.6 ensures that the neural net only changes in the close vicinity of the winner neuron. The algorithm is recursively applied to the input vectors until no noticeable changes in the adjustment of the reference vectors are observed.

For the implementation of the SOM in this book, the learning rate ϵ was set to 0.1 and one was chosen as the "effective width" (σ) of the Gaussian function in Equation 5.5.

Evaluation of the Global Colour Feature (CBIR)

The database used in this book consisted of 2,000 flower images (see Section 4.5.1). Each topological ordering process for the feature vectors required many iterations of the SOM-algorithm. Because these processes were quite time consuming when applied to the whole database, a sample set of 220 flower images was chosen from the database to evaluate the quality of the calculated image features. This set of images consisted of several representative images for each flower species. For visualisation purposes, the images were resized to thumbnails with a resolution of 40×30 pixels.

Figure 5.7 shows the results of the SOM for the sample images after 250 learning steps applied to the global colour feature. The learning process was already terminated after 250 steps, because there were no notable changes in the arrangement of the images. The aim behind the SOM application was to get a general idea about the quality of the chosen image features, not a detailed analysis. Furthermore, the chosen learning rate (ϵ) was quite high. As stated in Section 4.5.2, the flower images were quantised to 216 colours prior to histogram calculation. Hence, each input vector for the SOM consisted of 216 dimensions representing the colour histogram of a particular flower image. As can be seen, all images with a dominant dark background are clustered at the upper left part of the SOM. For a better illustration, the images belonging to the feature vectors related to a particular neuron on the lattice are depicted by stacks. Moving to the right, the background of the flower images become more greenish. Images with a dominant green background are clustered at the upper right corner. Images with a large red or orange blossom against a dark or green background are located in the upper area. The yellow flowers are clustered at the lattice centre. In general, images with a dark background are located on the left, whereas those with a background consisting of leaves are located at the right side of the lattice. There are two clusters of violet flowers located at the lattice centre: To the right are those with a greenish background, whereas to the left are those with a darker background. Flowers, photographed in front of the sky, are clustered in the lower right area of the SOM. Water lilies and other flowers depicted against a greenish-greyish background are mainly located at the lower left side, whereas those with a bright blue background are located in the lower right area of the SOM. There are some flowers that do not fit well within the ordering on the lattice. For example, the violet flower on the black background depicted in the lower left corner or the red flower in the lower right corner. After more learning steps the outliers might move to more adequate regions of the lattice.

All in all, the results revealed that images with similar global colour histograms are located at topological neighbourhoods, whereas those with different colour features are distributed throughout the lattice. These results support the suitability of the chosen global colour feature for image retrieval in the CBIR approach.

Figure 5.7: SOM visualisation for the global colour feature after 250 learning steps.

Evaluation of the Global Shape Feature (CBIR)

Input vectors for the SOM are required to have the same dimensionality. This prerequisite was not fulfilled for the global shape features. As stated in Section 4.5.3, the shape features consisted of the eccentricity, the solidity, the compactness and the bounding box calculated for each segmented blossom. Since the flower images contained different numbers of blossoms, the feature vectors for the single images have different dimensions. Thus, the shape distances of a sample set of images were visualised with the result viewer (see Figure 5.2). The results revealed that for each query, the most similar images were within the best 24 matches. However, there were also some outliers within the 24 nearest neighbours which are due to poor segmentation results (see Section 4.5.3). Compared to the global colour features, the results of the visualisations of the global shape features with the result viewer show more outliers. This emphasises the higher discrimination power of the global colour features, which is in line with the outcome of the Shannon entropy (see Chapter 4.6).

Evaluation of the Global Texture Feature (CBIR)

For the evaluation of the global texture features, calculated from the grey level co-occurrence matrix (GLCM) (described in Section 4.5.4), additionally a second sample set consisting of 170 greyscale images was created. Those images showed dominant texture features like coarseness, contrast, and directionality. The images were taken from the categories cages, fences, ladders, radiator grills, granular structures, and flowers. The second sample set was created, because in contrast to colour and shape, texture is not as dominant a feature of the flowers in the database. This makes the evaluation of the global texture features more difficult, because it can hardly be seen if images with similar texture features are clustered together. If, on the other hand, an image set has dominant texture features it is easier to evaluate the similarities and dissimilarities between the images. For comparison, also the global texture features of the 220 representative flower images were evaluated with the SOM.

Figure 5.8 shows the result of the SOM for the 170 sample images after 250 learning steps applied to the global texture features. The input vectors for the SOM were four-dimensional, consisting of the four texture features calculated from the co-occurrence probabilities (entropy, contrast, correlation and homogeneity) (see Section 4.5.4).

Figure 5.8: SOM visualisation of an example texture database (170 samples) after 250 learning steps.

The results revealed that the granular structures are clustered in the upper left half of the SOM. The coarser structures are arranged around the finer ones. From top to bottom, image content becomes more detailed. The flower images can be found in the middle left and the upper right area of the SOM. Whereas flower images with dominant blossoms are primarily arranged at the left part, posies, with more than one blossom, are located mainly in the upper right part of the lattice. Flower hedges photographed against a wall or those that completely fill out the images, are grouped on the right side of the lattice centre or at the outer right part, respectively. Images with more directional structures are mainly located at the lower area of the lattice. More coarse structures, like ladders and bricks, are clustered at the central lower part of the lattice. Finer structures, like cages and radiator grills, are located at the lower right part.

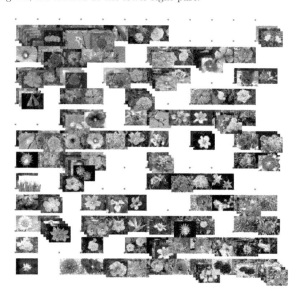

Figure 5.9: SOM visualisation of the global texture feature for the representative flower set after approximately 7,000 learning steps.

Figure 5.9 shows the results of the SOM for the 220 sample flowers after 7000 learning steps applied to the global texture features. Again, the input vectors for the SOM were four-dimensional, consisting of the four texture features calculated from the co-occurrence probabilities (i.e., entropy, contrast, correlation and homogeneity) (see Section 4.5.4). It can be seen that the images with a heterogeneous background (consisting of leaves and branches) are mainly located at the right (especially in the lower right area), whereas those with a more homogeneous background are preferably located at the left side of the lattice. Jagged flowers can mainly be found in the centre. Again, flower hedges are mainly located at the lower right part of the lattice. Flowers photographed against a black background are distributed throughout the lattice, depending on the shape and nature of the blossom. As stated above, the evaluation of the texture features for the flower images is quite difficult, because the flowers do not show obvious texture features, like directionality, entropy, inertia, coarseness and so on.

The results support the suitability of the global texture features for image retrieval. However, the discrimination power of the texture feature is weaker compared to the colour features: The clustering of texture images on the SOM lattice revealed more outliers, e.g., the image of a fence in the upper right area (see Figure 5.8). These results are conform to the outcome of the Shannon entropy, where the colour feature revealed a higher discrimination power than the texture feature (see Section 4.6).

Evaluation of the Tile-Based Colour Feature (VBIR)

The evaluation of the tile-based colour feature with the SOM requires input vectors with a dimension of 3456, because the images are divided into 16 tiles, represented by a 216 bin colour histogram (see Section 4.5.2). Thus, the evaluation of the tile-based colour features with the SOM is a complex task and requires extensive computing time. Figure 5.10 shows the results for the evaluation of the tile-based colour feature after 20,000 learning steps. The result reveals a clear structuring of the different flower images. Images with a dominant dark background are arranged in the lower left part of the lattice. Large-sized yellow flowers photographed against a background consisting of dark green leaves are grouped on the right, small-sized ones in the centre and large-sized flowers with a brighter green background on the left part of the lattice. The orange flowers are all clustered at the centre. Images, photographed against the sky are all located at the upper right corner. Below, a cluster of flowers against a greyish background can be found. Flowers with a background of dominant light green leaves are mainly located in the upper left corner of the lattice. They compose different sub-clusters, depending on the size and colour of the blossom: For example, all red flowers are grouped together. Violet flowers against a dominant dark background compose a cluster on the central left position of the lattice. Those photographed against a wall are located closer to the lattice centre.

A comparison of the SOM visualisations for the global (see Figure 5.7) with the tile-based colour features (see Figure 5.10) shows several differences. The images with a black background are more distributed for the tile-based features. In case of global features, all images with a dominant black background are clustered together, because black dominates the other colours. Large-sized flowers are clustered together for both features, because the influence of the background colours in the histogram is small. The yellow flowers compose one central cluster in case of global features, but two cluster for the tile-based features (for small and large-sized blossoms). Additionally, the large-sized violet flowers are clustered for the global colour features, but they are distributed throughout the lattice (depending on the background) for the tile-based colour features. The flowers photographed against the sky are clustered together for both types of features, emphasising the dominant role of

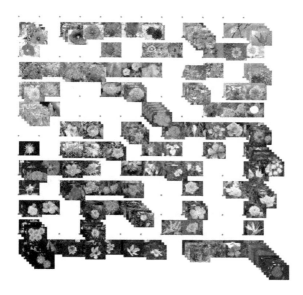

Figure 5.10: SOM visualisation of the tile-based colour feature after 20,000 iterations.

the blue colour. In case of the tile-based features, the images are more distributed, because some images contain large-sized flowers (for example, the sunflower), which covers multiple image tiles. For the global colour features on the other hand, the images containing the sky are staggered at one neuron in the lattice, because blue is the dominant colour.

All in all, the results support the suitability of the tile-based colour histograms for image retrieval, which has already been demonstrated by other researchers. For example, the adequacy of quantised colour histograms, calculated for 16 non-overlapping image tiles, was demonstrated by Luo and Nascimento (2004).

Evaluation of the Tile-Based Shape Feature (VBIR)

The evaluation of the tile-based shape features with the SOM was not feasible, because the feature vectors for each tile may have different dimensions. Here, the same reasons as for the global shape feature apply. The tile-based shape feature distances were also not visualised with the result viewer (see Section 5.3.1). The reason is that the result viewer was implemented as a quite simple visualisation tool for the feature distances stored in the database. Since the shape features were not separately calculated for each image tile (see Section 4.5.3), the visualisation according to tile-based shape features does not make sense without any post-processing of the data. This is the only feature which was neither evaluated nor visualised.

Evaluation of the Tile-Based Texture Feature (VBIR)

Because the suitability of the global texture features had already been proved by using a separate test database of 170 images, the evaluation of the tile-based texture features was performed on the sample database of 220 flower images. This allowed to evaluate whether the tile-based texture features reliably represent the similarity between flower images. Each greyscale image was represented by a 64-dimensional feature vector, i.e., the textures features for 16 tiles, each one consisting of the four features calculated from the local co-occurrence probabilities (i.e., entropy, contrast, correlation and homogeneity) (see Section 4.5.4).

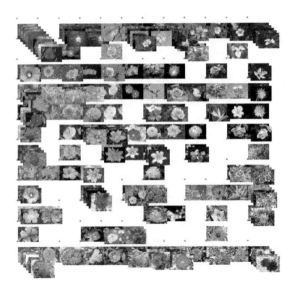

Figure 5.11: SOM visualisation of the tile-based texture features (after 250 learning steps).

Figure 5.11 shows the result of the SOM for the sample image set after 250 learning steps applied to the tile-based texture features. The result reveals an adequate clustering of the flowers according to blossom and background. The flowers with a relatively consistent background are located at the upper half of the lattice, whereas those with an inconsistent background are distributed throughout the lower part of the lattice. The yellow water lilies are all clustered at the top of the SOM, the roses with dark green leaves in the background can all be found in the lattice centre, whereas jagged flowers are located at the right side. Small blossoms with a relatively dominant dark background are arranged at the upper central and right part, whereas large-sized star-shaped flowers are located at the central and lower left parts of the lattice. The lower right part of the SOM is mainly populated by flowers photographed against a relative bright, mainly inconsistent background. Among these images, those photographed against the earth or against a wall, are clustered, respectively. Posies and hedges against an irregular background (e.g., earth, leaves or branches) are clustered in the right area of the lattice.

A comparison of the global texture features (see Figure 5.9) with the tile-based features (see Figure 5.11) shows some differences: The small-sized flowers depicted on a black background are mainly distributed on the top of the lattice for the tile-based features, whereas they are more clustered for the global texture features. For the tile-based texture features, the small flowers are more located at the upper half, the larger-sized flowers in the central, and the posies and hedges are mainly at the lower part of the lattice. For the global texture features the small flowers are more distributed throughout the lattice (depending on the background). The same is true for the large-sized flowers. The posies and hedges are also located at the upper right and centre right areas of the lattice. Additionally, the flowers with heterogeneous background are more distributed, forming two clusters in the case of the tile-based features compared to the global features. Also, the jagged flowers are clustered in the lattice centre for the tile-based features, but they are more distributed throughout the lattice for the global features.

The distribution of flowers of the same species against various backgrounds over the whole lattice, and the clustering of similar flowers photographed against similar backgrounds on the lattice, supports that the tile-based texture features, independently calculated from the local co-occurrence probabilities of each tile, are suitable for image retrieval.

5.4   Conclusions

The results of the feature evaluations of the applied global and tile-based features for colour and texture with the SOM confirmed the suitability of both feature types for the retrieval of flower images. Images with similar colour and texture features are clustered in neighbouring areas of the SOM. Both features are evaluated on a representative image set from the flower database (see Section 4.5.1). For the global texture features, a second database of 170 greyscale images with dominant texture features was created, which alleviates the feature evaluation in regard to the flower images. The clustering of the colour features revealed less outliers than for the texture features, which confirmed the dominant discriminative power of the colour feature for the retrieval of flower images (see Section 4.6). Because of the different number of blossoms in the single flower images, the shape features have high variances in their feature vector dimensions and can therefore not serve as an input for the SOM. Thus, the result viewer, a visualisation tool for feature distances was implemented. It depicts the 24 most similar images to a given query on the basis of the pre-calculated shape distances. The visualisations corroborate the suitability of the global shape features for image retrieval: The most similar images to a given query were within the best 24 matches. Although, there were some outliers among the best matches due to poor segmentation results (see Section 4.5.3). These results support the better discrimination power of the colour feature revealed by the Shannon entropy (see Section 4.6). The result viewer reveals no information on the structure of the image subset, e.g., which images are clustered together and how their distances are related to the query and the other images of the database. Furthermore, it is not possible to deduce general statements about the whole database from the image subset. For these purposes, the hyperbolic multidimensional scaling method (HMDS) can be applied. It presents the data images arranged in a hyperbolic space and allows a comfortable navigation in the data set.

Let us now - at least partly - consider again the main aspects of the previous chapters: A database of 2,000 flower images was created. Suitable colour, shape and texture features for image retrieval were chosen. These features were calculated for each database image, once as global features (i.e., on the data of the whole image) and once as tile-based features (i.e., for each of 16 non-overlapping image tiles). The global features are used for Content-Based Image Retrieval (CBIR), where the user-relevance feedback is provided by mouse clicks. The tile-based features, on the other side, are required for the new Vision-Based Image Retrieval (VBIR) approach. In VBIR, the user-relevance feedback is provided by the mouse and additionally by eye movements. The optimal weighting for the single features were determined by using the Shannon entropy. The appropriateness and suitability of the global and tile-based colour and texture features were evaluated with the self-organizing map (SOM). The global shape distances were visualised with the result viewer. For each feature, another distance metric was applied to calculate the pairwise distances between images or between all corresponding tiles of an image pair. These pre-calculated distances were stored in a database.

This chapter concludes the description of the preliminary work. The chosen global and tile-based image features and their corresponding distance functions were the subject of Chapter 4. After evaluating the quality of the selected image features and their distances in this chapter, and the determination of the optimal feature weights through the Shannon entropy in Section 4.6, all fundamentals for the following steps are provided: The empirical experiments and the implementation of the models for the different retrieval approaches are described in Chapter 6 and 7. The discussion of the results and perspectives for future work is subject of Chapter 8.

Chapter 6

Image Retrieval Experiments

After establishing the preliminaries for the present research and explaining the design and the differences between the new VBIR and the general CBIR approach to image retrieval in the previous chapters, both approaches are put into practice, i.e., experiments are conducted so that the approaches can be compared and evaluated as to performance.

In order to provide a valid basis for the comparison of the new vision-based approach with a general content-based approach, two experiments were designed. In experiment I the retrieval performances of the new VBIR and a general CBIR approach were directly compared. In order to exclude the influences of other factors on retrieval performance, the experimental setup for both approaches was designed as similar as possible: The images were presented using the same retrieval scenario and the participants had to accomplish identical tasks. The differences concerned the additional on-line processing of eye movements in the VBIR system, as well as the way features were calculated, i.e., globally versus tile-based (see Section 4.5). These differences relate to the technical implementations and were hidden from the participants in the experiment.

Because of the high computational time for the single retrieval processes, the number of retrieval steps for each query image in the CBIR and VBIR conditions were limited in order to test both approaches on a set of eight representative query images from the flower database. Thus, an additional experiment was designed, where participants ranked the retrieval results of both approaches according to their overall impression of similarity to the corresponding query images. This experiment had two purposes: For one, it provided subjective estimations of the quality of the retrieval results. For another, it allowed to evaluate the degree of similarity between the retrieval results and the query images for each approach, in cases where the query image was not found within the limited number of retrieval steps.

6.1 Experiment I: CBIR versus VBIR

In order to evaluate the suitability of the new eye-tracking based approach to image retrieval (*VBIR*), its performance was compared with a system using the established techniques of Content-Based Image Retrieval (*CBIR*). For a reliable comparison, both systems operated on the same database, used the same colour, shape and texture features as well as the corresponding distance functions, and the participants were given identical instructions. The only differences were that in the VBIR condition, a fixation map (see Section 3.5.1) was calculated online from participants' eye movements in order to weight the different image tiles for image retrieval (see Section 4.4.1), and that tile-based calculated image features were used instead of global ones (see Section 4.5). Through the additional recording of eye movements in the VBIR condition, relevant parts of the image can be automatically identified by the system. By increasing the weights for the image features calculated from the relevant image areas, the retrieval process should be significantly improved, leading to a higher retrieval rate and lower retrieval times.

6.1.1 Method

Participants

Altogether 30 students of Bielefeld University participated in experiment I (14 females, 16 males). Their age was between 25 and 35 years. The majority of the participants had no prior experiences with eye-tracking experiments. They had normal or corrected visual acuity. No pupil anomalies or colour blindness were found. Each participant received an honorarium of 6 € for his or her participation in the experiment.

Materials

The image database used for the retrieval experiment consisted of 2,000 flower images (see Section 4.5.1 for more details). From the database, eight start configurations were selected randomly, each consisting of a query and six flower images (see Appendix). All images of the different start configurations are depicted in higher resolution in the Appendix. The images were presented on a computer screen with a resolution of 1024×768 pixels ($31.3^o \times 25.0^o$ of visual angle) and a refresh rate of 80 Hz (see Figure 6.1). The experimental layout was identical for both approaches: The query image was presented in the centre at the top of the screen (from position (364,50) upper left corner to position (652,250) lower right corner). Below the query image, six database images were depicted, arranged in a grid of two rows and three columns. The horizontal space between two database images and the vertical space between two rows was 40 pixels (1.37^o and 1.39^o of visual angle, respectively). The vertical distance between the first row and the query image was 50 pixels (1.74^o of visual angle). Between the left edge of the screen and the first database image of each row was a space of 40 pixels (1.37^o of visual angle). All images were 288×200 ($9.7^o \times 6.9^o$ of visual angle) pixels in size. The experiment was designed with the VDesigner (see Chapter 3.5).

Apparatus

For the experiment, the SMI Eyelink I eye tracker (see Section 3.3.2) was used to record participants' eye movements. Participants were seated about 60 cm from a 20-in colour

Figure 6.1: Screenshot of the retrieval scenario. The query image is depicted at the top. The database images are arranged in a grid of two rows and three columns. The image chosen by the participant is surrounded by a red frame.

monitor. The VBIR approach required an exact recording of gaze positions. Hence, the participants' head was stabilised by using a chin rest (see Figure 6.2). In order to guarantee a constant viewing position and distance for all participants, the chin rest was also used in the CBIR approach, even though eye movements were not recorded.

Procedure

The participants were tested individually. Prior to the start of the experiment, they were provided with written instructions, explaining the task they had to complete. After reading the instructions, participants adjusted the chin rest so that the screen centre was at eye level. Randomly, half of the participants were assigned to the CBIR and the other half to the VBIR condition. Participants were instructed to find the query image in the database by successively clicking on that image out of the six displayed database images that they assumed to be most similar to the query image (see Figure 6.1). Participants had to choose the images according to their overall impression of similarity. After the participants had chosen an image by clicking on it (it was marked with a red frame to signal that the computer has registered the mouse click (see Figure 6.1)), the program calculated the distances of the selected image to all other images in the database. In case of the CBIR condition, the distance between an image pair was calculated as the sum of the distances for the global colour, shape and texture features. In case of the VBIR condition, first a fixation map (see Section 3.5.1) for the selected image was calculated online from the recorded eye movements, leading to an importance value for each image tile (see Section 4.4.1). The overall distances were then calculated as the average of the colour, shape and texture distances between all 16 corresponding tiles, where the 16 feature distances were weighted by the corresponding importance value from the fixation map. The global (CBIR), as well as the tile-based (VBIR) colour, shape and texture distances were weighted by the optimal feature weights calculated from the distance histograms using the Shannon entropy (see Section 4.6). The six images from the database most similar to the clicked image were then presented on the screen. They were ordered according to increasing distance from top to bottom and left to right. Each image was presented only once, i.e., if the top six images included an image that had already been displayed, the next undisplayed image from the retrieval list was shown. The computational time for finding the six most similar images from the database to the clicked one was around 22 seconds in the VBIR approach. The time was so long, because in the VBIR system more calculations had to be performed for each image pair since the distances between all sixteen tiles had to be considered. A delay loop was added to the CBIR scenario to ensure that the computational time for one retrieval step was identical for both approaches. The retrieval loop ended, when the query image was found or when the maximum number of retrieval steps was reached.

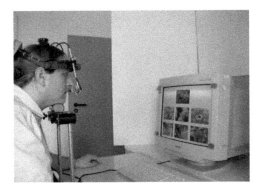

Figure 6.2: Participant using the VBIR system in experiment I.

Altogether, the experiment consisted of eight start configurations. For each query image, there was a maximum of 10 retrieval steps allowed to find it. The number of steps to find a query image was limited in order to test both approaches on a representative selection of query images. The start configurations were presented to the participants in a random order. This order was identical in the CBIR and VBIR condition, respectively. Additionally, for each retrieval process, the positions of the six images in the start configuration varied. Whenever a query image had been found or the maximum number of steps had been reached without finding the query image, the next start configuration was presented to the participant and the retrieval process started anew.

In case of CBIR, the experiment started right away. In case of the VBIR scenario, first the eye tracker was set up and calibrated for each participant. During the calibration, par-

Figure 6.3: Screenshot of the VBIR test image. The purpose of the test image is to validate the quality of the calibration. The actual gaze position is marked by a white square on the screen. Previous positions of the white rectangle are depicted by black circles.

ticipants had to fixate successively nine calibration markers at different screen positions. After the calibration, a test image was centred on a white background (see Figure 6.3). The actual gaze position was depicted on the screen by a small white rectangle. When the participant moved the eyes, the new gaze position was marked by the rectangle and a black circle was drawn on the previous position. Through this online presentation of gaze positions, the quality of the calibration could be validated. There were also two black boxes at the upper left side of the test screen. By gazing at the top one and pressing the left mouse button, the VBIR system was started. A fixation on the bottom box and a simultaneous mouse click started a drift correction for the re-calibration of the eye tracker.

Participants of experiment I were not informed about how the program calculates the image distances, nor about the image features that were used for the distance calculation. Participants in the VBIR approach were also not informed about the fixation map that was calculated from their eye movements to adjust the weights for the tile-based feature distances. After every second retrieval process, a re-calibration of the eye tracker in form of a drift correction was performed in the VBIR condition, in order to compensate for possible displacements of the headset due to slight head movements. For both retrieval approaches, the number of the query images and the depicted database images, as well as the positions of the selected images and the reaction times were recorded during the experiment. In the VBIR system additionally the fixation information was stored. The differences between the two retrieval approaches are summarised in Table 6.1.

6.1.2 Results and Discussion

After the experiment the participants were asked about their preferred retrieval strategies. Most of them had focussed on the colour information. According to their intuition, participants first tried to match colour and shape information. Only in cases where this

	CBIR	VBIR
Feature Calculation	Global	Tile-Based
Relevance Feedback	Mouse Click	Eye Movements and Mouse Click
Recorded Data	Query - and Database Images, Positions of Selected Images, Reaction Time	Query- and Database Images, Positions of Selected Images, Reaction Time

Table 6.1: The differences between the CBIR and VBIR retrieval conditions.

information was not sufficient for the similarity estimation, they also considered other features like background information, overall impression and contrast. Participants usually changed their retrieval strategies during the experiment. A few also counted the number of blossoms at the beginning of the experiment.

In order to draw further conclusions from the experiment, the recorded data was subjected to a deeper analysis with regard to the number of retrieved images and reaction time. For all subsequent statistical analysis, the α-level for the significance of effects is set to $p = 0.05$.

Number of Retrieved Images

As can be seen from Table 6.2, the number of retrieved images in the VBIR is higher than in the CBIR approach, i.e., 31 to 14 images, respectively. The highest number of retrieved images in the VBIR approach is four and the lowest is one. On average, each participant found 2.07 of eight query images. In the CBIR approach on the other hand, the highest number of retrieved images is two, whereas the lowest is zero. On average, 0.93 query images were found (see Figure 6.4).

A statistical analysis of the number of retrieved images for the two different retrieval approaches reveals that the participants found significantly more images in the VBIR than in the CBIR approach ($t(29) = 3.885$; p=0.001). Most participants using the CBIR system (11 out of 15) found query image 342, two participants retrieved image number 1431, whereas only one succeeded for image 380 (see Table 6.3). The reason for the high probability of retrieval for image 342 is due to the similar image 162 (a white blossom on a black background) in the corresponding start configuration (see Appendix). When participants choose image 162 from the start configuration, query image 342 is retrieved in the following step, because the database does not contain many images with a white blossom against a black background.

Image 1431 has a large-sized, dominant red blossom and a background with many leaves and part of the ground. There is also a flower (image 1463) with a dominant red blossom and a colour distribution similar to the query in the corresponding start configuration (see Appendix). By choosing this image in the first step and successive

Participant (CBIR)	Images Found	Participant (VBIR)	Images Found
1	1	16	3
2	2	17	1
3	1	18	1
4	1	19	1
5	1	20	3
6	0	21	2
7	1	22	3
8	1	23	4
9	0	24	3
10	0	25	1
11	1	26	2
12	2	27	2
13	1	28	2
14	1	29	2
15	1	30	1
$\sum$	**14**	$\sum$	**31**

Table 6.2: Number of images found listed separately for the participants using the CBIR (1-15) and VBIR (16-30) system.

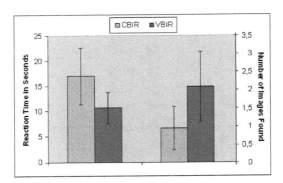

Figure 6.4: Average reaction time (in seconds) and number of images found for the CBIR and VBIR approach.

selection of images with dominant red blossoms, query image 1431 can be found within 10 retrieval steps. In image 380, the blossom is much smaller and the background is more heterogeneous. The colour histogram is much more distributed and the flower has a common shape. This makes it more difficult to retrieve the image within 10 retrieval steps. Table 6.3 shows also for each retrieved image in the CBIR approach the probability of retrieval (PR) and the average number of retrieval steps the participants needed to find it (AvgNS).

Query Image	PR (CBIR)	AvgNS (CBIR)	PR (VBIR)	AvgNS (VBIR)
63	$\frac{0}{15}$	-	$\frac{0}{15}$	-
342	$\frac{11}{15}$	2	$\frac{13}{15}$	4.31
380	$\frac{1}{15}$	8	$\frac{2}{15}$	7
626	$\frac{0}{15}$	-	$\frac{5}{15}$	5.6
715	$\frac{0}{15}$	-	$\frac{4}{15}$	4.75
1431	$\frac{2}{15}$	4.5	$\frac{6}{15}$	4.83
1569	$\frac{0}{15}$	-	$\frac{0}{15}$	-
1600	$\frac{0}{15}$	-	$\frac{1}{15}$	7

Table 6.3: All query images, their image number as well as their probability of retrieval (PR) and the average number of required retrieval steps (AvgNS) in the CBIR and VBIR approach. The query images are depicted in the Appendix.

In the following, some scan paths from the VBIR approach for various query images are depicted and analysed. In the visualisations, fixations are depicted by circles whereas saccades are illustrated by lines. The diameter of the circle is proportional to the fixation duration.

Almost all the VBIR participants found image 342 (i.e., 13 out of 15), but they required more retrieval steps than the participants in the CBIR approach. Typical scan paths for this image are shown in Figures 6.5 - 6.8. In the following, Q denotes the query and the letters from A to F the database images from left to right and top to bottom (see Figure 6.5). Figure 6.5 shows the scan path of participant 26 during the first retrieval step for query image 342. The scan path starts with a central fixation (marked by a red circle). This is due to a preceding drift correction with a central marker position. The participant shortly fixated the query and immediately directed the gaze to the database images at the centre, before he focussed on image D (the white blossom on the black background). Then the participant directed the gaze to the query for a longer period of time, to check details of the flower image. The cumulative fixations on the query and on image D of this participant are conform to the findings that humans have to fixate regions of particular objects being important for the estimation of image similarity (see Section 3.2.4). Before the gaze was directed back to image D, the participant shortly checked the other database images. Thus, his attention was directed only for a small period of time to regions of dissimilar images (see Section 3.2.6). The last fixation, marked by a violet circle, was again on image D. The orange flower (image F) was not fixated at all. Conceivably, this participant recognised through peripheral vision that this flower was not important (see Section 3.2.2). As can be seen from Figure 6.5, his focus was on the yellow-white coloured flower in image D and not on the dark background. Because more images in the database consisted of flowers with a dominant white colour mixed with other colours, the number of possible candidates is higher than in the CBIR approach.

In the second step (see Figure 6.6) the retrieved images are all flowers depicted against a dark background. The focus was first on the query, then on image B. Conceivably, this participant checked in his peripheral vision the importance of the four images. After shortly jumping back to the query for two fixations, the participants' gaze was directed successively to image E and D, then to A and finally, back to B. Then the participant repeated this fixation pattern, conceivably, to compare the flowers again after receiving more information about the single database images. There were several regions in the different images the participant had to check for similarity. Thus, the participants' gaze was subsequently directed to these regions. This might be necessary, because it was not clear in advance, which database image was most similar to the query. In the second "loop" the gaze was first directed from the query to image E, from there to image B, followed by fixation on image D and A and finally back to the selected image. The last fixation was on the orange flower in the first row (image C).

In the third step (see Figure 6.7), there were many more fixations than in the steps before. Additionally, the participant focussed on the four database images that depict a white flower on a dark background. In general, fixation density is influenced by the amount of semantic information in a region and the total fixation time is longer for visually and

Figure 6.5: Eye movements of participant 26 for the retrieval of the query image 342 (step 1).

Figure 6.6: Eye movements of participant 26 for the retrieval of the query image 342 (step 2).

semantically important regions (see Section 3.2.4). Conceivably, the participant had to check several regions for image similarity, so that he directed his gaze subsequently to the different regions for a relatively long period of time (see Section 3.2.6). Obviously, the participant had difficulties in selecting the most similar image, because these four images were all quite similar to the query, so that he had to check image details. Furthermore, there were saccades between all four database images and the query. This shows that the participant "jumped" between all five images to compare feature details. The final fixation was on image C, which was finally chosen.

Figure 6.7: Eye movements of participant 26 for the retrieval of the query image 342 (step 3).

In the last step (see Figure 6.8), the participant focussed on the images in the first row from right to left. Images B and C were focussed once. Conceivably, the participant could realise quite fast that the images are not similar to the query. There was no focus on the query at the beginning. Probably, the participant had already an exact impression of the query in mind. Interestingly, the participant directed his gaze shortly back to the query, when he has gazed at the first image (which is the correct one). After that, the focus was again on image A and then on image D, before returning to the correct one. The short fixation on image D served to check the similarity between the shape features of the flowers in the query and in image D.

More participants retrieved image 1431 in the VBIR than in the CBIR approach (see Table 6.3). The reason is that participants primarily focussed on the central tiles. These tiles fully cover the blossom. There is no background information covered by the central tiles that deteriorated image retrieval. Thus, images with large-sized red blossoms in the centre are preferably retrieved from the database, which restricted the search space and led to improved retrieval performance.

Image 715 was found four times in the VBIR approach, while it could not be retrieved at all in the CBIR approach. One reason could be that the database contained many images of red blossoms with green leaves in the background. As can be seen from Figure 6.9, the participants' focus was on the blossom as it is the most important part of a flower. In general, task-related knowledge determines fixation location and durations when viewing natural scenes (see Section 3.2.3). The focus on the blossom narrowed the search space, because now the VBIR system retrieved images with a large-sized red flower in the image centre, whereas the background information was ignored. This means that the additional eye movements significantly improved the retrieval performance. Even though the images of the start configuration are quite dissimilar to the query, the participant

Figure 6.8: Eye movements of participant 26 for the retrieval of the query image 342 (step 4).

managed to find the query. Figure 6.9 shows the scan path for participant 23 during the first step for the retrieval of image 715. As can be seen, the fixations were mostly focussed on image A and F. There were mainly "jumps" from the selected image to the query image and between the selected image and image A. The background of both images was not considered. Only in case of the yellow flowers (image B and D), the participant also gazed on the background. There were also "jumps" between both images. Again, all images were fixated several times, conceivably, to compare image details.

Figure 6.9: Eye movements of participant 23 for the retrieval of the query image 715 (step 1).

In the second retrieval step (Figure 6.10), the query image and image B and E were intensively fixated. The fixation pattern reveals that the participant judged image similarity by comparing fine image details (see Section 3.2.6). Again, also the more dissimilar images were focussed several times, probably to make sure that all image details were considered. There were many "jumps" between image A, B and the query, because these images were quite similar to the one chosen in step 1 (see Figure 6.9). Later, the focus was directed towards image B, E and the query. Conceivably, at that time, the participant had already decided to select one of those images.

Figure 6.10: Eye movements of participant 23 for the retrieval of the query image 715 (step 2).

In the final retrieval step (see Figure 6.11), the participant changed the focus between the query and the correct image. Image B, located between the query and the correct database image, was only shortly fixated.

Both, the sunflower image (image 63) as well as image 1559, the small white flowers on the ground, was neither found in the CBIR nor in the VBIR approach (see Table 6.3). The sunflower image was photographed in front of a blue sky. No image of the corresponding start configuration has a blue background. Because participants usually preferred colour and shape features, the focus was clearly on the blossom and not on the sky (see Figure 6.12). Image C was selected as the most similar image. Conceivably, for participant 17, colour played the dominant role for the selection of the most similar image from the start configuration. As a consequence, the system preferably retrieved large-sized yellow flowers on a green background. Thus, the retrieval of the sunflower image within ten steps was impossible, even though in the VBIR approach participants managed to navigate to flowers with large-sized yellow blossoms.

Image 1559 is quite inhomogeneous. The small white blossoms are photographed against a mainly brown, but quite unstructured background. Participants usually focussed

Figure 6.11: Eye movements of participant 23 for the retrieval of the query image 715 (step 3).

Figure 6.12: Eye movements of participant 17 for the retrieval of the query image 63 (step 1).

on the big blossom and its surrounding in the query image (see Figure 6.13). Because of the small size of the white flowers, fixated tiles of the blossom also contained a lot of background, even though participants tried to focus on the petals and to ignore the background. Hence, for the similarity calculations, also much noise was considered, resulting in poor retrieval results, which prevented the user from a target-oriented navigation in the database. The main focus was on image F, which depicts a white flower with a similar size and number of petals. Consequently, small white blossoms were retrieved in the following steps.

Figure 6.13: Eye movements of participant 28 for the retrieval of the query image 1569 (step 5).

Figure 6.14: *Original image 1569.*

Figure 6.15: *Segmentation result for image 1569 (see Figure 6.14).*

In the CBIR approach, the inhomogeneous background of image 1569 (see Figure 6.14) resulted in a widely distributed colour histogram leading to many false positives in the retrieval process. Furthermore, the segmentation result was a small star-shaped flower (see Figure 6.15). This shape of the blossom occurred frequently in the images of the database. As a consequence, the shape features matched those of many other database images: Probably another reason for the poor retrieval performance in the VBIR approach, since the colour and shape features were the predominant features, because they received higher feature weights (see Section 4.6).

Average Reaction Time

As a second variable, the average reaction time has been analysed (see Figure 6.4). The statistical analysis reveals that the average reaction time of the participants in the CBIR is significantly higher than in the VBIR approach ($t(29) = 3.82$; $p=0.001$). The mean of the average reaction times for CBIR is 16.96 s and 10.66 s for VBIR (see Figure 6.4). The standard deviation is 5.58 and 3.09 s in case of CBIR and VBIR, respectively. One reason for the higher average reaction times in the CBIR approach could be that it is more difficult to control the retrieval system, because only a coarse relevance feedback by mouse click is considered. In cases where no image out of the six actually presented ones strikes as more similar to the query than the others, it became more difficult for the participants to select the most similar one. Thus, once the retrieval resulted in a set of irrelevant images, it became more difficult for the participant to redirect the system to more relevant results.

In the VBIR scenario, on the other hand, even if the retrieved images were very dissimilar to the query image, it was possible to use the eye movements, focussed on important image regions, to navigate to a more similar set of images. Then, also the reaction time decreased, because in the course of the retrieval process the presented images became more similar to the query. Conceivably, in general, at least one of the flowers in the VBIR approach seemed to be obviously more similar to the query than the others. This may have prevented the participants from time-consuming comparisons of similar image pairs. In the CBIR approach on the other hand, more often database images were dissimilar to the query, resulting in a long-standing selection process. This process seems to be more time consuming than the selection of a candidate from a set of similar images.

6.2   Experiment II: Evaluation of the Retrieval Results

As described above, the maximum number of retrieval steps to find a query image in experiment I was limited to a maximum of 10 retrieval steps in order to test both retrieval approaches on a set of eight query images. The results were evaluated according to the number of retrieved images and the average reaction time. For the evaluation of the retrieval success, those trials were not considered, where the participants did not successfully retrieve the query image within the maximum of 10 steps. In order to evaluate the similarity of the retrieval results of both approaches to the corresponding query in cases, where the query was not retrieved, a second experiment was designed. In this experiment participants had to rate the retrieval results of both approaches according to their overall impression of similarity to the corresponding query images. The approach with the highest number of retrieved images, rated as more similar to the query images is taken to be the better one. This experiment has two further advantages: For one, the retrieval results were evaluated by using a similarity criterion that was not applied in experiment I . For another, the retrieval results were evaluated in a cognitively adequate way that is, according to human measures of similarity. Thus, the aim of experiment II was to evaluate the retrieval performances of both approaches by ranking the retrieval results of both approaches according to the participants' overall impression of similarity to the corresponding query images.

6.2.1   Method

Participants

A group of fifteen students from different departments at Bielefeld University was recruited for this experiment (7 females, 8 males). None of these students took part in the retrieval experiment I (see Section 6.1). They received an honorarium of 4 € for their participation.

Materials

The participants were presented the retrieval results and the corresponding query images from experiment I, each with a resolution of 288×200 pixels ($9.7^o \times 6.9^o$) on a 20-in screen with a resolution of 1024 by 768 pixels ($31.3^o \times 25.0^o$) and a refresh rate of 80 Hz (see Figure 6.16). The query image was shown in the centre of the upper half of the screen. Below the query image, two images were depicted side-by-side, the corresponding retrieval results of experiment I. In cases the query was not found within the limit of 10 retrieval steps, the retrieval result was the image that was chosen by the participant in the last retrieval step. In case of retrieval success, it was the query image.

There was a slider below each retrieved image with a scale ranging from 0 to 100. The value represented the subjective degree of similarity between the retrieved image and the query image. Zero meant "not similar" at all, whereas 100 represented identity. Additionally, there was a white box below each slider. The selected similarity value was additionally displayed in the box and changed dynamically with slider movements. The computer for experiment II was the same one used for experiment I in order to hold constant the appearance of the images. The overall size of the frame (see Figure 6.16) was 800×700 pixels ($24.5^o \times 22.8^o$).

Altogether 120 retrieval pairs from experiment I had to be evaluated: All in all, 15 participants took part in the VBIR and CBIR experiment, where each participant had to retrieve eight query images.

Procedure

All participants were tested individually. Prior to the experiment, the participants were provided with written instructions explaining the tasks they had to complete.

Each participant had to evaluate 120 image pairs (see above), presented in blocks of eight retrieval pairs from the participants of the CBIR and VBIR approach having the same order of start configurations. The order of the eight retrieval pairs as well as the order of the participants from experiment I was chosen randomly. It was only guaranteed that the same query image did not appear in two successive steps. For each cycle, the position of the retrieval results from both approaches were chosen randomly.

The participants' task was to evaluate the similarity of the two retrieved images (depicted in the lower half of Figure 6.16) to the query image (upper half) by moving the slider with the mouse until the value appeared in the white box, representing participants' overall impression of similarity. The entry in the box was automatically updated, when

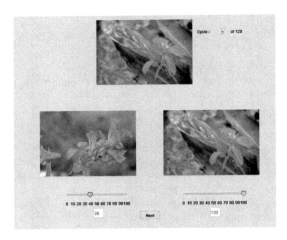

Figure 6.16: Screenshot of experiment II. The query image is depicted in the centre on the top of the screen. Below are the corresponding result images from the CBIR and VBIR experiment.

the slider was moved, which made it easier for the participants to adjust the slider value exactly. When both retrieved images had been rated, participants had to click on the "Next"-button at the bottom of the page (see Figure 6.16) and another query image as well as the corresponding pair of retrieval results were shown. This procedure was repeated until all 120 pairs of retrieval results had been evaluated. A counter in the upper right corner showed the number of trials (out of 120) that had already been accomplished (see Figure 6.16).

The names of the query, CBIR, and VBIR result images as well as the corresponding slider values for the retrieval results were recorded in a log file. The number of retrieved images from the VBIR and CBIR approach, which received higher similarity values, was counted. Additionally, the overall sum and the average slider ratings, separated by retrieval approach, were stored in a second log file.

In interviews after the experiment, the participants stated that they mostly relied on colour and shape (mainly the petals) information when they judged image similarity. Some of them emphasised colour, others shape information. The participants, who focussed more on shape information gave higher ratings if the flowers had similar shape, but different colours. Participants also considered background information or the overall impressions only, if they could not match the colour or shape information. One participant additionally considered the bright-dark contrast of the images. Another one considered the number of flowers for the first passes, but changed his strategy later and focussed more on the overall impression. One participant also paid attention to the orientation of the petals.

6.2.2   Results and Discussion

The results of experiment II are summarised in Table 6.4. The second and the third column of Table 6.4 shows, for each participant, the number of times the retrieval results of the CBIR or VBIR approach received the highest slider values in the 120 pairwise comparisons, respectively. In case of equal ratings, neither the VBIR nor the CBIR value were incremented. As can be seen from Table 6.4, all participants rated the retrieval results of the VBIR approach as more similar to the query images than those of the CBIR approach. The highest difference between the two values shows participant 15, who preferred the retrieval results of the VBIR approach more than twice as often. The smallest difference between the two approaches is six for participant 8.

In order to evaluate if there are significant differences between the slider ratings of the VBIR and CBIR approach, a χ^2 test had to be calculated. The result showed a highly significant difference between the slider ratings of the CBIR and VBIR retrieval results, i.e., significantly more result images from the VBIR approach received higher slider values than from the CBIR approach $(\chi^2(1) = 113.0; p < 0.01)$.

The third and the fourth column of Table 6.4 contain the average slider values calculated over all ratings for the CBIR and VBIR approach, respectively. The comparison of means using the t-test revealed that the average slider values significantly differed between the CBIR and VBIR approach $(t(14) = 26.399; p < 0.01)$. The sample means are 34.51 and 49.6, and the standard deviations are 9.57 and 10.46 for the CBIR and VBIR approach, respectively.

Additionally, the distances between the retrieval results and the corresponding queries are computed from the feature values stored in the database. This allows the comparison of the subjective similarity estimations (provided by participants' slider settings) with the objectively calculated feature distances. The correlation between the slider ratings for the CBIR results and the CBIR distances from the database is significant (r=-0.571; p < 0.01). Also the correlation between the slider ratings for the VBIR results and the calculated VBIR distances is significant (r=-0.767; p< 0.01). Both results revealed that there is a negative correlation between the slider ratings and the calculated features distances, i.e., high slider values correlate with small feature distances. This demonstrates that the subjective slider ratings correspond to the objective feature distances. The results emphasised the importance of carefully selected image features for the quality of the system's retrieval performance. When designing retrieval systems, image features should be preferred that correlate highly with human judgement of similarity (Neumann & Gegenfurtner, 2006).

The results also support the participants' statements in the interviews after the experiments that they usually focussed on the colour and shape features of the flowers, whereas the background was less important for the evaluation of image similarity. Focussing on the tiles containing important features and simultaneous masking of non-relevant regions by the assignment of small weights, makes the VBIR approach superior to the CBIR approach. Thus, tile-based features in combination with a fixation map from eye movements seem to catch human judgement of similarity better than the global features. But

Participant	CBIR	VBIR	Equal Ratings	CBIR Avg	VBIR Avg
1	39	67	14	34.68	46.56
2	38	70	12	37.36	55.06
3	36	72	12	23.58	37.75
4	32	74	14	50.06	65.11
5	28	42	50	19.85	31.34
6	33	70	17	21.38	36.61
7	34	62	24	28.63	42.86
8	48	54	18	29.65	42.91
9	37	72	11	40.46	54.5
10	43	66	11	40.17	55.89
11	38	71	11	37.24	55.64
12	40	66	14	24.56	40.22
13	36	70	14	40.35	58.38
14	37	69	14	49.61	63.03
15	32	77	11	40.0	58.16
ϕ	36.73	66.8	16.47	34.51	49.59

Table 6.4: Number of retrieval results rated higher for the CBIR and VBIR approach, specified for each participant. The fourth column indicates how often the retrieval results received equal slider values. Avg signifies the average slider values calculated over all ratings.

this holds only when attention is concentrated on several tiles and not spread over the whole image: The advantage of the tile-based features disappears, when all image tiles are considered.

All in all, the results of the slider experiment support the benefit of considering user relevance, especially the attention patterns, for image retrieval: The retrieval results of the VBIR approach received significantly higher similarity values than those of the CBIR approach. This is also the case, when the query could not be found within the limited number of retrieval steps. Additionally, the outcome of the experiment provides evidence for the correspondence of the numerically calculated feature distances with the subjectively provided similarity ratings. This shows clearly that the chosen image features (see Section 4.5) and optimal feature weights (see Section 4.6) are suitable for the retrieval of flower images and reflect reliably users' similarity estimations. Thus, the focus of the distance calculation on important image regions by analysis of the eye-movement patterns significantly improves the retrieval performance and meets more closely the demands of humans, even though, viewed objectively, the approach for locally calculated image features seems to be less promising.

The final part of this book is concerned with the implementation and verification of computer models for image retrieval. These models try to reproduce participants' behaviour for image retrieval on the basis of the empirical results presented in this chapter. The combination of empirical experiments and computational simulations of the observed effects help to understand the processes underlying image retrieval.

Chapter 7

Computer Models of Image Retrieval

7.1　The Motivation of Computer Simulations

Generally, computer simulations are applied in many research fields to complement empirical studies. In empirical studies, the collected data is subjected to qualitative and quantitative, mainly statistical analysis, to relate the experimental observations (*dependent variables*) to the systematically varied parameters (*independent variables*) (e.g., Sichelschmidt & Carbone, 2003). Based on the analytical results, the experimental observations can be interpreted and conclusions can be derived. However, it is not clear whether the conclusions drawn from a particular experiment are also valid in a more general context.

In order to enhance our understanding of complex processes, a more or less formal *model* (i.e., algorithmic descriptions of the suggested interpretations of the experimental data) can be implemented that attempts to simulate the empirical observations. The comparison of the results between the empirical data and the model reveals information about the adequacy of the computational simulation. If there are discrepancies, then the model is incomplete or partially incorrect (i.e., one or more essential aspects had not been taken into consideration). Through additional experiments and measurements an optimised model can be developed, which again would have to be tested. These steps can be repeated until a satisfactory model has been found. In return, also the initial premises and the suggested interpretations of the empirical data that led to the generation of the model, can be verified.

Usually, computer simulations can also be parameterised in order to test the influence and the interactions of the different parameters on the model output and to fine tune the model to optimal results. The high performance of modern computers allows the implementation of sophisticated models that can perform even complex mathematical calculations in an appropriate period of time.

The repeating loop of experimental data acquisition, interpretation and its successive validation through modelling, is a promising strategy leading to a better understanding of the complex processes underlying human behaviour. Exactly these are the premises and motivations for the implementation of the models developed in this book.

The computer simulations in this chapter address two main questions: For one, how can the image retrieval experiments (see Chapter 6) be adequately modelled? For another, what is the optimal linear combination weight for different feature maps resulting in the highest correlation with participants' attention distributions calculated from the recorded eye movements during the retrieval experiments?

In the following, the different image retrieval models are described first. After that, the saliency map based model is explained in more detail.

7.2 Computer Simulation I: The Image Retrieval Models

In this book, we deal with two different retrieval approaches: First, the new attention-based approach using locally calculated image features (for each image tile) and user-relevance feedback by eye movements and mouse clicks (VBIR) (see Section 4.4). Second, an approach based on globally calculated image features and relevance feedback by mouse clicks (CBIR) (see Section 4.5). These differences must also be considered for the implementation of the corresponding retrieval models.

Another difference is in the intention of the two models. The two CBIR models apply different distance functions to select the most similar image, called *reference image*, from the set of the six actually retrieved images (see Figure 6.1). For the retrieval of the most similar images from the database the same distance function is used for both approaches (see Table 7.5). Though, the question is which of the two models reflects more closely the human selection process of the reference images. For the three VBIR approaches on the other hand, a particular distance function is used to select the most similar image from the actual retrieved images (see Table 7.5). Here, a constant selection criterion for the reference image is assumed over all models. In contrast, the distance functions applied for the retrieval of the six similar images from the database are different for the three models (see Table 7.5). Thus, the main question behind the VBIR models is, which techniques do most closely reflect the retrieval of similar images from the database. The different retrieval functions of the VBIR models could not be tested in the eye-tracking experiment (see Section 6.1), because each approach would have required a separate experiment. In the model, the importance of each image tile is calculated using the colour information of the image (see Section 7.2.3) instead of the participant's gaze patterns. This algorithmic approach allows variations in the tile weighting scheme. Furthermore, the insights from the eye-tracking experiment were integrated into the model design. For example, the lower bounds for weight vectors in the AVBIR model (see Section 7.2.6). Since the gaze patterns as well as the tile weightings are the central concepts behind the VBIR system, which directly influences the retrieval of the most similar images from the database (not the selection of the reference image), the focus of the modelling approaches to VBIR are on different distance functions for the retrieval process.

Beside these differences, the two retrieval approaches share the same design and follow the same common retrieval steps: The user selects successively the most similar image from a set of six database images (see Figure 6.1), until the query is found or the maximum number of retrieval steps is reached (see Section 6.1). Found means in this context that once the query was among the six retrieved database images, all models terminated the current retrieval process and continued with the next start configuration. When all eight queries had been found, the models stopped and the total and average number of retrieval steps were displayed. Thus, the design and the workflow for the models are identical. The differences are in regard to the applied distance functions and the integration of user-relevance feedback in the retrieval process. The design and the common steps of the image retrieval models are the subject of the next section. The differences are the topic of the following sections.

7.2.1 Common Steps in the Modelling Approaches to Image Retrieval

All models start by reading the first start configuration (i.e., the query image and the six randomly selected database images). The database images are displayed as a matrix of two rows and three columns on the screen (see Figure 6.1). The query is located at the top. The arrangement of the images in all models and in the experiments (see Section 6.1) is identical. Then, the image out of the six start images is selected, which has the smallest distance to the query image. The distances between the images of the start configuration and the query image are calculated using the different distance functions of the various retrieval models. The image with the smallest distance to the query serves as a new *reference image*. It is marked with a white rectangle in the upper left corner. Now, six database images with the smallest distances to the reference image are retrieved from the database and displayed on the screen. Again, the different retrieval models use different weighting schemes to calculate the feature distances between the query and the database images, which are the subject of the following sections. These two steps repeat, until the query image is found.

As in the experiment, each image is presented only once: If the top six images include an already displayed one, the next undisplayed image from the retrieval list is selected. The whole process repeats for all eight start configurations. The number of retrieval steps required to find the query images is stored in a log file. Figure 7.1 shows the program flow chart of the common steps of the different computational modelling approaches to image retrieval.

The detailed descriptions of the different computational models are subject of the following sections, starting with the models for Content-Based Image Retrieval (CBIR).

7.2.2 Computational Modelling Approach to CBIR

Two models for Content-Based Image Retrieval are implemented in this book: For one the CBIR and for another, the CBIR_MLP model which are described in detail in this section.

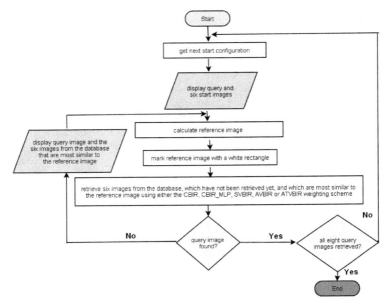

Figure 7.1: Program flow chart of the common steps of the different computational modelling approaches to image retrieval. The differences between the models regard the determination of the reference image and the distance functions applied to retrieve similar images from the database.

The CBIR Model

The CBIR experiment (see Section 6.1) is based on the pre-calculated global feature distances (see Section 4.5). In order to be as close as possible to the experiment, the CBIR model also operates on the global feature distances. The reference image in the CBIR model is selected from the actual set of the six retrieved database images (see Figure 6.1) according to:

$$D(qi, db) = w_c * D_c(qi, db) + w_s * D_s(qi, db) + w_t * D_t(qi, db) \qquad (7.1)$$

where $D_c(qi, db)$, $D_s(qi, db)$ and $D_t(qi, db)$ are the pre-calculated global colour, shape and texture distances, respectively, between the query (qi) and database (db) image (see Section 4.5). W_c, w_s and w_t are the optimal weights for the colour, shape and texture features, calculated from the distance histograms using the Shannon entropy (see Section 4.6). Equation 7.1 is also used to compute the six images from the database that are most similar to the reference image. These images are shown and the process repeats until the query is found.

The CBIR model was evaluated by running the model with the eight start configurations from the experiments (see Appendix) and counting the number of retrieval steps needed to find all query images. The retrieval results of the CBIR model (see Table 7.6) show that five out of eight queries are found within the maximum of 10 retrieval steps. The outcome does not correspond to the results of the empirical experiments, where the participants found on average 0.93 query images in the CBIR experiment (see Section 6.1.2). In contrast to general CBIRS, where the aim is to retrieve similar images to a provided query (see Section 1.2.6), the task in this book is to find the identical image from a set of 2,000 flower images (see Section 4.5.1). For the retrieval of identical images, the information of the whole image is important. This could be the reason for the high performance of the CBIR model, because it is the only computational model that is based on global image features. Furthermore, the results show that the chosen features describe reliably the image content.

The discrepancies between the results of the CBIR model and experiment show that the model does not reflect adequately the retrieval processes applied by humans. Thus, it should be further optimised to reflect human measures of similarity for the retrieval of flower images more closely and therefore to produce results that are more conform to the outcome of the empirical CBIR experiment. These considerations led to the implementation of a modified CBIR model, called CBIR_MLP.

The CBIR_MLP Model

The CBIR_MLP model applies a *multi-layer perceptron* (MLP) to select the reference image from the set of retrieved database images. Before the model is described in more detail, the MLP is first introduced.

Multi-Layer Perceptron (MLP)

A perceptron (j) is a model of an artificial neuron. It sums up several input values ($x_1, x_2, ..., x_n$) and offsets the result against some activation function ($f(net_j)$), finally producing a single output value (y) (see Figure 7.2). The summation of the weighted input is decribed by:

$$net_j = \sum_{i=1}^{n} x_i w_i \qquad (7.2)$$

where w_i are the corresponding weights and $i = 1, ..., n$ are the number of inputs. An activation function ($f(net_j)$), in general a fermi or hyperbolic tangent function, is applied to the sum to produce the output (y): $y = f(net_j)$. The activation function is defined as:

$$f(net_j) = \begin{cases} 1, \ if \ \sum_{i=1}^{n} x_i w_i \geq t_j \\ 0, \ \text{otherwise} \end{cases} \qquad (7.3)$$

A single perceptron can only calculate linearly separable binary functions. A universal function approximator can be realised by the grouping of several perceptrons. Instead of speaking about a group, one could refer to a single layer. Several of those layers can form a so-called *multi-layer perceptron* (MLP), which is a more powerful classificator (see

Figure 7.3). The first and last layer of an MLP are called *input layer* and *output layer*, respectively. Any others - as encapsulated by those mentioned - are referred to as *inner* or *hidden layers*. Each neuron of one layer is directly connected to each neuron of the subsequent layer. The multiple layers are usually interconnected in a *feed-forward* way.

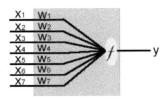

Figure 7.2: Scheme of a perceptron: The concept of perceptron depicts systems that map a number of inputs ($\vec{x}$) to an output value (y) (from [23]).

One of the main problems in designing a MLP is to choose the correct numbers of perceptrons for the single layers. If the number of perceptrons is too small, the output may be imprecise. On the other hand, if the number is too high, a high amount of training may be required.

The MLP learns the correct weights through a training process. The training data is split into training- and validation data. The MLP learns only from the training data. There are two training processes: *Supervised* and *unsupervised* learning. In case of supervised learning, the correct output value for each training sample is known in advance. In case of unsupervised learning, this information is missing and the learning is realised via clustering. For the MLP in this book, supervised learning is used. Hence, for each input sample, the output of the net is compared with the desired output value from the training set. The difference is back-propagated through the single layers. According to the difference, the weights are adjusted a little each time, in order to reduce the error between the net's output and the correct values of the training set. The training set is repetitively presented to the net, until the error for all input vectors falls below a pre-specified threshold. Then the correctness of the adapted weights can be tested by running the net with the validation data and measuring the error.

Applying the MLP in the CBIR_MLP Model

The MLP, implemented in this book, consists of four layers: 48 neurons in the input layer, two hidden layers with 12 and six neurons, and one output neuron (see Figure 7.4). The input vectors consist of the normalised global colour (16 dimensional), shape (4 dimensional) and texture (4 dimensional) features of the query and database image, respectively (see Section 4.5). The output is a value between zero and one, reflecting the similarity between the actual query and database image. Different net architectures were

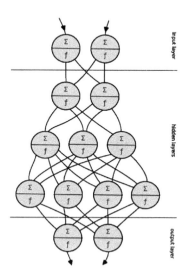

Figure 7.3: Scheme of a multi-layer perceptron (MLP).

tested, where the chosen one revealed the best compromise between the amount of training time and optimisation of the generalisation performance. The training set for the MLP are the similarity estimations between flower pairs provided by the participants in the slider experiment (see Section 6.2). There, participants had to evaluate the similarity of the corresponding retrieval results of the CBIR and VBIR experiment to their respective query by moving a slider in the range from zero to 100. Zero meant not similar at all, whereas 100 stood for identity. All participants had to evaluate the same 120 retrieval pairs. From these data, 189 training sets for the MLP were generated by taking the average slider ratings for each image pair. Additionally, a second evaluation experiment was performed, where ten participants had to rate the similarities between the database images and the corresponding queries for the eight start configurations, resulting in a set of 48 additional training examples. The people participating in the second evaluation experiment were not identical to those of experiment II (see Section 6.2). Here again, the average ratings were chosen as similarity values for each image pair. Altogether, there were 237 similarity estimations, where 200 were used as training examples and 37 as a test set to evaluate the MLP. The training of the MLP comprised 300,000 steps until the average error for the training set was below 0.28.

In order to evaluate how closely the MLP approaches human similarity estimations, the selection probability for the single database images of the eight start configurations

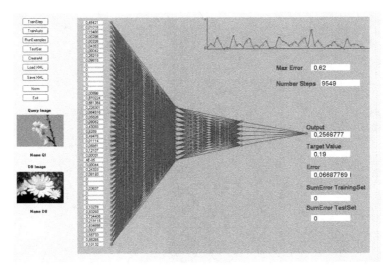

Figure 7.4: Multi-layer perceptron with 48 input neurons, two hidden layers and one output neuron. The inputs are the global colour, shape and texture features (normalised between 0 and 1) of the query and database image, respectively.

was calculated from the decisions made by the participants in retrieval experiment I (see Table 7.1). In the majority of the cases, the users prefer one database image over the others. In case of query image 63, 626 and 715, two database images receive identical values of 43% and 33%, respectively.

For comparison, Table 7.2 shows the similarity results of the MLP computed for all image combinations from the eight start configurations. The outcome of the MLP corresponds in three out of eight queries to the selections of the participants in the retrieval experiments (i.e., for query 626, 380 and 1431). For these queries, the MLP assigns the highest similarity values to the database images with the highest selection probability in experiment I. Note that the training data for the start configurations are from participants who are not identical to those of the retrieval experiments (see Section 6.1). For image 342, the MLP prefers image 290 and 162 over the other images, which also corresponds to the participants' preferences (see Table 7.1). For the other queries, the database images preferably selected by the participants are within the top three results of the MLP. As can be seen from Table 7.1 and Table 7.2: In cases where the MLP does not prefer the user selected database image, it assigns higher similarity values to those images, having a higher probability of being chosen by the users, whereas those with low percentage values also receive low similarity values. For the sunflower (image 63), no similar images are in the training set. Thus, the slider ratings of the participants show high variations (see Table 7.3). Hence, the MLP cannot learn the correct similarity value for this image and

QI	DB1	DB2	DB3	DB4	DB5	DB6
63	43 (54)	3 (610)	7 (540)	0 (1918)	43 (1018)	3 (1221)
626	33 (1891)	13 (909)	10 (24)	3 (427)	7 (161)	33 (338)
342	0 (1052)	10 (290)	7 (1738)	0 (1971)	83 (162)	0 (1107)
715	33 (778)	17 (1317)	3 (75)	7 (1962)	7 (211)	33 (1471)
380	3 (429)	97 (353)	0 (1457)	0 (650)	0 (69)	0 (1133)
1431	0 (879)	57 (1463)	37 (1225)	3 (356)	3 (243)	0 (1965)
1569	13 (1352)	10 (1930)	13 (1764)	10 (1582)	0 (18)	53 (759)
1600	3 (1660)	3 (917)	0 (772)	57 (518)	7 (1672)	30 (31)

Table 7.1: The selection probabilities (in %) for each database image from the eight start configurations, calculated from the decisions made by the participants in the retrieval experiments. The number in the brackets are the image numbers (from 1 to 2,000). The first number in each table field shows the percentage of participants, who chose the corresponding database image as most similar to the query image in the same row.

QI	DB1	DB2	DB3	DB4	DB5	DB6
63	0.52 (54)	0.02 (610)	0.69 (540)	0.63 (1918)	0.25 (1018)	0.58 (1221)
626	0.58 (1891)	0.21 (909)	0.31 (24)	0.09 (427)	0.19 (161)	0.16 (338)
342	0.13 (1052)	0.71 (290)	0.21 (1738)	0.03 (1971)	0.59 (162)	0.32 (1107)
715	0.26 (778)	0.85 (1317)	0.72 (75)	0.25 (1962)	0.13 (211)	0.09 (1471)
380	0.09 (429)	0.72 (353)	0.41 (1457)	0.45 (650)	0.02 (69)	0.48 (1133)
1431	0.1 (879)	0.46 (1463)	0.27 (1225)	0.01 (356)	0.01 (243)	0.25 (1965)
1569	0.05 (1352)	0.52 (1930)	0.74 (1764)	0.4 (1582)	0.01 (18)	0.48 (759)
1600	0.63 (1660)	0.62 (917)	0.07 (772)	0.49 (518)	0.59 (1672)	0.03 (31)

Table 7.2: Similarity estimations between the query and database images of the eight start configurations calculated by the MLP. The number in the brackets are the image numbers (from 1 to 2,000). The first number in each table field shows the percentage of similarity between the query and database image calculated by the MLP. A value of 1 corresponds to 100% and a value of 0 to 0% similarity.

Query	Database Image	P1	P2	P3	P4	P5	P6	P7	P8	P9	P10
63	54	19	71	5	30	67	11	46	16	59	16
63	610	0	12	24	0	20	60	0	38	13	6
63	540	6	28	0	20	39	0	42	14	9	8
63	1918	9	16	0	0	31	0	39	15	12	9
63	1018	7	14	16	20	51	0	42	18	6	12
63	1221	0	27	0	0	35	11	15	4	0	9

Table 7.3: The user selected similarity values for the sunflower image (image 63). P1 to P10 are the abbreviations for participant one to ten.

assigns the user preferred image (image 54) only the fourth highest similarity value (see Table 7.2). However, the similarity value of 0.52 is quite high.

All in all, the results show that the MLP cannot exactly replicate users' similarity estimations from the retrieval experiments, because of the high variations in the users' similarity rankings. The ranking of the similarities between flower pairs is very subjective: Some users evaluate the similarity according to colour, others according to shape or by a combination of different features. Participants reported that the majority of flower pairs were quite different. Furthermore, they had difficulties to find suitable indications for similarity ratings. Consequently, they often did not know how to position the sliders correctly and mostly assigned only low similarity values.

Nevertheless, the comparison of the results in Table 7.1 and Table 7.2 shows that the MLP can at least approximate the user decisions from the training examples. This motivates the application of the MLP in the CBIR_MLP model to simulate humans' similarity estimation during image retrieval. In the CBIR_MLP model, the reference image is selected by the MLP from the actual set of six database images. The six most similar images to the reference image are calculated as described in the CBIR model (see Equation 7.1).

Table 7.6 shows the results of the CBIR_MLP model for the eight start configurations. Altogether, 761 retrieval steps are necessary to retrieve the eight query images. On average, 95.12 steps are needed. No query is retrieved within ten retrieval steps. Here, the outcome of the model is inconsistent with the results from experiment I (see Section 6.1), where most participants found query 3 (image 342) within the limit of ten retrieval steps (see Table 6.3). In the CBIR_MLP model, 108 retrieval steps are necessary to retrieve query image 342. The reason is that the MLP selects image 290 instead of image 162 from the start configuration (see Appendix). The database contains many large-sized red blossoms depicted on different backgrounds. Thus, the model puts more emphasis on the blossom than on the background (because red is a dominant global colour feature): The model's retrieval performance degrades. In contrast, for query 2 (image 626) and 4 (image 715), the CBIR_MLP model needs 14 and 15 retrieval steps, respectively. This is quite close to the maximum number of ten retrieval steps. For these images, more similar images may have been in the training set, so that the MLP selects more similar images. Again, the sunflower required the highest number of retrieval steps. Here, the MLP clearly selects the rather dissimilar reference images because of missing training samples.

This conlcudes the description of the CBIR models. In experiment I, also the new attention-based approach to image retrieval (VBIR) was investigated. The modelling of this approach need other techniques, which are the subject of the following sections.

7.2.3 Object-Oriented Cognitive Visual Attention Approach (OOCVA)

In experiment I, the importance of each image tile in the VBIR approach for the actual retrieval process was calculated online from participants' eye movements (see Section 6.1). For the VBIR models we need an alternative way to calculate the average attention values for each image tile, because the online fixation patterns of the participants are not available. A solution for this problem is the *object-oriented cognitive visual attention approach* (OOCVA) to image retrieval.

OOCVA is a modified implementation of the cognitive visual attention (CVA) approach (Bamidele, Stentiford & Morphett, 2004). CVA is based on the theory of surround suppression in primate V1, an area of the visual cortex (Nothdurft, Gallant & Van Essen, 1999). The core idea is that high values of visual attention are assigned to pixels when randomly selected neighbouring pixel configurations do not match identical positional configurations at other randomly selected pixels in the image (see Figure 7.5). Thus, image regions without predominant features, like anomalous objects, edges or boundaries, receive high attention values.

The correspondence between image regions with high attention values predicted by the original CVA model (Barmidele, Stentiford & Morphett, 2004) and regions of visual interest was investigated by recording participants' eye movements when looking at the images (Oyekoya & Stentiford, 2004a). Even though the results varied considerably between the participants, it was shown that participants' gaze within the first two seconds of image presentation was directed towards regions with high visual attention values. Additionally, frequent saccades occurred between highlighted areas.

In order to adapt the CVA to flower images, the attentional values in the OOCVA approach (in contrast to the CVA approach) are only calculated for those image pixels, which have been assigned as foreground (i.e., blossoms) by the Lazy-PNN segmentation algorithm described in Section 4.5.3. The algorithm terminates when the visual attention values for all foreground pixels have been calculated.

The implementation of the OOCVA approach to image retrieval is described as follows. Given two preliminaries:

(a) For each image pixel $x = (x_1, x_2)$ a corresponding p-dimensional feature vector $a = (a_1, a_2, .., a_p)$ is given. For example: $a = (r, g, b)$ in case of RGB colour values.

(b) Define a function F such that $a = F(x)$ for each image pixel x and corresponding feature vector a.

Then, the OOCVA approach works as follows:

(1) Select image pixel $P = (x, y) \in I\!\!N^2$ starting from upper left to lower right.

(2) Continue, if $P(x, y)$ is a foreground pixel. Otherwise goto (1).

(3) Initialise the loop variable ($loop = 0$) and the visual attention score $VA(P) = 0$.

(4) Select the neighbourhood N_P within distance ϵ to pixel P: $(x', y') \in N_P$, $\quad if \quad |x - x'| < \epsilon$ and $|y - y'| < \epsilon$ (see Figure 7.5). Select randomly a set of m points from N_P, denoted as $S_P = \{P'_1, P'_2, P'_3, ..., P'_m\}$.

(5) Select randomly a second pixel Q in the image.

(6) Create the same neighbourhood configuration around pixel Q, i.e., $P - P'_i = Q - Q'_i$ for $i = 1, ..., m$ (see Figure 7.5). This neighbourhood configuration is denoted by $S_Q = \{Q'_1, Q'_2, Q'_3, ..., Q'_m\}$.

(7) $loop \rightarrow loop + 1$. If $loop > t$ then goto (1).

(8) Compare the colour configuration around P with the same pixel configuration around Q and test for a mismatch, i.e., $|F(P) - F(Q)| > \delta$ and $|F(P'_k) - F(Q'_l)| > \delta$, $\quad \forall k, l = 1, ..., m$.

(9) If there is a mismatch, increment the visual attention score $VA(P)$ for image pixel P and goto (5). Otherwise goto (4).

The motivation behind keeping the mismatching neighbourhood is that once such a configuration is generated, it is likely that it also mismatches identical neighbourhoods in other areas of the image. Thus, the rise of the visual attention scores is accelerated if the process is not interrupted by a subsequent match. The value for the threshold δ depends on the chosen image features. For the OOCVA implementation in this book, only the RGB colour information is used. The threshold (δ) is set to 80 in order to find high differences in RGB colour values. It means that if the sum of the differences in the red, green and blue component between a pixel pair is above 80, then a mismatch is detected. Typical parameters for the algorithm are: $\epsilon = 3$, $m = 3$ and $t = 100$. These values provide good results for the flower images. For objects with other scales, probably other values have to be selected. Higher values for t improve the level of confidence in the details of the visual attention map.

The OOCVA approach uses knowledge about scene objects, because it focusses on the pixels of the segmented areas. As stated in Section 3.2.2 this knowledge influences fixation placement.

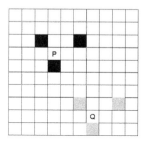

Figure 7.5: Neighbourhood configuration for pixel P and pixel Q. The parameters for the OOCVA approach are $m = 3$, $t = 100$ and $\epsilon = 3$. The neighbourhood (N_P) of pixel P is marked by the red square. The neighbourhood configuration S_P of pixel P and S_Q of pixel Q are indicated by black and grey squares, respectively.

Figure 7.6: *Original flower image.*

Figure 7.7: *Calculated visual attention map (the brighter the pixel, the higher is the attention score). As can be seen, pixels on the boundary and in the flower centre receive higher values.*

The OOCVA approach assigns high values of visual attention to image pixels P that archive high mismatching scores over a range of t neighbouring pixel sets S_P. This means, pixels with features rarely present elsewhere in the image (e.g., anomalous objects, edges or boundaries), receive high attention scores, whereas those with common features get small values. Exemplarily, an original flower image and its visual attention map are shown in Figures 7.6 and 7.7. As can be seen, pixels on the boundary and in the flower centre receive higher values. The attention scores are finally normalised to values between zero and one. This is analoguous to the fixation maps (see Section 3.5.1) in the VBIR experiment (see Section 6.1), where an attention value in the range between 0 and 1, calculated from the recorded fixation data, is assigned to each pixel. Hence, the average attention values (Φ_i) for each image tile i in the VBIR models can be calculated analogously, using the data from the OOCVA approach:

$$\Phi_i = \frac{1}{M} \sum_{(x,y) \in tile_i} \overline{VA}(x,y), \quad i = 1, ..., 16 \qquad (7.4)$$

where M is the number of pixels in tile i (in the VBIR approach of this book, each tile has a dimension of 72×50 pixels) and $\overline{VA}(x, y)$ is the normalised visual attention score for pixel (x, y) belonging to tile i. The average attention values can then serve as the corresponding weights for the colour, shape and texture features of each tile i. Thus, the difference between the tile weighting scheme for the VBIR experiment and the two VBIR models is that in case of the experiment, the weights are calculated from the fixation data, whereas in the models, the visual attention scores are determined from the results of the OOCVA approach.

In the following, the differences in the weighting schemes for the retrieval of the most similar images from the database between all three VBIR models are explained in more detail.

7.2.4 Computational Modelling Approaches to VBIR

In the VBIR experiment, the image features were calculated locally, i.e. seperately for each image tile (see Section 4.4). Additionally, fixation maps (see Section 3.5.1) were calculated online from participants' eye movements during image retrieval, which were used to adjust the importance of the different image tiles for the actual retrieval task at hand. For the model, the online fixation patterns of the participants are not available. Instead, the attention values for each image tile are calculated by using the OOCVA approach (see Section 7.2.3).

For the computational modelling approach to VBIR, the distances between all corresponding tiles of the query and database images are considered. This approach suggests three different weighting schemes for the single image tiles, resulting in three distinct modelling approaches to VBIR:

(1) **SVBIR** (**S**imple **VBIR** model): All feature distances between corresponding tiles of the query and database image are equally weighted by a constant C.

(2) **AVBIR** (**A**ttention Based **VBIR** model): The feature distances between corresponding tiles of the query and database image are weighted by the average attention value, derived from the OOCVA approach (see Section 7.2.3).

(3) **ATVBIR** (**T**hresholded version of the **AVBIR** model): Only those image tiles are considered for the distance calculation that received the highest average attention values in the OOCVA approach (see Section 7.2.3).

The approach behind the ATVBIR model is quite different from those of the other two VBIR models. Whereas for the SVBIR and AVBIR models the focus is on the overall impression of the images (all image tiles are considered for the distance calculation), the ATVBIR model uses only the most important tiles (i.e., those that received much attention) for the distance calculation and discards the less important ones. The motivation behind the implementation of the ATVBIR model was to investigate, if the focus on important image tiles, while concurrently discarding tiles receiving a small amount of attention, leads to a better retrieval performance than the consideration of the overall image information.

All three models have the same design and rely on the pre-calculated tile-based colour, shape and texture features (see Section 4.5). The only differences are the variable weighting schemes between corresponding tiles of the query and the database image. The performance of the different models can then be compared among each other with regard to the required retrieval steps to find a query image and the number of times, the query has been found within ten retrieval steps.

The expectations are that the AVBIR performs better than the SVBIR model, because in the AVBIR model the image areas are weighted by the corresponding average attention values (Φ_i), i.e., more important regions receive higher weights than unimportant ones. In the ATVBIR approach only the most important areas are considered for the distance calculation, whereas tiles receiving a small amount of attention are discarded. Thus, the ATVBIR model is expected to provide the best results when the discarded tiles contain unimportant information. Otherwise, the AVBIR approach should lead to a better retrieval performance.

The next section explains the simplest model (SVBIR) in more detail.

7.2.5 The Simple VBIR Model (SVBIR)

The SVBIR model is the simplest computational model for Vision-Based Image Retrieval (VBIR). In the SVBIR model, the distance between an image pair is calculated as the sum of the tile-based feature distances equally weighted by a constant C. Thus, the distance between an image pair results in:

$$D^{SVBIR}(qi, db) = \frac{1}{16} \sum_{i=1}^{16} D(qi_i, db_i) \, C \tag{7.5}$$

where i represents the number of the image tile, and qi and db are the query and database image, respectively. $D(qi_i, db_i)$ is the image feature distance between corresponding image tiles i in the query and database image:

$$D(qi_n, db_n) = w_c * D_c(qi_n, db_n) + w_s * D_s(qi_n, db_n) + w_t * D_t(qi_n, db_n) \tag{7.6}$$

where $n = 1, ..., 16$ are the image tiles and $D_c(qi_n, db_n)$, $D_s(qi_n, db_n)$, and $D_t(qi_n, db_n)$ are the pre-calculated colour, shape and texture distances between the corresponding tiles n of the query (qi) and database (db) image, respectively (see Section 4.5). w_c, w_s and w_t are the optimal weights for the colour, shape and texture features, calculated from the distance histograms using the Shannon entropy (see Section 4.6). In the SVBIR model developed in this book, the constant C in Equation 7.5 is set to 1.0.

7.2.6 The Attention Based VBIR Model (AVBIR)

In contrast to the SVBIR model, where all image tiles are equally weighted, the distances between corresponding tiles of the query and database image in the AVBIR model are multiplied with weights depending on the results of the OOCVA approach (see Section 7.2.3). The weighting scheme in the AVBIR model is most similar to the one in the VBIR experiment (see Section 6.1). The only difference between the model and the experiment (see Section 6.1) is that the weights in the experiment resulted from the average fixation map values for each image tile, calculated from the recorded fixation data (see Section 4.4). Because participants' fixation patterns changed with each retrieval step, the weighting scheme in the empirical experiment varied dynamically. In the AVBIR model on the other hand, the tile weights depend on the results of the OOCVA approach (see Section 7.2.3). The OOCVA approach uses the RGB colour information of the foreground pixels. Since the colour values of the database images do not change, the attention values from the OOCVA approach can be pre-calculated and thus they are constant for each database image.

How can the tile-based weights in the AVBIR model be determined from the average attention values $\Phi(i)$ (see Equation 7.4) of the OOCVA approach? The average attention values resulting from the OOCVA approach and the fixation map values are within the interval from zero to one (see Section 7.2.3). This means that image tiles receiving high values of attention are weighted by one, whereas those receiving no attention at all, get a weight of zero. For an even partition of the feature weight range over the 16 image tiles, the interval between zero and one is evenly divided into 16 parts, resulting in intervals of $\frac{1.0}{16} = 0.06$. This value determines the nuances in the tile-based feature weights: The feature distances of the tile with the highest average visual attention value $\Phi(i)$ is multiplied with a weight of 1.0, the tile with the second highest value with 0.94, the third one with 0.88 and so on. This continues until the value of 0.34 is reached for the tile with the 12th highest average attention value. To reduce the influence of image tiles with a small average value of visual attention, the weight vector for the features cannot be smaller than 0.34, i.e., the feature distances for the five tiles with the lowest average attentional values are all multiplied by a weight vector of 0.34. Smaller values would result in false positives, because the multiplication of high distances with small weight vectors results in small distance values. The minimum value of 0.34 was determined experimentally by running the model with different tile weights and counting the number of retrieval steps needed to find all eight query images. Thus, the list of *bounding weight vectors* results into:

$$\theta = [1.0, 0.94, 0.88, 0.82, 0.76, 0.7, 0.64, 0.58, 0.52, 0.86, 0.04, 0.34, 0.34, 0.34, 0.34, 0.34]$$
(7.7)

The experimental determination of a smallest lower bound for weight vectors to control the influence of factors for the overall distance calculation is a common practice in Computer Science (Lowe, 2004; Shi & Malik, 2000).

The bounding weight vectors guaranteed that the pre-calculated tile-based distances were not distorted by a multiplication with an improper weight value. Although, in cases, where the average attention value $\Phi(i)$ of an image tile i, calculated by the OOCVA approach, is higher than the corresponding lower bound value $\theta(i)$, the features of tile i would receive feature weights that are lower than the attention values. In order to provide a weighting scheme that is as close as possible to the average attention values calculated from the OOCVA approach (see Section 7.2.3), the corresponding values for $\Phi(i)$ and $\theta(i)$ are compared and the maximum is chosen. This guaranteed that image tiles with high attention values still receive the appropriate feature weights.

Thus, the distance between an image pair in the AVBIR model is determined according to:

$$D^{AVBIR}(qi, db) = \frac{1}{16} \sum_{i=1}^{16} (1 - D(qi_i, db_i)) \, max(\Phi(i), \theta(i)) \tag{7.8}$$

where $D(qi_n, db_n)$ is calculated according to Equation 7.6. $\Phi(i)$ is calculated according to Equation 7.4: For all image tiles the average attention values ($\Phi(i)$) and the corresponding entries from the bounding weight vectors list θ are compared and the highest value is chosen as the final weight.

7.2.7   The Thresholded Based VBIR Model (ATVBIR)

The ATVBIR model is quite similar to the AVBIR model. The only difference between the two models is that the similarity is not calculated for all 16 tiles, but only for the $\kappa < 16$ tiles with the highest average attention value ($\Phi(i)$). This means that only important tiles (which receive high average visual attention values in the OOCVA approach) are considered, whereas unimportant ones are weighted by zero. As stated in Section 7.2.4, the motivation behind this model was to investigate, if the focus on important tiles, while concurrently discarding those receiving only a small amount of attention, leads to a better performance than the retrieval of images according to the overall image information. In the ATVBIR model developed in this book, κ is set to seven. This value was determined experimentally by running the model with different values for κ and counting the number of retrieval steps needed to find all eight query images (see Table 7.4). The value of κ with the lowest number of retrieval steps needed to find all eight query images, is chosen as the optimal value. Thus, the overall similarity between the query image (qi) and a database image (db) in the ATVBIR model is calculated according to:

$$D^{ATVBIR}(qi, db) = \frac{1}{\kappa} \sum_{i \in I(\kappa)} (1 - D(qi_i, db_i)) \, max(\Phi(i), \theta(i)) \tag{7.9}$$

where $I(\kappa)$ is the set of κ tiles having the highest average attention values ($\Phi(i)$) calculated according to Equation 7.4.

7.2.8   Random Modelling Approach to Image Retrieval

For a comparison of the performances of the CBIR and VBIR models described above, with a retrieval process based on a random selection of database images, a fifth model was implemented: The random modelling approach to image retrieval.

Like the computational modelling approaches to CBIR and VBIR, this model starts by reading the first start configuration, i.e., the query image and the six database images, and

κ	1	2	3	4	5	6	7	8	sum	average
4	33	5	24	22	54	10	72	14	234	29.25
5	20	6	5	6	41	4	6	33	121	15.12
6	12	4	5	6	46	4	18	7	102	12.75
7	21	5	5	5	12	5	12	17	82	10.25
8	20	5	3	4	10	5	120	25	192	24.00
9	29	5	3	4	11	5	115	6	178	22.25
10	9	5	2	5	8	5	66	26	126	15.75
11	10	4	4	5	9	5	134	25	196	24.50
12	7	4	2	5	25	27	22	28	120	15.00
13	8	4	4	5	10	45	31	17	124	15.50
14	74	4	4	5	12	45	94	19	257	32.12
15	19	4	2	4	14	29	87	17	176	22.0
16 (AVBIR)	54	5	4	5	7	20	20	8	123	15.38

Table 7.4: Number of retrieval steps required to find the queries of the different start configurations (1 to 8) in the ATVBIR model, depending on the number of image tiles (κ) considered for distance calculation. For $\kappa = 7$ the sum and the average number of retrieval steps reached a minimum. For $\kappa = 16$, all image tiles are considered for the distance calculation. This corresponds to the distance calculation applied for the AVBIR model (see Equation 7.8).

displays them on the screen (see Figure 6.1). Then, iteratively six images are randomly selected from the database. No feature distances are considered for image retrieval. Each image is presented only once, i.e., if the actually retrieved images included an already displayed one, another image was randomly selected from the database. The retrieval terminates, when the actual set of retrieved images contains the query image. The whole process repeats for all start configurations. The model counts the number of retrieval steps required to find the query images in a log file.

The six different modelling approaches to image retrieval are summarised in Table 7.5.

7.2.9 Modelling Results

The results of the six different computational modelling approaches to image retrieval are summarised in Table 7.6. Each row lists the results for a particular retrieval approach. The columns labelled with numbers from one to eight contain the number of retrieval steps needed to find each of the eight query images. The query images are depicted

Model	Equation for the calculation of the reference image (RI)	Equation for the calculation of the similar images from the database
CBIR	$min_{k=1,...,6}(w_c * D_c(qi, db^k) + w_s * D_s(qi, db^k) + w_t * D_t(qi, db^k))$	$D(qi, db) = w_c * D_c(qi, db) + w_s * D_s(qi, db) + w_t * D_t(qi, db)$
CBIR_MLP	MLP Results	$D(qi, db) = w_c * D_c(qi, db) + w_s * D_s(qi, db) + w_t * D_t(qi, db)$
SVBIR	$min_{k=1,...,6}(\frac{1}{16}\sum_{n=1}^{16} D(qi_n, db_n^k))$	$D^{SVBIR}(qi, db) = \frac{1}{16}\sum_{n=1}^{16} D(qi_n, db_n)\, C$
AVBIR	$min_{k=1,...,6}(\frac{1}{16}\sum_{n=1}^{16} D(qi_n, db_n^k))$	$D^{AVBIR}(qi, db) = \frac{1}{16}\sum_{n=1}^{16} sim(qi_n, db_n)\, max(\Phi(i), \theta(i))$
ATVBIR	$min_{k=1,...,6}(\frac{1}{16}\sum_{n=1}^{16} D(qi_n, db_n^k))$	$D^{ATVBIR}(qi, db) = \frac{1}{\kappa}\sum_{n\in I(\kappa)} sim(qi_n, db_n)\, max(\Phi(n), \theta(n))$
Random	Random	Random

Table 7.5: Overview of the distance functions for the retrieval of the reference image and the six database images for the different computational models. Qi is the actual query image and db^k is image k from the actual set of database images, with $k = 1, ..., 6$. The tile number is denoted by n.

in the Appendix. Furthermore, each row contains the sum and the average number of retrieval steps over all start configurations separated for each model. The random model was executed 20 times to get representative data. The average values for the random model can be found in row six. Because the retrieval steps for the CBIR, CBIR_MLP, SVBIR, AVBIR and ATVBIR are deterministic, each execution of these models provide the same results.

At first glance, when focussing on the sum and average column of Table 7.6, the numerical results are as expected: The random approach required the highest number of steps to find the query images. The total sum of retrieval steps needed is 1382, the average is 172.75. The CBIR model shows much better results, with a total sum of 262 retrieval steps and 32.75 on average. The CBIR_MLP approach required more steps than the CBIR approach (761 in total and 95.12 on average). The number of retrieval steps needed for each query is higher for the CBIR_MLP model. The overall retrieval steps for the CBIR_MLP models are between those of the CBIR and Random model. Nevertheless, the results are closer to the CBIR than to the Random model. All VBIR models outperformed the two CBIR approaches. The SVBIR approach has a total sum of 145 and an average of 18.13 steps. The AVBIR approach performed considerably better with a total sum of 123 steps, and 10.25 steps on average. As expected, the smallest number of overall retrieval steps were required in the ATVBIR approach: 82 steps in total and 10.25 on average.

A deeper analysis of the results shows that there are major differences between the retrieval behaviour of the six computational models with regard to the single query images. It can be seen that the ATVBIR model does not perform optimally on each query image.

Model	1	2	3	4	5	6	7	8	Sum	Average
CBIR	200	12	3	9	15	5	10	8	262	32.75
CBIR_MLP	320	14	108	15	162	62	40	40	761	95.12
SVBIR	84	4	2	10	5	5	25	10	145	18.13
AVBIR	54	5	4	5	7	20	20	8	123	15.38
ATVBIR	21	5	5	5	12	5	12	17	82	10.25
Random ϕ	175	157	191	160	150	163	219	167	1382	172.75

Table 7.6: Number of retrieval steps needed to retrieve the query images for all eight start configurations, listed for the different modelling approaches. The random model was executed 20 times to get representative results. The images of the start configurations (1-8) are depicted in the Appendix. In the experiments (see Chapter 6) the maximum number of retrieval steps to find the query images was limited to 10. The probability of retrieval for the eight query images in experiment I (see Section 6.1) can be found in Table 6.3.

Only for three (query 1, 4 and 6) out of eights queries, this model required the minimal number of retrieval steps compared with the other models. In the SVBIR approach, most of the query images (i.e., six out of eight) are found within the limit of ten retrieval steps. Followed by the CBIR and AVBIR approach with retrieval success in five out of eight queries. In the CBIR model, queries 3, 4, 6, 7 and 8 are retrieved in less than ten steps. The AVBIR approach succeeded for queries 2, 3, 4, 5 and 8. In the ATVBIR model four images were found within ten retrieval steps. In the CBIR_MLP approach no query was retrieved within the maximum number of ten retrieval steps. However, the number of retrieval steps for query 2 and 4 are close to ten. The Random approach trails far behind the rest of the models.

Only for the first query image, the sunflower, the number of retrieval steps needed drops sharply from the Random to the ATVBIR model. There is no similar image in the corresponding start configuration. Thus, the first reference image is quite dissimilar to the query. By using the global features, it is difficult to navigate to other images with different colour distributions. In the AVBIR approach on the other hand, the focus is on large-sized yellow flower images, which restricts significantly the search space. With regard to query 3, the corresponding start configuration includes a similar image. Furthermore, only a few images in the database depict large-sized white flowers against a dominant black background: A reason for the good retrieval performance in all models (except for CBIR_MLP). The result is also consistent with the outcome of the experiments (see Section 6.1), where the majority of participants in both approaches retrieved this image within the limit of ten retrieval steps. In case of query 2, the flower is quite small and it is depicted on a relatively inconsistent background. Thus, a lot of background information is considered for the calculation of the global image features, resulting in a poor retrieval performance for the second query image in the CBIR model. In the other models, the focus is mainly on the flower, and the unimportant background information is nearly ignored through the tile-based approach. Because all VBIR models put the highest emphasis on the four central tiles, they all perform nearly equal. For query image 3 and 5, the CBIR_MLP model results in a high number of retrieval steps. The reason is that for query image 3, the net selects image 290 instead of image 162 (see Appendix) in the first step. This points the system into a detrimental direction resulting in the high number of retrieval steps. If the MLP had chosen image 162, the query would appear in the next set of retrieved database images. Similar reasons hold for query 5. Here, the detrimental decision occurs later in the retrieval process. Once the detrimental decision was made, it is relatively difficult in the CBIR approach to direct the system to another set of retrieval results. The performance of the VBIR models improve from SVBIR to ATVBIR, because of the decreasing number of image tiles considered for the distance calculation. Since the flowers are only distributed over roughly five tiles, the ATVBIR approach performs better than the other VBIR approaches.

All in all, the CBIR models show advantages when the flower consists of a dominant large-sized blossom depicted on a relatively homogeneous background. Then the information of the flower is sufficiently represented in the global image features and the retrieval is successful. If the flowers are small-sized and depicted on an inhomogeneous background, the VBIR models clearly outperform the CBIR approach: The focus lies on the image tiles containing important flower information, whereas the background is only partially considered. These findings are in particular illustrated by the retrieval results for query 8. Because of the high variance in the participants' similarity ratings, the MLP can only approximate the humans' decision process for similarity estimation. This is the reason, why it performs much worse than the CBIR approach.

For further statistical analysis, the Wilcoxon signed-ranks test, a nonparametric method for paired samples, is applied to the results, because of the small sample size of only eight query images. Parametric methods, like t-tests, normally require sample sizes of 15 or more samples. Even though the MLP cannot handle the high variances in users' similarity estimations, the outcomes of the CBIR_MLP model are closer to the results of the participants in the experiments than those of the CBIR model. This regards not only the number of images retrieved, but also the number of images found within the limit of ten retrieval steps. In the experiment (see Chapter 6.1), the participants of the CBIR approach retrieved on average around one image, the maximum was two images. The CBIR_MLP model did not retrieve any images within ten retrieval steps, but came very close to the limit for two images (see Table 7.6). The CBIR model on the other hand retrieved five out of eight queries (see Table 7.6) and performed better than the participants in the VBIR approach (see Section 6.1). Thus, the CBIR model is not an adequate simulation for the human retrieval performances and is therefore not considered for the further statistical analysis.

The results show that there are significant differences in the retrieval performances be-

Model	Z	Asymptotic Significance
CBIR_MLP-Random	-1.472	0.141
SVBIR-Random	-2.521	0.012
AVBIR-Random	-2.524	0.012
ATVBIR-Random	-2.521	0.012
SVBIR-CBIR_MLP	-2.521	0.012
AVBIR-CBIR_MLP	-2.521	0.012
AVBIR-SVBIR	-0.564	0.573
ATVBIR-CBIR_MLP	-2.524	0.012
ATVBIR-SVBIR	-0.339	0.735
ATVBIR-AVBIR	-0.734	0.863

Table 7.7: The results of the Wilcoxon signed-ranks test for the different modelling approaches.

tween the random and the other retrieval models: The Random model is significantly inferior to the other models (Wilcoxon $Z = -2.521$; $p = 0.012$). Only for the CBIR_MLP model, there are no highly significant differences to the results of the Random model (Wilcoxon $Z = -1.472$; $p = 0.141$). There are also significant differences between the CBIR_MLP and all VBIR models (Wilcoxon $Z = -2.521$; $p = 0.012$). This result is consistent with the outcomes of the empirical experiments (see Chapter 6.1), where the participants in the VBIR experiment clearly outperformed those of the CBIR system. As stated above, the VBIR experiment is most closely approximated by the AVBIR model. The results of the Wilcoxon signed-ranks test show also that there are no significant differences between the retrieval performances of the three VBIR models.

The reason for the non-significant results could be caused by the heterogeneity of the flower database. The sample set of eight queries is quite small. Thus, the retrieval result for each query has a strong influence on the results of the Wilcoxon signed-ranks test. It would be interesting to investigate if the focus on the most important image tiles shows no significant effect, because the database consists only of images from one domain. The application of the models on a more diverse image database would probably lead to different results.

The results of the CBIR_MLP model show that it approximates the retrieval strategies applied by humans. The CBIR model based on the global features shows retrieval results that do not reflect participants' results in the experiment, because it retrieves more images than the participants in the experiment (0.93 on average). Here, the CBIR_MLP model reflects closer the experimental results. For two images, the CBIR_MLP approach needs just a little more than 10 retrieval steps. The MLP cannot totally approximate humans' similarity estimations. As stated above: Participants provided similarity ratings of a high variance. Most of them stated that the flowers, they had to evaluate, were quite dissimilar. Also, some participants use only a small scale between the interval from 0 to 100, wheras others make use of the whole interval. As stated above, participants apply strategies for image retrieval that are not approximated by the algorithmic implementation of the models. They seem to use, among others, subjective decisions, experiences or cultural knowledge to evaluate the similarity of flowers. An in-depth analysis of all these aspects and their implementation into algorithmic descriptions would go beyond the scope of this book. Thus, for the retrieval models implemented in this book, the problem of image retrieval is reduced to a plausible mapping of similar database images to a query based on information about the distribution of visual attention on flower images. The suggested approaches can only be accounted as a first step towards the realisation of retrieval models that closely reflect human behaviour during image retrieval. More sophisticated simulations require a deeper investigation of the underlying processes and an extensive re-engineering of the model concepts.

7.3   Computer Simulations II: Saliency Map Model

The second type of computer simulations applied in this book make use of the eye movements recorded in experiment I (see Section 6.1). For several images from the flower database (see Section 4.5.1), human fixation maps, computed from participants' eye movements, are compared with the corresponding overall saliency maps (Itti, Koch & Niebur, 1998), which code topographically salient image regions over the entire visual scene. The following sections describe in detail how overall saliency maps are calculated.

7.3.1   The Saliency-Based Model of Visual Attention

The saliency-based model of visual attention is widely used to detect the most salient, and thus, unique features of the environment, by simulating the ability of the visual system to detect salient regions of a scene at the expense of other regions. There exist real time implementations of the model (Ouerhani, Hügli, Burgi & Rüdi, 2002), which, because of the model's universality, are applied to many research fields, like Computer Vision and Robotics.

The basic idea behind the saliency-based model of visual attention by Itti and Koch (2001) is that uniform regions along some image dimensions are uninformative, whereas distinct ones are informative. The implementation of the saliency-based model of visual attention consists of three main steps (see Figure 7.8): The calculation of the single (bottom-up) *feature maps* and their transformation into the corresponding *conspicuity maps*, which highlight areas of the images that strongly differ from their surrounding according to the applied image features. Finally, the single conspicuity maps are linearly combined into the overall *saliency map*. Regions with high saliency values attract attention.

Even though a weighted linear combination of three important features (i.e., spatial orientation, intensity and colour) seems to be sufficient to predict salient regions that correlate with human perception, complicated scenes or complete simulation of gaze patterns require more image features (Parkhurst et al., 2002). Furthermore, the quality of the saliency map can be improved by considering knowledge-based information, for example, visual properties of the objects in a scene (Rao et al., 2002). Even though the saliency maps are a promising model for visual attention, there are some drawbacks:

(1) Saliency maps are calculated on orientation, intensity and colour features, but it is still unclear whether those features play a central role in the determination of fixation locations. Recently, the saliency-based approach to visual attention has received some empirical support: An eye movement study revealed a correlation between the saliency map and a human fixation map, derived from participants' eye movements when viewing natural and synthetic colour images (Ouerhani, von Wartburg, Hügli & Müri, 2003).

(2) Not only the stimulus (bottom-up information), but also the knowledge about scene objects and meaning (top-down information) influences fixation positions. The top-down factors for fixation location are insufficiently incorporated in the saliency-based model of visual attention. Additionally, the direction of the initial saccade is influenced by scene information perceived during the first fixation (Henderson, Weeks & Hollingworth, 1999). Recent work applies accumulated statistical knowledge of the visual features (Navalpakkam & Itti, 2006b) to tune bottom-up maps for optimal target detection. In another work, the influence of bottom-up cues, task knowledge and target influence on the guidance of attention are modelled in a biologically plausible manner (Navalpakkam & Itti, 2005).

The single steps in the implementation of saliency maps are the topic of the following sections, starting with the feature maps.

Feature Maps

As described above, the first step is the pre-attentive calculation of primitive image features in a parallel manner over the entire visual field. In general, $n = 3$ primitive features, i.e., intensity, colour and orientation are computed from the images resulting in 42 feature maps. Similar to the *feature integration theory* (see Section 2.8.3), the single feature maps represent different elementary features of a visual scene. The difference between the two approaches is that the feature maps do not code the characteristics of a feature at the corresponding image position, but rather the local *conspicuity* of the feature compared to the sorrounding image regions.

As already mentioned in Section 2.5, the cells in the laterale geniculate nucleus (LGN) and the primary visual cortex have an antagonistic receptive field. These cells detect locations that stand out from their surround. In the saliency-based model, the centre-surround is implemented as the difference between fine and coarse scales. Computing the

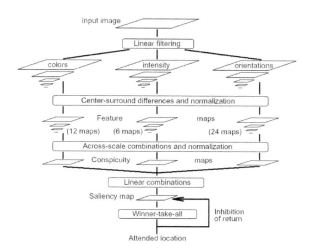

Figure 7.8: General architecture of the saliency-based model of visual attention (from Itti, Koch & Niebur, 1998).

differences between several scales yields to a multiscale feature extraction. In the model, eight spatial scales of the image are created using Gaussian pyramids, which progressively low-pass filter and subsample the image. Thus, the following subsamples of the original image are created: $288 \times 200, 144 \times 100, 72 \times 50, 36 \times 25, 18 \times 13, 9 \times 7, 5 \times 4$ and 3×2. Through *interpolation*, a scaled image can be tranformed back into the original size. Interpolation means in this context the enlargement of an image, in which missing image pixels are calculated from the average of the surrounding image points. In the resized images, the lack of information becomes apparent as blurring. At the same time, information about the surrounding image region is coded at every image position. The size of this region depends on the scaling factor: Higher scaling factors result in larger image regions.

By using intensity, colour and orientation, altogether seven centre-surround differences can be calculated: Contrast for bright-dark, red-green, blue-yellow, as well as edge orientations of $0°, 45°, 90°$ and $135°$. Each contrast calculation is performed for six different scales: The pixel values of a centre scale $c \in \{2, 3, 4\}$ are compared to the corresponding pixel in the surround at scale $s = c + \delta$, with $\delta \in \{3, 4\}$. A centre-surround calculation between a centre of scale 3 and a surrounding of scale 7, for example, calculates the contrast between a 3×2 centre and a 36×25 surrounding. The across scale difference, denoted by $\ominus$ in the following, consists of an interpolation to the final scale and subsequent point-by-point substraction.

The calculation of the feature maps for intensity, colour and orientation are the subject of the following sections.

Intensity

First, an intensity image (I) is calculated from the red (R), green (G) and blue (B) channels of the input image:

$$I = (R + G + B)/3.0 \tag{7.10}$$

The intensity contrast models the neurons sensitive to either dark centres to bright surrounds or bright centres to dark surrounds (see Section 2.5). It is computed as a set of six maps $I(c, s)$ with $c \in \{2, 3, 4\}$ and $s = c + \delta, \delta \in \{3, 4\}$:

$$I(c, s) = |I(c) \ominus I(s)| \tag{7.11}$$

where $\ominus$ are the centre-surround differences between a centre (with a fine scale c) and a surrounding with a coarse scale s.

Colour

The calculation of the colour saliency models the *colour-opponent cells* in the visual cortex (see Section 2.5). Colour-opponent cells have an antagonistic centre-surround receptive field (see Figure 2.10): Their centre is excited by one colour and inhibited by another and an opposite reaction in the surround. Such opponencies exist for the red/green, green/red, blue/yellow and yellow/blue colour pairs in the primary visual cortex. Thus, first four broadly-tuned colour channels are created:

- Red: $R = r - (g + b)/2$

- Green: $G = g - (r + b)/2$

- Blue: $B = b - (r + g)/2$

- Yellow: $Y = (r + g)/2 - |r - g|/2 - b$

To account for the four colour-opponency pairs (see above), maps $RG(c, s)$ and $BY(c, s)$ are created from the different scales of the red, green, blue and yellow colour channels:

$$RG(c, s) = |(R(c) - G(c)) \oplus (G(s) - R(s))| \tag{7.12}$$
$$BY(c, s) = |(B(c) - Y(c)) \oplus (Y(s) - B(s))| \tag{7.13}$$

where $c \in \{2, 3, 4\}$ and $s = c + \delta, \delta \in \{3, 4\}$. The overall colour conspicuity map results from a linear combination of the two colour-opponency maps.

Orientation

The orientation saliencies are calculated from the intensity image (I) by applying *Gabor Pyramids* $O(\sigma, \theta)$, where ($\sigma \in [0..8]$) is the scale and ($\theta \in 0^o, 45^o, 90^o, 135^o$) are the orientations. Gabor Filters are described in detail in Section 1.2.3. Thus, the different orientation feature maps are calculated according to:

$$O(c, s, \theta) = |O(c, \theta) \oplus O(s, \theta)| \tag{7.14}$$

Integration of Different Feature Maps

In total, 42 feature maps are calculated: Six for intensity, 12 for colour and 24 for orientation. The integration of the different feature maps is carried out in three steps: The single feature maps are first normalised. Then they are combined into three conspicuity maps for intensity, colour and orientation. The three conspicuity maps are finally combined into the overall saliency map (see Figure 7.8).

The values of the single feature maps are first normalised to the interval between 0 and 1, to adjust scale differences between the single features. Then, a second normalisation (N) is applied to each feature map. The result of N is that feature maps with a small number of peaks are promoted, whereas maps with a high number of comparable peaks are suppressed (see Figure 7.9). This guarantees that high conspicuities in a few feature maps are not overlapped by noise or low conspicuities in other maps (Itti, Koch & Niebur, 1998). The normalisation N can be realised by applying a 2D *Difference-of Gaussian* kernel (DoG) on the feature maps (Itti & Koch, 2001b). This filter intensifies local conspicuities that differ clearly from their surroundings:

$$N_2(K) = |K + DoG(K) - C_{inh}|_{\geq 0} \qquad (7.15)$$

where K is the feature map. Uniform local minima are inhibited by subtraction of the constant C_{inh}. For maps scaled between 0 and 1, C_{inh} is set to 0.02 (Itti & Koch, 2001b). The substraction can lead to negative values in the feature maps. By taking the absolute value ($|...|_{\geq 0}$), all negative values are set to zero. Reapplications of Equation 7.15 and normalisation lead to a clear segregation of strong saliences in the feature maps. According to Itti and Koch (2000), the convolution with the DoG is a coarse model for the activation and inhibition processes in the cortex.

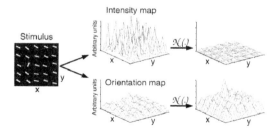

Figure 7.9: Normalisation of the feature maps (from Itti, Koch & Niebur, 1998). Feature maps with a small number of peaks are promoted, whereas maps with a high number of comparable peaks are suppressed.

Then, the single feature maps are combined into three conspicuity maps for intensity ($\bar{I}$), colour ($\bar{C}$) and orientation ($\bar{O}$) (see Figure 7.8). The combination of the single feature maps is implemented by across-scale addition ($\oplus$) (by reducing each feature map to scale four followed by a point-by-point addition). Similar features compete for saliency, whereas different ones contribute independently to the overall saliency (Itti, Koch & Niebur, 1998). This motivates the calculation of three single conspicuity maps and their individual normalisation.

In the final step, the three conspicuity maps are normalised and linearily combined into the overall saliency map S (see Figure 7.11):

$$S = w_i N(\bar{I}) + w_c N(\bar{C}) + w_o N(\bar{O}) \tag{7.16}$$

where w_i, w_c and w_o are the corresponding weights for the single features, i.e., intensity, colour and orientation. An increased saliency in a single feature map leads automatically to an increase of the saliency in the overall map. The maximum in S defines the most salient image region, to which the focus of attention should be directed. The most salient regions are successively selected by a *winner-take-all* network (Itti, Koch & Niebur, 1998).

Figure 7.10: The first row shows the original image and its computed overall saliency map. The lower row depicts the fixation map and the comparison map.

Human Fixation Map and Overall Saliency Map

The human fixation map is derived from the human eye movements recorded in the VBIR experiment (see Section 6.1). It is calculated as described in Section 3.5.1.

The idea behind the saliency map model is, to compare the human fixation map, based on the fixation information, with the saliency map computed by the saliency-based model of visual attention. As described above, the three different conspicuity maps are linearly combined into an overall saliency map (see Equation 7.16). Thereby, each (bottom-up) conspicuity map is associated with a set of (top-down) weights (w_i, w_c and w_o). The top-down component used, derives knowledge from the human gaze patterns by iteratively determining the feature weights for the single bottom-up maps (see Figure 7.12) that maximise the correlation between the human fixation and the overall saliency map. Why is this top-down component necessary? Pomplun (2006) investigated participants' eye movements when they had to find a previously shown small search target somewhere in a large display. He demonstrated that in natural and complex displays, visual search is guided by top-down control based on low-level search features. The low-level features considered were intensity, contrast and predominant spatial frequency and orientation. This is also true for image retrieval: Top-down factors influenced participants' gaze patterns in the retrieval experiment (see Section 6.1). For example, when participants gazed at the database images (see Figure 6.7), they did not only look for striking regions but also tried to match them with the information gathered from the query. Through the comparison of the overall saliency map with the human fixation map, the model "integrates" the top-down information from participants' gaze patterns into the corresponding feature weights (w_i, w_c and w_o).

Such an optimisation of the correlation between the human fixation and overall saliency map by top-down information emphasises the attended regions more than the unattended ones. Thus, important regions, who attract users' attention, are faster detected.

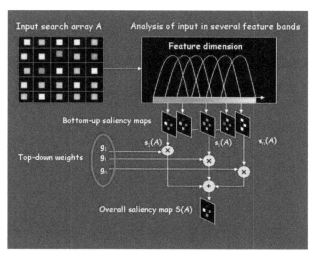

Figure 7.11: General architecture of the saliency-based model of visual attention (from Navalpakkam & Itti, 2006).

Analogous to the Shannon entropy (see Section 4.6), the optimal weight combination reflects the importance of each feature (i.e., intensity, colour and orientation) for the computation of the overall human attention distribution.

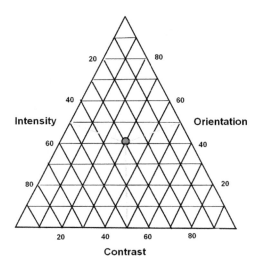

Figure 7.12: The triangle for choosing the different weights for the single conspicuity maps. The red dot marks the weight combination $w_i = 50$, $w_c = 50$ and $w_o = 50$.

Subjective Comparison

In order to evaluate subjectively the correlation between the human fixation map and the overall saliency map, a *comparision map* is calculated (Ouerhani, von Wartburg, Hügli & Müri, 2004) (see Figure 7.10 and 7.13). This map uses the RGB colour triplet, where:

$$R = \textit{value of the human attention map}$$
$$G = 0$$
$$B = \textit{value of the saliency map}$$

Red regions indicate high human attention values, but low values in the saliency map. Blue regions represent pixels with high values in the saliency map, but absense of attention in the human fixation map. Magenta regions indicate correlated values in the human and saliency map.

Objective Comparisons

For an objective comparison of the human and saliency map, the correlation coefficient is calculated according to:

$$\rho = \frac{\sum_{(x,y)}(M_h(x,y) - \mu_h)(M_s(x,y) - \mu_s)}{\sqrt{(\sum_{(x,y)}(M_h(x,y) - \mu_h)^2)(\sum_{(x,y)}(M_s(x,y) - \mu_s)^2)}} \tag{7.17}$$

where μ_h and μ_s are the mean values of the human map (M_h) and saliency map (M_s), respectively. The correlation is calculated for different saliency maps (M_s), resulting from different weight combinations w_i, w_c and w_o (see Equation 7.16).

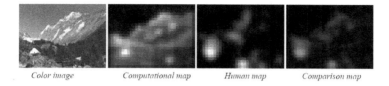

Color image   *Computational map*   *Human map*   *Comparison map*

Figure 7.13: The original image, its computed overall saliency map, the human and the comparison map (from Ouerhani, von Wartburg, Hügli & Müri, 2004).

7.3.2   Results of the Saliency Map Model

The results for two example images (see Table 7.8 and 7.9) reveal that there are high variations in the correlation values and slight differences in the optimal weighting scheme between the single flower images. Nevertheless, the results demonstrate clearly the dominance of the colour channel over intensity and orientation. In order to get high correlation values between the human attention map and the corresponding overall saliency map, colour should receive a weight above 70%. The optimal weight for intensity is between 10-30%, whereas orientation should be associated with weights between 0-20%. Table 7.8 shows the correlation between the human fixation map and the overall saliency map for different weight combinations in case of image 1225. The correlation values are quite high, showing that there are strong similarities between the image regions receiving high attention in the human fixation and overall saliency map. As can be seen from Figure 7.14 (b), participants preferably fixate the blossom (particularly the centre). Only little attention is directed toward the background in the lower right area. The optimal weight combination for image 1225, which shows the highest correlation to the human fixation map, is (w_i = 13, w_c=85, w_o=2) for intensity, colour and orientation. In the following, the weight combinations are presented as a triple consisting of the weights for intensity, colour and orientation. Also the combination (10,80,10) shows a quite high correlation. When the weight for colour gets below 70%, the correlation drops significantly, for example in case

Image	Intensity (w_i)	Colour (w_c)	Orientation (w_o)	Correlation (ρ)
1225	13	85	2	0.611636700068136
1225	10	80	10	0.610202835010455
1225	33	33	33	0.52306031910075
1225	60	40	0	0.51497990818908
1225	5	20	75	0.319464429430311

Table 7.8: Correlation values between the human fixation map and the overall saliency map for different weight combinations for image 1225.

of (60,40,0). Figures 7.15 and 7.16 illustrate the differences in the overall saliency maps when colour receives lower or higher weights, respectively. The single bottom-up conspicuity maps can be found in Figure 7.14. The colour map (see Figure 7.14 (d)) shows high attention values for the whole blossom area, which reflect already the flowers' shape. Only a few attention blobs are located on the background. The results of the intensity and orientation map on the other hand, show attention dots or edges as parts of the flower borders. Here the intensity and orientation differences are most prevalent. A comparison of the single conspicuity maps with the human fixation map explains the dominance of the colour feature: The overlap between areas of high attention in the human fixation and the colour conspicuity map receives a maximum, leading to a high value for w_c. Figure 7.14 shows also that the highligted areas in the conspicuity maps and the human fixation map are restricted to the blossom. Thus, the correlation value is quite high.

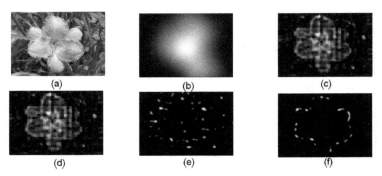

Figure 7.14: The results of the saliency model for image 1225: (a) Original image, (b) average human fixation map, (c) overall saliency map (10,90,0), (d) colour conspicuity, (e) intensity conspicuity and (f) orientation conspicuity.

Table 7.9 shows the correlation values for different weight combinations for image

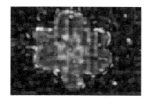

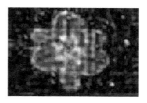

Figure 7.15: *Saliency map of image 1225 (33,33,33).*

Figure 7.16: *Saliency map of image 1225 (30,65,5).*

Image	Intensity (w_i)	Colour (w_c)	Orientation (w_o)	Correlation (ρ)
778	0	95	5	0.318381874800017
778	0	80	20	0.316252777104215
778	5	75	20	0.314625101931079
778	33	33	33	0.267709029129873
778	5	20	75	0.187096944772978

Table 7.9: Correlation values between the human fixation map and the overall saliency map for different weight combinations for image 778.

778. Compared to image 1225, the correlation values between the overall saliency map and the human fixation map are smaller. The optimal weight combination is (0,95,5). Other combinations with high correlation values are (0,100,0) and (0,90,10). Figure 7.17 depicts the human fixation map, as well as the different conspicuity maps for image 778. Figure 7.17 (b) shows that humans fixate preferably the flower, especially the centre. In the conspicuity maps on the other hand, the flower centre receives low attention values, because it consists of a relatively homogeneous black area. The petals get high attention values for the colour feature. As can be seen from Figure 7.17, there are also blobs of high attention in the background, especially for intensity and orientation. This is the reason for the relatively low correlation value between the human fixation map and the overall saliency map. Again, colour is the dominant feature. If the weight for colour gets below 70%, the correlation drops significantly, for example in case of (33,33,33).

Table 7.10 shows the optimal weight combinations and the corresponding correlation values between the human fixation map and the overall saliency map for 20 images from the start configurations (see Appendix A). The outcomes confirm the results described above: Colour is the most important feature. It should receive a weight of at least around 70%. Intensity is the second important feature with weights between 10% to 30%. The least important one for flower images is orientation with weights in the interval between 0% to 20%. Table 7.11 shows the mean and standard deviation for the single features

Image	Intensity (w_i)	Colour (w_c)	Orientation (w_o)	Correlation (ρ)
24	30	65	5	0.632158417917597
31	0	100	0	0.491966460761374
54	4	84	12	0.545164255921715
69	10	70	20	0.23002524418382
162	10	80	10	0.716476300530291
290	10	90	0	0.431393965465445
353	2	98	0	0.501885824190969
518	30	70	0	0.315872238099545
540	15	70	15	0.326719482928673
650	10	90	0	0.546680166589919
759	13	86	1	0.474625748653614
778	0	95	5	0.318381874800017
909	20	80	0	0.309693298472969
1221	15	70	15	0.288933133132566
1225	13	85	2	0.611636700068136
1463	4	82	14	0.311604358754086
1471	20	70	10	0.315201270810674
1582	5	90	5	0.335530208397559
1738	10	70	20	0.475792990358998
1891	2	98	0	0.282658332280641

Table 7.10: Correlation values between the human fixation map and the overall saliency map for the optimal weight combinations for 20 images from the start configuration. The images are depicted in the Appendix.

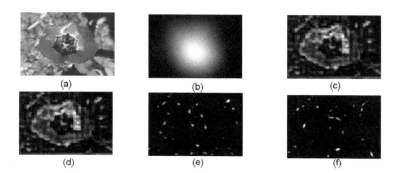

Figure 7.17: The results of the saliency model for image 778: (a) Original image, (b) average human fixation map, (c) overall saliency map (0,100,0), (d) colour conspicuity, (e) intensity conspicuity and (f) orientation conspicuity.

Feature	M	SD
Intensity	11.15	8.7856
Colour	82.15	11.2075
Orientation	6.7	7.1532

Table 7.11: Mean (M) and standard deviation (SD) for the intensity, colour and orientation values depicted in Table 7.10.

(i.e., intensity, colour and orientation). The mean values reflect the importance of each feature. As can be seen, the standard deviation for colour is quite high.

In Itti and Koch (2001b) different combination strategies for the single conspicuity maps were evaluated using three databases of natural images. The result revealed the poorest performance for the simple normalised summation of the single maps. In a second approach, *supervised learning* was applied to determine an optimal weight combination for the single conspicuity maps for a given class of images. This may model the biological processes in animals when they are trained to detect a particular target. The application of the supervised learning on a set of images depicting a red can photographed from different viewpoints, revealed the dominance of the colour channel and a suppression of the intensity and horizontal orientation channels. These findings correspond to the results mentioned above. The disadvantage of supervised learning is that it leads to specialised systems with poor generalisation abilities.

The results for the correlations, depicted in Table 7.8 and 7.9, are in correspondence to those reported in Ouerhani, Wartburg, Hügli and Müri (2004), who found high correlation values around 0.6 for the best matches, whereas low matches between the human fixation and the saliency maps result in correlation values around 0.1.

The comparison of the human fixation and the single conspicuity maps shows that the attention distribution in the colour map reflects most closely that of the human fixation maps. Intensity and orientation are less important. The framework implemented for this model allows to investigate other features, which may be more relevant to model human attention on natural flower images than intensity and orientation.

Chapter 8

Conclusions and Outlook

In the preceding chapters it was demonstrated how the consideration of users' gaze behaviour, obtained from eye-tracking data, can significantly improve the retrieval performance when searching for images in a flower database. By using an eye tracker as a rapid and natural interface for relevance feedback, the search can be directed towards information of increasing relevance and therefore leading to results that reflect closer participants' interest.

In the Vision-Based Image Retrieval (VBIR) system developed in this book, the user provides feedback through eye movements and mouse clicks. Semantically important image regions receive much attention, manifested by a higher number of fixations and increasing fixation durations. By increasing the weights for the locally calculated image features of semantically important regions, more relevant images are retrieved in the next retrieval step. The adequateness of the attention-based retrieval technique was evaluated by comparing the VBIR with a standard CBIRS, where the user provides feedback by clicking on the most similar images. In the CBIRS, similar images are retrieved according to the distances in the globally calculated features. In order to test the retrieval approaches on a set of eight queries, the number of retrieval steps was limited to a maximum of ten in the experiment.

Compared to the standard CBIR approach, participants retrieved more images using the VBIR system. Additionally, the time to select the most similar image from the actual set of retrieved images was shorter in the VBIR approach. The correspondence of the retrieval results of both approaches to the users' estimation of similarity, especially in those cases, where the queries were not found, was evaluated with a second experiment. In this experiment participants ranked the similarity between the retrieval results of both approaches to the corresponding queries according to their subjective impression of similarity. The empirical findings revealed significantly higher similarity values for the retrieval results of the VBIR approach. This may be one reason for the longer reaction times in the CBIR approach: When none of the retrieved images is similar to the query, participants needed more time to come to a decision, because they had difficulties to find adequate indications for their similarity ratings. Furthermore, participants' subjective similarity estimations comply with objectively calculated feature distances, i.e., high similarity values correlate with small feature distances. Furthermore, once the participants navigated to a set of dissimilar images, it was much more difficult in CBIR than in VBIR to return to more similar images. The outcomes of the experiment also revealed major differences in the results for the single query images of the eight start configurations: In general, the CBIR approach shows good results, when the blossom is quite large and the background is homogeneous. Here, the object features "dominate" the global feature vectors. In case of small-sized blossoms and inhomogeneous backgrounds on the other hand, the VBIR approach performs much better. With targeted gaze patterns, the important (local) features can be "emphasised", whereas unimportant ones can be "suppressed". This leads to better performances of the VBIR system compared to the CBIR approach, where the unimportant information (noise) is part of the globally calculated image features.

This study confirmed that visual perception is a complex process below conscious awareness (Pelz et al., 2000). Participants had difficulties to specify exactly their evaluation criteria for image similarity. The majority evaluated image similarity according to colour or shape information. Only when images were quite similar in regard to colour and shape, they also considered background information or the overall image impression. Therefore, introspective reports alone are of limited use to understand human similarity decisions. In day-to-day tasks, such as estimating the similarity between image pairs, participants tend to describe only large-scaled goals (for example, "search for a flower of the same colour"). Details about the strategies applied to accomplish the day-to-day tasks do not reach consciousness (Pelz et al., 2000). Thus, the monitoring of eye movements during image retrieval allows to investigate the underlying processes of human similarity evaluation.

Besides the implementation of a new approach to image retrieval, this book proposed methods to calculate the optimal feature weights as well as to evaluate the quality of the extracted image features. The Shannon entropy, calculated from the feature distance histograms, revealed the dominance of colour for the retrieval of flower images. The self-organizing map (SOM) arranges the images on a 2D grid according to their feature values: Images with similar features are clustered, whereas those with dissimilar features are scattered throughout the grid. Thus, two automatic techniques are available that allow to compute the optimal weighting and to evaluate the features before system application. In case of inconsistencies, optimisations can be developed, which again would have to be tested. This repeating optimisation process is also one of the main ideas behind computer simulations (see Section 7.1).

The knowledge from the experiments has been used to implement several image retrieval models. In the simplest CBIR model, the images are retrieved according to distances in the global image features. This model outperformed the participants' retrieval success in the experiment. This result clearly shows that humans apply, besides image features, other similarity measures for the evaluation of flower images, which are not sufficiently reflected by the model's parameters. An evaluation of the selection probabilities for the single database images of the eight start configurations revealed that there are commonalities among the different participants: In the majority of cases, the participants prefer one database image over the others. These findings led to the idea, to extend the original CBIR model by a multi-layer perceptron (MLP) that approximates the preferences in human similarity decision processes. Thus, the MLP was trained with similarity estimations between flower pairs provided by several participants. These estimations were very subjective: Some users evaluated the similarity according to features (especially colour or shape), other considered also background information or a combination of different measurements. Participants reported that the majority of flower pairs were quite different. Furthermore, they had difficulties to find suitable indications for similarity ratings. Thus, they often did not know how to position the sliders correctly and mostly assigned only low similarity values. Because of these high variations, it is not possible to predict the similarity estimations from one participant from the ratings of another. The MLP was evaluated by comparing its similarity estimations for all image combinations of the start configurations with the selection probabilities of the participants from the retrieval experiment. The outcome revealed that the MLP cannot exactly replicate users' similarity estimations from the retrieval experiments, because of the high variations in participants' similarity rankings.

Because of the partial correspondence of participants' selection probabilities with the MLP similarity estimations, the neural net was integrated in the original CBIR model to choose the reference images from the actual retrieved set of database images. No query from the start configuration could be found by the modified CBIR model within the maximum of ten retrieval steps. The outcome of the model reflects closer the retrieval performances of the participants in the experiment than does the original CBIR model. But again, although the results are much better than those of the random model, the modified model did also not simulate human retrieval performances satisfactorily. This shows that the MLP did not correctly approximate users' similarity estimations. The reason is in the unsteadiness and variability of participants' similarity estimations, which cannot be handled by the classical MLP approach. A solution for these problems could be accomplished through two improvements: For one, the classical MLP algorithm could be optimised to better handle high variations in the input data. For another, the participants should given better indications for providing similarity estimations, either by using more heterogenous images or by introducing a reference value to which the similarity estimations should be directed. This should lead to lower variances in humans' similarity estimations, which could be easier handled by an automatic learning algorithm.

The three VBIR models differ in regard to the weighting scheme for the single image tiles. In the simplest model (SVBIR), the single tiles are weighted by a constant. In the two other VBIR models, all tiles are either weighted by an attention value resulting from the OOCVA approach (AVBIR) or by just considering the tiles with the highest attention values (ATVBIR). The results are as expected: ATVBIR performed best with regard to the average number of image steps required to find the query. The simplest model found the highest number of images (six out of eight), but required nearly twice as much retrieval steps to find all eight query images. AVBIR, which most closely reflects the VBIR approach, retrieved five out of eight images.

All in all, the results of the different retrieval models revealed that they can only approximate the processes underlying image retrieval. These processes are so diverse and subjective that they can hardly be expressed in an algorithmic form. Much more research is necessary to better understand the processes underlying image retrieval and similarity estimation so that (more adequate) models can be implemented that closer reflect human behaviour. Here, the recording and analysis of human gaze patterns can provide helpful insights into visual retrieval and comparison processes ("eyes are a window to the mind").

A second model made use of the recorded eye movements in the retrieval experiments. From the eye-movement data, human fixation maps were calculated. Furthermore, three bottom-up (i.e., intensity, colour and orientation) maps were computed from the images and linearly combined into a single overall saliency map. The model integrates top-down information by iteratively determining the feature weights that maximise the correlation between the human fixation and the overall saliency map (see Section 7.3.1). The corresponding weights reflect the importance of the intensity, colour and orientation features for the computation of the overall human attention distribution. The outcome of the model revealed that there are high variations in the correlation values and small differences in the weight combinations between the single flower images. Nevertheless, the model demonstrates the dominance of the colour feature. In order to get a high correlation between the human fixation map and the overall saliency map, it should at least receive a weight of 70%. The optimal weight for intensity is between 10-30%, whereas the orientation should be associated with weights in the interval from 0% to 20%.

This result substantiates the prominent role of the colour feature for the retrieval of flower images, which is in accordance with the findings of Gegenfurtner and Rieger (2000). A model that optimally describes human attention distribution when looking at flower images should emphasise the colour features. Thus, not only salient points in the flower images that preferable attract attention can be more easily detected, but also more biologically motivated attention patterns could be investigated in more detail. A retrieval system or model focussing on the colour component should therefore lead to a better performance. These outcomes are conform with the results of the Shannon entropy, where colour also received the highest emphasis (see Section 4.6).

The results of the saliency model are also important for many industrial applications. For example, in Robotics and Computer Vision, saliency maps are used to detect scene objects or to control stereo cameras. By using weight combinations for the single conspicuity maps that are derived from human attention patterns, more human-like machines can be developed. These machines can then more closely imitate the effective human classification between foreground and background objects, maximising target detection speed. Furthermore, under certain circumstances a complete generation of a world-model of the environment can be avoided, in that only interesting parts of the image are analysed. This results in a reduction of information processing enabling real-time image analysis even with photos from complex environments.

Based on these promising results of the basic image retrieval scenario, which starting points for further research on this paradigm seem to be most interesting and important?

- **Image database and image domains**: The VBIR approach is tested on a homogeneous database of 2,000 flower images. The focus on one image domain complicates the retrieval process since the images are quite similar according to particular image features. Even though there are many application areas with images from limited domains (e.g., medical images), image collections are usually heterogenous (e.g., photographs from the last vacation). Thus, the techniques developed in this book should be tested on a larger, more heterogeneous image database.

- **Analysis of other gaze parameters**: The eye tracker provides a lot of data that enables predictions about refixations (as a measure of interest in the image), saccade speed (decreases prior to image selection), pupil diameters (increases for hard-to find images) and unconscious pre-attentive vision (Oyekoya, 2007). The consideration of further parameters may lead to better and more reliable retrieval performances.

- **Region-based subdivision of images:** The task in this experiment was to find the identical image in a set of 2,000 flower images. In classical CBIRS, the user provides a query and the system retrieves all similar images from the database. Here, a fixed subdivision of the image into 16 tiles is not adequate. A better and more flexible approach would be to first extract the important regions and then to weight the single regions according to their received attention.

- **Variations in the display size**: The retrieval scenario was designed to fit within a screen resolution of 1024×768 pixels ($31.3^o \times 25.0^o$ of visual angle). Thus, participants could to some extent see image details in the visual periphery without the need to focus on image regions that are of particular relevance. Various display sizes may also yield different results. The images could be presented on a bigger computer screen or a projection field, or fewer images could be displayed simultaneously. Then images are of bigger size so that participants have to gaze at important image regions. This would probably lead to even better retrieval results in the VBIR approach.

- **Storage of relevance feedback**: The eye movements and mouse clicks are not stored in the VBIR system to continuously improve the retrieval performance. Therefore, the system has to relearn the weighting for the different tiles for each retrieval session. From the collected data a retrieval profile could be generated for each user or image category. Since images from the same category show similar eye movement patterns (Jaimes, Pelz, Grabowski, Babcock & Chang, 2001), the system can learn from previous recorded data to improve its retrieval performance and to apply retrieval techniques that are closer to human similarity requirements. There exist already retrieval systems that remember relevant results of each query, for example, the *iFind* system (Lu, Hu, Zhu, Zhang & Yang, 2000).

- **Flexible extensions**: Ideal would be a system, where new images can be provided by the user and easily be integrated into the database. This process usually requires a recalculation of image features as well as the distances between all new image combinations in the database. This feature is not provided by traditional systems. Furthermore, sometimes a randomly retrieved image should be added to the actual set of retrieval results allowing the user to navigate out of a retrieval loop. This technique is, for example, applied in the *EyeVisionBot* system (Scherffig & Diebner, 2005).

Before the techniques described in this book can be applied in day-by-day applications, the eye-tracking technology has to be improved substantially. Although eye-tracking techniques have made a significant progress over the last years, much smaller, cheaper and more accurate devices are necessary in the near future. These smaller eye-tracking systems or small cameras embedded in screens or laptop lids record users' eye movements and enable a more natural human-machine interface. The application ranges for theses systems will be manifold: Input assistance systems for handicapped people, natural operation environment of computer systems, cataloguing applications and mobile phones. The deeper study of eye movements and the possible application fields, as well as the acceptance by users, will be of paramount importance for the development of future eye-tracking systems. The tracking of the eyes in more natural environments establish better insights in visual perception processes. This very promising research direction will attract many activities over the next years.

Up-to-date, nobody uses CBIRS for his or her private image collections, because of their high expenses, non-intuitive handling and cumbersome installation. Hence, private users apply image annotations or simple programs without retrieval facilities to manage their image collections. A system which is widely applicable, extensible, easy to install and provides an intuitive operation will attract users' interest. Additionally, the subjective differences in the perception of image content have to be considered: Simple statistical analysis of eye movements, like clustering, summation and differentiation as user-relevance feedback are insufficient for identifying interests and more robust methods are needed, i.e., machine learning techniques. Hereby, the spreading of more powerful computer hardware allows to implement more complex and storage intensive applications.

Today we live in a cross-medial world. It is not sufficient for entrepreneurs to manage images, audio, video or other media alone. Rather, the capturing, managing, storing, preserving, conversion and delivering of different data is of higher concern. This led to *Enterprise-Content-Management Systems* (ECMS), which provide these features as all-in-one solutions or as single, stand alone packages. Thus, the future of CBIRS will not be as a stand-alone application, but rather as method combined with other techniques like EMCS systems or *Virtual Reality* (VR).

This work has established many new insights in a wide and only recently established research field of combining CBIR and eye-tracking techniques as relevance feedback for image retrieval. The experimental results, as well as the different models for image retrieval can serve as a motivation for further research to investigate the cognitive processes underlying image retrieval and similarity estimations. The first results are very promising, but a lot of interesting research and hardware development is still waiting to be done.

The outcome will be a better understanding of human behaviour and the development of natural and intuitive human-machine interfaces.

References

Adelson, E.H. & Bergen, J.R. (1991). The plenoptic function and the elements of early vision. In M.S. Landy & J.A. Movshon (Eds.), *Computational Models of Visual Processing*, 3–20. Cambridge, MA: MIT Press.

Altmann, G. T. & Kamide, Y. (2004). Now you see it, now you don't: Mediating the mapping between language and the visual world. In J.M. Henderson & F. Ferreira (Eds.), *The interface of language, vision, and action: Eye Movements and the visual world* (347–386). New York: Psychology Press.

Antes, J.R. (1974). The time course of picture viewing. *Journal of Experimental Psychology*, 103, 62–70.

Awater, H. (2002). *Perception of visual space at the time of saccadic eye movements*. Dissertation. Ruhr-Universität Bochum, Bochum, Germany.

Bach, J. et al. (1996). Virage image search engine: An open framework for image management. *Proceedings of the SPIE, Storage and Retrieval for Image and Video Databases IV*, San Jose, CA, 76–87.

Baeza-Yates, R. & Ribeiro-Neto, B. (1999). *Modern Information Retrieval*. New York: ACM Press, Addison-Wesley.

Bamidele, A., Stentiford, F.W.M. & Morphett, J. (2004). An attention based approach to content based image retrieval. *BT Technology Journal*, 22, 151–160.

Barrow, H.G. & Tannenbaum, M.J. (1986). Computational approaches to vision. In K.R. Boff, L. Kaufman & J.P. Thomas (Eds.), *Handbook of perception and human performance* (38.1-38.70). New York: Wiley.

Bauckhage, C., Käster, T., Pfeiffer, M. & Sagerer, G. (2003). Content-Based Image Retrieval by Multimodal Interaction. *Proceedings of the 29th Annual Conference of the IEEE Industrial Electronics Society*, Roanoke, VA, 1865–1870.

Beck, J. (1972). Similarity grouping and peripheral discriminability under uncertainty. *American Journal of Psychology*, 85, 1–19.

Beck, J. (1973). Similarity grouping of curves. *Perceptual and Motor Skills*, 36, 1331–1341.

Beck, J. (1982). Textural segmentation. In J. Beck (Ed.), *Organization and Representation in Perception* (285–317). Hillsdale: Erlenbaum.

Beck, J., Sutter, A. & Ivry, A. (1987). Spatial frequency channels and perceptual grouping in texture segregation. *Computer Vision Graphics Image Processing*, 37, 299–325.

Beckmann, N, Kriegel, H.-P., Schneider, R. & Seeger, B. (1990). The R^*-Tree: An efficient and robust access method for points and rectangles. *Proceedings of ACM SIGMOD International Conference on Management of Data*, Atlantic City, NJ, 322–331.

Biederman, I. (1995). Visual object recognition. In S.M. Kosslyn & D.N. Osherson (Eds.), *An invitation to cognitive science. 2nd edition, Visual Cognition.* (121–165). Cambridge: MIT Press.

Biederman, I., Mezzanotte, R. J. & Rabinowitz, J. C. (1982). Scene Perception: detecting and judging objects undergoing relational violations. *Cognitive Psychology,* 14, 143–177.

Del Bimbo, A. & Pala, P. (1997). Visual Image Retrieval by Elastic Matching of User Sketches. *IEEE Transactions on Pattern Analysis and Machine Intelligence,* 19, 121–132.

Del Bimbo, A. (1999). *Visual information retrieval.* San Francisco: Morgan Kaufmann Publishers.

Bishop, C.M. (1995). *Neural networks for pattern recognition.* Oxford: Oxford University Press.

Boff, K.R. & Lincoln, J.E. (1988). *Engineering data compendium-human perception and performance.* Harry G. Armstrong Aerospace Medical Research Laboratory, Wright-Patterson Airforce Base, Ohio.

Boring, E.G. (1942). *Sensation and perception in the history of experimental psychology.* New York: Appleton-Century-Crofts.

Brodatz, P. (1966). *Textures: A Photographic Album for Artists and Designers.* New York: Dover Publications.

Buswell, G.T. (1935). *How people look at pictures: A study of the psychology of perception in art.* Chicago: University Press.

Campbell, F.W. & Robson, J.G. (1968). Application of Fourier analysis to the visibility of gratings. *Journal of Physiology,* 197, 551–566.

Campbell, N.W., Mackeown, W.P.J., Thomas, B.T. & Troscianko, T. (1997). Intepreting image databases by region classification. *Pattern Recognition,* 30, 555–563.

Canosa, R.L., Pelz, J.B., Mennie, N.R. & Peak, J. (2003). High-level aspects of oculomotor control during viewing of natural-task images. In B.E. Rogowitz & T.N. Pappas (Eds.), *Proceedings IS&T/SPIE 15th Annual Symposium on Electronic Imaging: Human Vision and Electronic Imaging VIII.,* 5007, 240–251.

Carson, C., Thomas, M., Belongie, S., Hellerstein, J.M. & Malik, J. (1999). Blobworld: A system for region-based image indexing and retrieval. In D.P. Huijsmans, A.W.M. Smeulders (Eds.), *Proceedings Int. Conf. on Visual Information Systems, Lecture Notes in Computer Science* (509–516). Amsterdam: Springer Verlag.

Chang, S.K. & Hsu, A. (1992). Image Information Systems: Where do we go from here? *IEEE Transactions on Knowledge Data Engineering,* 4, 431–442.

Chen, Y., Nixon, M. & Thomas, D. (1995). Statistical geometrical features for texture classification. *Pattern Recognition,* 28, 537–552.

Christ, S.E., McCrae, C.S. & Abrams, R.A. (2002). Inhibition of return in static and dynamic displays. *Psychonomic Bulletin & Review,* 9, 80–85.

Chun, M.M. (2000). Contextual cueing of visual attention. *Trends in Cognitive Sciences*, 4, 170–178.

Clermont, T. (2001). VDesigner: Eine visuelle Programmiersprache und ihre Entwicklungsumgebung. *Diplomarbeit*, Technische Fakultät, Universität Bielefeld.

McConkie, G.W. (1979). On the role and control of eye movements in reading. In P.A. Kolers, M.E. Wrolstad & H. Bouma (Eds.), *Proceedings of visual language* (1, 37–48). New York: Plenum Press.

Cords, R. (1927). *Graefes Arch. Opthalm.*, Vol. 118, p. 118.

Cornsweet, T.N. & Crane, H.D. (1973). Accurate two dimensional eye tracker using first and fourth Purkinje images. *Journal of the Optical Society of America*, 63, 921.

Cox, I.J., Miller, M.L., Omohundro, S.M. & Yianilos, P.N. (2000). The bayesian image retrieval system, PicHunter: Theory, implementation and psychophysical experiments. *IEEE Transactions on Image Processing*, 9, 20–37.

Czepa, N. (2005). The earth mover's distance as a metric for image retrieval. *Kurze schriftliche Zusammenfassung, Seminar Bilddatenbanken.* University of Magdeburg. Retrieved Month 5, 2006, from
http : //www.iti.cs.uni − magdeburg.de/iti_db/lehre/proseminarws0506 − 1/emd_schriftlich.pdf

Daugman, J.G. (1980). Two-dimensional Spectral Analysis of Cortical Receptive Filed Profiles, *Vision Res*, 20, 847–856.

Davis, L.S. (1979). Shape matching using relaxation techniques. *IEEE Transactions on Pattern Analysis and Machine Intelligence*, PAMI-1, 60–72.

Delorme, A., Richard, G. & Fabre-Thorpe, M. (2000). Ultra-rapid categorization of natural scenes does not reply on color cues: A study in monkeys and humans. *Vision Research*, 40, 2187–2200.

Diepen, P.M.J. van, de Graef, M. & d'Ydewalle, G. (1995). Chronometry of foveal information extraction during scene perception. In J.M. Findlay, R. Walker & R.W. Kentridge (Eds.), *Eye movement research: Mechanisms, processes and applications* (349–362). Amsterdam: Elsevier.

Diepen, P.M.J. van, Wampers, M. & d'Ydewalle, G. (1998). Functional division of the visual field: Moving masks and moving windows. In G. Underwood (Ed.), *Eye guidance in reading and scene perception.* Oxford: Elsevier.

Duchowski, A.T. (2003). *Eye Tracking Methodology: Theory and Practice.* London: Springer.

Eakins, J.P. & Graham, M.E. (1999). Content-based image retrieval, a report to the JISC Technology Applications Programme, *Institute for Image Data Research, University of Northumbria at Newcastle.* Retrieved Month 5, 2004, from
http : //www.unn.ac.uk/iidr/report.html

Epstein, R. & Kranwisher, N. (1998). A cortical representation of the local visual environment. *Nature*, 392, pp. 598–601.

Epstein, R., Graham, K.S. & Downing, P.E. (2003). Viewpoint-specific scene representations in human parahippocampal cortex. *Neuron*, 37, pp. 865–876.

Essig, K., Ritter, H. & Pomplun, M. (2004). Application of a Novel Neural Approach to 3D Gaze Tracking: Vergence Eye-Movements in Autostereograms. In K. Forbus, D. Gentner & T. Regier (Eds.), *Proceedings of the 26th Annual Meeting of the Cognitive Science Society*, Chicago, Illinois, 357–362.

Essig, K., Pohl, S. & Ritter, H. (2005). EyeDataAnalyser - A general and flexible visualisation and analysation tool for eye tracking data-files. *Proceedings 13th European Conference on Eye Movements ECEM 13*, Bern, Switzerland.

Essig, K. & Ritter, H. (2005). Visual-Based Image Retrieval (VBIR) - A new approach for natural and intuitive image retrieval. *Proceedings 13th European Conference on Eye Movements ECEM 13*, Bern, Switzerland.

Equitz, W.H. (1989). A new vector quantization algorithm. *IEEE Transactions on Acoustics, Speech and Signal Processing*, 37, 1568–1575.

Faller, A. (1995). *Der Körper der Menschen: Einführung in Bau und Funktion*. Stuttgart: Thieme Verlag.

Faloutsos et al. (1994). Efficient and effective querying by image content. *Journal of Intelligent Information Systems*, 3, 231–262.

Friedman, A. (1979). Framing pictures: The role of knowledge in automatized encoding and memory for gist. *Journal of Experimental Psychology: General*, 108, 316–355.

Gabor, D. (1946). Theory of communication. *J. IEEE*, 93, 429–459.

Gassovskii, L.N. & Nikol'skaya, N.A. (1941). Mobility of the eye during fixation. *Problemy Fiziol. Optiki*, 1, 173.

Gegenfurtner, K.R. & Kiper, D.C. (2003). Color vision. *Annual Review of Neuroscience*, 26, 181–206.

Gegenfurtner, K.R. & Rieger, J. (2000). Sensory and cognitive contributions of color to the perception of natural scenes. *Current Biology*, 10, 805–808.

Gevers, T. (2001). Colour in image search engines. In M.S. Lew (Ed.), *Principles of visual information retrieval*, London: Springer Verlag.

Gibson, J.J. (1950). *The perception of the visual world*. Boston: Houghton Mifflin.

Goldstein, E.B. (1996). *Sensation and perception*. Pacific Grove: Brooks/Cole Publishing Company.

Gonzalez, R.C. & Woods, R.E. (2002). *Digital image processing (2nd ed.)*. New York: Prentice Hall.

Goren, C.C., Santy, M. & Wu, R.W.K. (1975). Visual following and pattern discrimination of face-like stimuli by newborn infants. *Pediatrics*, 56, 544–549.

Gotlieb, C.C. & Kreyszig, H.E. (1990). Texture descriptors based on co-occurence matrices. *Computer Vision, Graphics, and Image Processing*, 51, 70–86.

Gouras, P. (1991). Colour Vision. In E.R. Kandel, J.H. Schwartz & T.M. Jessell (Eds.), *Princinples of neural science* (3. Edition, 467–480). New York: Elsevier.

De Graef, P., Christiaens, D. & d'Ydewalle, G. (1990). Perceptual effects of scene context on object identification. *Psychological Research*, 52, 317–329.

Grecu, H., Cudalbu, C. & Buzuloiu, V. (2005). Towards gaze-based relevance feedback in image retrieval. *International Workshop on Bioinspired Information Processing: Cognitive modeling and gaze-based communication*, Lübeck, Germany.

Groner, R., Walder, F. & Groner, M. (1984). Looking at face: Local and global aspects of scanpaths. In A.G. Gale & F. Johnson (Eds.), *Theoretical and Applied Aspects of Eye Movement Research* (523–533). New York: Elsevier.

Haindl, M. (1991). Texture synthesis. *CWI Quart*, 4, 305–331.

Hallett, P.E. (1986). Eye movements. In K.R. Boff, L. Kaufman & J.P. Thomas (Eds.), *Handbook of perception and human perfomance* (10.1–10.112). New York: Wiley.

Haralick, R., Shanmugam, K. & Dinstein, I. (1973). Textural features for image classification. *IEEE Transactions on Systems, Man and Cybernetics*, 3, 6, 610–621.

Haralick, R. (1979). Statistical and structural approaches to texture. *Proceedings of the IEEE*, 67, 5, 786–804.

Haralick, R. & Bosley, R. (1973). Texture features for image classification. *Third ERTS Symposium, NASA SP-351*, 1219–1228.

Haralick, R. & Shapiro, L.G. (1992). *Computer and Robot Vision*. Boston: Addison-Wesley.

Hartigan, J.A. & Wong, M.A. (1979). Algorithms AS136: A k-means clustering algorithm. *Applied Statistics*, 28, 100-108.

Helmholtz, H. von (1852). *Über die Theorie der zusammengesetzten Farben. Habil.*. Berlin.

Helmholtz, H. von (1925). *Helmholtz's Treatise on Physiological Optics (Vol. III)*, Translated from the Third German Edition. New York: Optical Society of America.

Henderson, J.M. (1992). Visual Attention and Eye Movement Control During Reading and Picture Viewing. In K. Rayner (Ed.), *Eye movements and visual cognition: Scene perception and reading* (260–283). New York: Springer-Verlag.

Henderson, J.M., McClure, K.K., Pierce, S. & Schrock, G. (1997). Object identification without foveal vision: Evidence from an artificial scotoma paradigm. *Perception & Psychophysics*, 59, 323–346.

Henderson, J.M. & Hollingworth A. (1998). Eye movements during scene viewing: An overview. In G. Underwood (Ed.), *Eye Guidance in Reading and Scene Perception* (269–283). New York: Elsevier.

Henderson, J.M., Weeks, P.A. & Hollingworth, A. (1999). Effects of a semantic consistency on eye movemenst during scene viewing. *J. Exp. Psychol. Hum. Percept. Perform,* 25, 210–228.

Henderson, J.M. & Hollingworth A. (1999a). High level scene perception. *Annual Review of Psychology,* 50, 243–271.

Henderson, J.M. & Hollingworth A. (1999b). The role of fixation position in detecting scene changes accross saccades. *Psychological Science,* 10, 438–443.

Henderson, J.M. (2003). Human gaze control during real-world scene perception. *Trends in Cognitive Sciences,* 7, 11, 498–504.

Henderson, J.M., Williams, C.C., Castelhano, M.S. & Falk, R.J. (2003). Eye movements and picture processing during recognition. *Perception & Psychophysics,* 65, 725–734.

Henderson, J.M. & Ferreira, F. (2004). Scene perception for psycholinguists. In J.M. Henderson & F. Ferreira (Eds.), *The Interface of Language, Vision and Action: Eye Movements and the Visual World* (1-58). New York: Psychology Press.

Hering, E. (1878). *Zur Lehre vom Lichtsinn.* Wien: Gerold.

Hollingworth, A., Schrock, G. & Henderson, J.M. (2001). Change detection in the flicker paradigm: The role of fixation position within the scene. *Memory & Cognition,* 29, 296–304.

Hu, M.K. (1962). Visual pattern recognition by moments. *IRE Transactions on Information Theory,* 8, 351–364.

Irwin, D.E. (1992). Visual Memory within and across Fixations. In K. Rayner (Ed.), *Eye movements and visual cognition: Scene perception and reading* (146–165). New York: Springer-Verlag.

Itti, L. & Koch, C. (2000). A saliency-based search mechanism for overt and covert shifts of visual attention. *Vision Research,* 40 (10-12), 1489–1506.

Itti, L. & Koch, C. (2001). Computational modelling of visual attention. *Nature Neuroscience Review,* 2, 194–204.

Itti, L. & Koch, C. (2001b). Feature combination strategies for saliency-based visual attention systems. *Journal of Electronic Imaging,* 10, 1, 161–169.

Itti, L., Koch, C. & Niebur, E. (1998). A model of saliency-based visual attention for rapid scene analysis. *IEEE Transactions On Pattern Analysis and Machine Intelligence,* 20, 1254–1259.

Jaimes, A., Pelz, J., Grabowski, T., Babcock, J. & Chang, S. (2001). Using human observers'
eye movements in automatic image classifiers. *Proceedings of SPIE Human Vision and
Electronic Imaging*, 4299, 373–384.

Javal, L.E. (1879). *Ann. Oculist*, 82, p. 242.

Jing, F., Zhang, B., Lin, F., Ma, W.-Y & Zhang, H.-L. (2001). A novel region-based image
retrieval method using relevance feedback. *Proceedings 3rd International Workshop on
Multimedia Information Retrieval*, 28–31.

Jing, F., Li, M., Zhang, H.J. & Zhang, B. (2002). Learning region weighting from relevance
feedback in image retrieval. *Proceedings of the 27th IEEE International Conference on
Acoustics, Speech, and Signal Processing (ICASSP)*, 4, 4088–4091.

Jones, J.P. (1985). *The two-dimensional structure and functional form of simple receptive fields
in cat striate cortex*. Dissertation. University of Pennsylvania, Philadelphia, PA.

Joos, M., Rötting, M. & Velichkovsky, B.M. (2003). Die Bewegungen des menschlichen
Auges: Fakten, Methoden, innovative Anwendungen. In G. Rickheit, T. Herrmann and
W. Deutsch (Eds.), *Psycholinguistics. An International Handbook* (142–168). Berlin: de
Gruyter.

Joseph, J.S., Chun M.M. & Nakayama, K. (1997). Attentional requirements in a "preattentive"
feature search task. *Nature*, 387, 805–807.

Julesz, B. (1981). Textons, the elements of texture perception, and their interactions. *Nature*,
290, 91–97.

Just, M.A. & Carpenter, P.A. (1987). *The Psychology of Reading and Language*. Newton: Allyn
and Bacon.

Kämpfe, T., Käster, T., Pfeiffer, M., Ritter, H. & Sagerer, G. (2002). INDI - Intelligent Database
Navigation by Interactive and Intuitive Content-Based Image Retrieval. *IEEE 2002 International Conference on Image Processing*, III, 921–924.

Kandel, E.R., Schwartz, J.H. & Jessell, T.M. (1995). *Essentials of neural science and behavior*.
East Norwalk: Prentice Hall International.

Kastner, S., Nothdurft, H.C. & Pigarev, I.N. (1999). Neuronal correlates of pop-out in cat
striate cortex. *Visual Neuroscience*, 16, 587–600.

Kastner, S., de Weerd, P. & Ungerleider, L.G. (2000). Texture segregation in the human visual
cortex: A function MRI study. *Journal of Neurophysiology*, 83, 2453–2457.

Käster, T. (2005). *Intelligente Bildersuche durch den Einsatz inhaltsbasierter Techniken*. Dissertation. Bielefeld University, Faculty of Technology.

Kato, T., Kurita, K., Otsu, N. & Hirata, K. (1992). A sketch retrieval method for full colour
image database - query by visual example. *Proceedings ICPR, Computer Vision and Application*, 530–533.

Kaukoranta, T., Fränti, P. & Nevalainen, O. (1999). A vector quantization by lazy pairwise nearest neighbor method. *Optical Engineering*, 38, 11, 1862–1868.

Kohonen, T. (1990). The self-organizing map. *Proceedings of IEEE*, 78, 1464–1480.

Krauskopf, J., Williams, D.R. & Heeley, D.W. (1982). Cardinal directions of color space. *Vision Res.*, 22, 1123–1131.

Krauzlis, R.J. (2005). The control of voluntary eye movements: New perspectives. *The Neuroscientist*, 11, 124-137.

Kruskal, J.B. (1964). Multidimensional scaling by optimizing goodness of fit to a nonmetric hypothesis. *Pychometrika*, 29, 1–27.

Kundu, A. & Chen, J.L. (1992). Texture classification using QMF bank-based subband decomposition. *CVGIP: Graph Models Image Process*, 54, 407–419.

Laaksonen, J., Koskela, M. Laakso, S. & Oja, E. (2001). Self-organizing maps as a relevance feedback technique in content-based image retrieval. *Pattern Analysis & Applications*, 4, 140, 140–152.

Lamme, V.A.F. (1995). The neuropsychology of figure-ground segregation in primary visual cortex. *Journal of Neuroscience*, 15, 1605–1615.

Land, E.H. (1977). The retinex theory of colour vision. *Sci. Am.*, 237, 108–128.

Land, M.F, Mennie, N. & Rusted, J. (1999). Eye movements and the role of vision in activities of daily living: Making a cup of tea. *Perception*, 28, 1311–1328.

Land, M.F. & Hayhoe, M. (2002). In what way do eye movements contribute to everyday activities? *Vision Research*, 41, 3559–3565.

Landy, M. S. & Graham, N. (2004). Visual perception of texture. In Chalupa, L. M. & Werner, J. S. (Eds.), *The Visual Neurosciences* (1106-1118). Cambridge, MA: MIT Press.

Lee, B.B., Martin, P.R. & Valberg, A. (1988). The physiological basis of heterochromatic flicker photometry demonstrated in the ganglion cells of macaque retina. *J. Physiol.*, 404, 323–347.

Lee, C., Ma, W.Y. & Zhang, H.J. (1998). Information embedding based on user's relevance feedback for image retrieval. *Proceedings of SPIE Multimedia Storage and Archiving Systems IV*,3846, 294-304.

Leek, E.C., Reppa, I. & Tipper, S.P. (2003). Inhibition of return for objects and locations in static displays. *Perception & Psychophysics*, 65(3), 388–395.

Lennie, P. (1998). Single units and cortical organization. *Perception*, 27, 889–935.

Levine, M.D. (1985). *Vision in Man and Machine*. New York: McGraw-Hill.

Levy, I., Hasson, U., Avidan, G., Hendler, T. & Malach, R. (2001). Center-periphery organization of human object area. *Nature Neuroscience*,4, 533–539.

Lew, M. S. (2001). *Principles of Information Retrieval*. London: Springer Verlag.

Li, F.F., VanRullen, R., Koch, C., & Perona, P. (2002). Rapid natural scene categorization in the near absence of attention. *Proceedings of the National Academy of Sciences*, 99, 9596–9601.

Lindsay, P.H. & Norman, D.A. (1972). *Human information processing*. New York: Academic Press.

Loftus, G.R. & Markworth, N.H. (1978). Cognitive determinants of fixation location during picture viewing. *Quarterly Journal of Experimental Psychology*, 35A, 187–198.

Loftus, G.R. (1985). Picture perception: Effects of luminance on available information and information-extraction rate. *J. Exp. Psychol. Gen.*, 114, 342–356.

Loftus, G.R., Kaufman, L., Nishimoto, T. & Ruthruff, E. (1992). Effects of visual degradation on eye-fixation durations, perceptual processing, and long-term visual memory. In K. Rayner (Ed.), *Eye Movements and Visual Cognition: Scene Perception and Reading* (203–226). New York: Springer Verlag.

Lowe, D.G. (2004). Distinctive image features for scale-invariant keypoints. *International Journal of Computer Vision*, 60, 2, 91-110.

Lu, Y., Hu, C., Zhu, X., Zhang, H.J. & Yang, Q. (2000). A unified framework for semantics and feature based relevance feedback in image retrieval systems. *Proceedings of 8th ACM International Conference on Multimedia (MM '00)*, Los Angeles, Calif, USA, 31-37.

Luo, J. & Nascimento, M.A. (2004). Content-based sub-image retrieval using relevance feedback. *Proceedings of the 2nd ACM Intl. Workshop on Multimedia Databases*, 2–9.

Ma, W.Y. & Manjunath, B.S. (1997). Edge flow: A framework of boundary detection and image segmentation. *Proceedings IEEE Conf. on Computer Vision and Pattern Recognition*, 744-749.

Ma, W.Y. & Manjunath, B.S. (1999). NETRA: A toolbox for navigating large image databases. *Multimedia Systems*, 7, 184–198. Berlin: Springer Verlag.

Mackworth, N.H. & Morandi, A.J. (1967). The gaze selects informative details within pictures. *Perception & Psychophysics*, 6, 547–552.

Maffei, L. & Fiorentini, A. (1973). The visual cortex as a spatial frequency analyser. *Vision Research*, 13, 1255–1267.

Mahoney, J.V. & Ullman, S. (1988). Image chunking defining spatial building blocks for scene analysis. In Z. Pylyshyn (Ed.), *Computation processes in human vision: An interdiscuiplinary perspective*. Norwood: Ablex.

Manjunath, B.S., Simchony, T. & Chellappa, R. (1990). Stochastic and deterministic networks for texture segmentation. *IEEE Transactions on Acoustic, Speech and Signal Processing*, 38, 1039–1049.

Manjunath B.S. & Ma, W.Y (1996). Texture Features for Browsing and Retrieval of Image Data. *IEEE Transactions on Pattern Analysis and Machine Intelligence*, 18, 837–842.

Mannan, S.K., Ruddock, K.H. & Wooding, D.S. (1995). Automatic control of saccadic eye movements made in visual inspection of briefly presented 2D images. *Spatial Vision*, 9, 363–386.

Mannan, S.K., Ruddock, K.H. & Wooding, D.S. (1996). The relationship between the locations of spatial features and those of fixations made during visual examination of briefly presented images. *Spatial Vision*, 10, 165–188.

Mannan, S.K., Ruddock, K.H. & Wooding, D.S. (1997). Fixations sequences made during brief examination of two-dimensional images. *Perception*, 26, 1059–1072.

Marr, D. (1976). Early processing of visual information. *Physological Transactions of the Royal Society London B*, 275, 483–519.

Marr, D. (1982). *Vision*. San Francisco: W.H. Freeman.

Mehtre, B., Kankanhalli, M. & Lee, W. (1997). Shape measures for content based image retrieval: A comparison. *Information Processing and Management*, 33, 319–337.

Morrison, R.E. (1984). Manipulation of stimulus onset delay in reading: Evidence of parallel programming of saccades. *Journal of Experimental Psychology: Human, Perception and Performance*, 10, 667–682.

Müller, H., Müller, W., Squire, D. McG., Marchand-Maillet, S. & Pun, T. (2000). Learning features weights from user behavior in Content-Based Image Retrieval. In S.J. Simoff & O.R. Zaiane (Eds.), *ACM SIGKDD International Conference on Knowledge Discovery and Data Mining (Workshop on Multimedia Data Mining MDM/KDD2000)*, 67–72. Boston, USA.

Müller, H., Müller, W., Squire, D.M., Marchand-Maillet, S. & Run, T. (2001). Performance evaluation in content-based image retrieval: Overview and proposals. *Pattern recognition Letters (special issue on image and video indexing)*, 593–601.

Navalpakkam, V. & Itti, L. (2005). Modelling the influence of task on attention. *Vision Research*, 45, 2, 205-231.

Navalpakkam, V. & Itti, L. (2006). Bottom-up and top-down influences on visual scanpaths, In B. Rogowitz, T. N. Pappas, S. Daly (Eds.), *Proc. SPIE Human Vision and Electronic Imaging XI (HVEI06)* (6057), San Jose:SPIE Press.

Navalpakkam, V. & Itti, L. (2006b). An integrated model of top-down and bottom-up attention for optimal object detection. *Proceedings IEEE Conference on Computer Vision and Pattern Recognition (CVPR)*, 2049-2056.

Navarrete P. & Ruiz-del-Solar J. (2002). Interactive face retrieval using self-organizing maps. *2002 Int. Joint Conf. on Neural Networks* (687 - 691), Honolulu, USA.

Nelson, W.W. & Loftus, G.R. (1980). The functional field during picture viewing. *Journal of Experimental Psychology: Human Learning and Memory*, 6, 391–399.

Neumann, D. & Gegenfurtner, K.R. (2006). Image retrieval and perceptual similarity. *ACM Transactions on Applied Perception*, 3, 1, 31–47.

Newhall, S.N. (1928). Instrument for observing ocular movements. *American Journal of Psychology*, 40, 628-629.

Niblack, W. et al. (1993). The QBIC project: Querying images by content using colour, texture, and shape. *Proceedings SPIE Storage and Retrieval for Image and Video Databases*, 1908, 173-181.

Niblack, W. et al. (1998). Updates to the QBIC system: Querying images by content using colour, texture, and shape. *Proceedings SPIE Storage and Retrieval for Image and Video Databases VI*, 3312, 150–161.

Nothdurft, H.-C., Gallant, J.L. & van Essen, D.C. (1999). Response modulation by texture surround in primate area V1: Correlates of 'popout' under 'anasthesia'. *Visual Neuroscience*, 16, 15–34.

Nothdurft, H.-C., Gallant J.L. & van Essen, D.C. (2000). Response profiles to texture border pattern in area V1. *Visual Neuroscience*, 17, 421–436.

Norton, D. & Stark, L. (1971). Scanpaths in eye movements during pattern perception. *Science*, 171, 308–311.

Ohm, J. (1928). Die Hebelnystagmographie. *Gradfes Arch Ophthal*, 120, 235-252.

Ohno, T. (1998). Features of eye gaze interface for selection tasks. *APCHI'98*, Japan, 176–181.

Oliva, A. & Schyns, P.G. (2000). Coloured diagnostic blobs mediate scene recognition. *Cognitive Psychology*, 41, 176–210.

Oliva, A. & Torralba, A., (2001). Modelling the shape of the scene: A holistic representation of the spatial envelope. *International Journal in Computer Vision*, 42, 145–175.

Oliva, A. & Torralba, A., (2003). Scene centered description from spatial envelope properties. In H.H. Bulthoff et al. (Eds.), *Lecture notes in computer science: Biologically motivated computer vision* (263-272). New York: Springer-Verlag.

Oliva, A., Torralba, A., Castelhano, C. & Henderson, J.M. (2003). Top-down control of visual attention in object detection. *IEEE Poreccedings of the International Conferecne on Image Processing*, 1, 253–256.

Olson, R.K. & Attnaeave, F. (1970). What variables produce similarity grouping? *The American Journal of Psychology*, 83, 1–21.

Ontrup, J. & Ritter, H. (1998). Perceptual grouping in a neural model: Reproducing human texture perception. Technical report, Technical Report SFB360-TR-98/6.

Ortega, M., Yong, R., Chakrabarti, K., Mehrotra, S. & Huang, T.S. (1997). Supporting similarity queries in MARS. *Proceedings of the 5th ACM International Multimedia Conference*, 403–413.

Ouerhani, N., von Wartburg, R., Hügli, H. & Müri, R. (2004). Empirical validation of the saliency-based model of visual attention. *Electronic Letters on Computer Vision and Image Analysis*, 3, 13–24.

Ouerhani, N., Hügli, H., Burgi, P.-Y. & Rüdi, P.-F. (2002). A real time implementation of the saliency-based model of visual attention on a SIMD architecture. *Proceedings of the 24th DAGM Symposium on Pattern recognition*. Lecture Notes in Computer Science, Springer Verlag, 2449, 282-289.

Oyekoya, O. & Stentiford, F.W.M. (2004a). Exploring human eye behaviour using a model of visual attention. *International Conference on Pattern Recognition 2004*.

Oyekoya, O. & Stentiford, F.W.M, (2004b). Eye tracking as a new interface for image retrieval. *BT Technology Journal*, 22, 161–169.

Oyekoya, O. & Stentiford, F.W.M. (2005). A performance comparison of eye tracking and mouse interfaces in a target image identification task. *2nd European Workshop on the Integration of Knowledge, Semantics & Digital Media Technology*.

Oyekoya, O. (2007). Eye Tracking: A Perceptual Interface for Content Based Image Retrieval, Dissertation. University College London

Parker, R.E. (1978). Picture processing during recognition. *Journal of Experimental Psychology: Human Perception and Performance*, 4, 284–293.

Parkhurst, D. et al. (2002). Modeling the role of salience in the allocation of overt visual attention. *Vision Res.*, 42, 107–123.

Pass, G., Zabih, R. & Miller, J. (1996). Comparing images using colour coherence vectors. *Proceedings ACM Conf. on Multimedia*, 65–73.

Peerson, E. & Fu, K.S. (1977). Shape discrimination using Fourier descriptions. *IEEE Tranactions on Systems, Man and Cybernetics*, 7, 170–179.

Pelz, J.B. & Canosa, R. (2001). Oculomotor behaviour and perceptual strategies in complex tasks. *Vision Research*, 41, 3587–3596.

Pelz, J.B. et al. (2000). Portable Eyetracking: A study of natural eye movements. In: B.E. Rogowitz & T.N. Pappas (Eds.), *Proceedings of the SPIE, Human Vision and Electronic Imaging V* (3959, 566–582). San Jose: SPIE.

Pentland, A., Picard, R.W. & Sclaroff, S.(1996). Photobook: Content-based manipulation of image databases. *International Journal of Computer Vision*, 18, 233–254.

Picard, R. & Minka, T. (1997). Interactive learning with a society of models. *Pattern Recognition*, 30, 565–582.

Pollatsek, A., Rayner, K. & Collins, W.E. (1984). Integrating pictorial information across eye movements. *Journal of Experimental Psychology: General*, 113, 426–442.

Pollatsek, A., Rayner, K. & Balota, D.A. (1986). Inferences about eye movement control from the perceptual span in reading. *Perception & Psychophysics*, 40, 123–130.

Pomplun, M. (1994). *Aufmerksamkeitsverteilung in ambigen Bildern und ein vielseitiges Programmpaket für Eyetracking-Experimente. Diplomarbeit.* Faculty of technology, Bielefeld University.

Pomplun, M. (1998). *Analysis and models of eye movements in comparative visual search.* Dissertation. Göttingen: Cuvillier.

Pomplun, M., Sichelschmidt, L., Wagner, K., Clermont, T., Rickheit, G. & Ritter, H. (2001). Comparative visual search: A difference that makes a difference. *Cognitive Science*, 25, 3–36.

Pomplun, M. (2006). Saccadic selectivity in complex visual search displays. *Vision Research*, 46, pp. 1886–1900.

Potter, M.C. (1976). Short-term conceptual memory for pictures. *Journal of Experimental Psychology: Human Learning and Memory*, 2, 509–522.

Puolamäki, K., Salojärvi, J., Savia, E., Simola, J. & Kaski, S. (2005). Combining Eye Movements and Collaborative Filtering for Proactive Information Retrieval. In: Marchionini, Moffat, Tait, Baeza-Yates, Ziviani (Eds.), *SIGIR 2005: Proceedings of the 28th Annual International ACM SIGIR Conference on Research and Development in Information Retrieval* (146–153). New York: ACM press.

Purves, D. et al. (2004) *Neuroscience (3rd ed).* Sunderland: Sinauer Associates.

Rao, R.P.N. et al. (2002). Eye movements in iconic visual search. *Vision Res.*, 42, 1447–1463.

Rayner, K. (1998). Eye Movements in reading and information processing: 20 years of research. *Psychological Bulletin*, 124, 372–422.

Reinagel, P. & Zador, M. (1999). Natural scene statistics at the center of gaze. *Network: Comp. Neural Syst.*, 10, 341–350.

Ren, M., Eakins, J.P. & Briggs, P. (2000) Human perception of trademark images: Implication for retrieval system design. *Journal of Electronic Imaging*, 9, 564–575.

Rensink, R.A., O'Regan, J.K. & Clark, J.J. (1997). To see or not to see: The need for attention to perceive changes in scenes. *Psychological Science*, 8, 368–373.

Richards, W. & Hoffman, D.D. (1985). Codon constraints on closed 2D shapes. *Computer Vision, Graphics, and Image Processing*, 31, 265–281.

Ritter, H., Martinetz, T. & Schulten, K. (1991). *Neuronale Netze (2nd ed).* Addison Wesley: Bonn.

Ritter, H. (1993). Parametrized self-organizing maps. *ICANN93-Proceedings* (568–577). Berlin: Springer.

Rötting, M. (2001). *Parametersystematik der Augen- und Blickbewegungen. Für Arbeitswissenschaftliche Untersuchungen.* Aachen: Shaker Verlag.

Rubner, Y. & Tomasi, C. (2001). *Perceptual metrics for image database navigation.* Dortrecht: Kluwer Academic Publishers.

Rui, Y., She, A. & Huang, T.S. (1998). A modified fourier descriptor for shape matching in MARS. In S.K. Chang (Ed.), *Image Databases and Multimedia Search.* Series on Software Engineering and Knowledge Engineering, World Scientific Publishing House in Singapore, 8, 165–180.

Rui, Y., Huang, T.S. & Chang, S.-F. (1999). Image Retrieval: Current techniques, promising directions, and open issues. *Journal of Visual Communications and Image Representation,* 10, 39–62.

Rui, Y., Huang, T.S., Mehrota, S. & Ortega, M. (1998). Relevance feedback: A power tool in interactive content-based image retrieval. *IEEE Trans. on Circuits Systems Video Technol. (Special Issue on Interactive Multi-Media Systems for the Internet).* Retrieved Month 2, 2002, from
http://www.ifp.uiuc.edu/~yrui/html/publication.html

Saida, S. & Ikeda, M. (1979). Useful visual field size for pattern perception. *Perception & Psychophysics,* 25, 119–125.

Salojärvi, J., Kojo, I., Simola, J. & Kaski, S. (2003). Can relevance be inferred from eye movements in information retrieval. *Proceedings of WSOM'03, Workshop on Self-Organizing Maps,* 261–266.

Salojärvi, J., Puolamäki, K. & Kaski, S. (2005). Implicit relevance feedback from eye movements. *ICANN 2005,* 11–15.

Salton, G. & McGill, M.J. (1988). *Introduction to Modern Information Retrieval.* McGrawHill, New York.

Samet, H. & Soffer, A. (1996). MARCO: Map retrieval by content. *IEEE Trans. on Pattern Analysis and Machine Intelligence,* 18, 783–798.

Santini, S. & Jain, R. (1999). Similarity Measures. *IEEE Transactions on Pattern Analysis and Machine Intelligence,* 21, 871–883.

Sayood K. (2000) *Introduction to Data Compression.* San Francisco: Morgan Kaufmann Publihers.

Scherffig, L. & Diebner, H.H. (2005). *It's in your eyes – gaze based image retrieval in context.* Karlsruhe: ZKM Institute for Basic Research.

Schomaker, L., de Leau, E. & Vuurpijl, L. (1999). Using pen-based outlines for object-based annotation and image-based queries. *Lecture notes in Computer Science,* 1614, 585–592.

Schor, C.M. & Ciuffreda, K.J. (1983). *Vergence eye movements: Basic and clinical aspects*. Butterwoth: Boston.

Sebe, N., Lew, M.S. & Huijsmans, D.P. (1999). Multi-scale sub-image search. *Proceedings of ACM Intl. Conf. on Multimedia (Part II)*, 79–82.

Sebe, N. & Lew, M. (2001). Texture features for content-based retrieval. In M.S. Lew (ed.), *Principles of Visual Information Retrieval*, (51–85). London: Springer.

Shannon, C.E. (1948). A mathematical theory of communication. *The Bell System technical Journal*, 27 (3), 379–423 and 623–656.

Shi, J. & Malik, J. (2000). Normalized cuts and image segmentation. *IEEE Transactions on Pattern Analysis and Machine Intelligence*, 22, 888–905.

Sibert, L.E. & Jacob, R.J.K. (2000). Evaluation of eye gaze interaction. *Proceedings of the SIGCHI conference on Human factors in computing systems*, The Hague, The Netherlands, 281–288.

Sichelschmidt, L. & Carbone, E. (2003). Experimentelle Methoden. In G. Rickheit, T. Herrmann & W. Deutsch (Eds.), *Psycholinguistik. Ein internationales Handbuch* (115–124). Berlin, New York: de Gruyter.

Sietmann, R. (2003). Licht ins Darknet, Multimedia suchen und finden. *c't Magazin für Computertechnik*, 8, 80–81.

Sillito, A.M., Grieve, K.L., Jones, H.E., Cudeiro, J. & Davis, J. (1995) Visual cortical mechanisms detecting focal orientation discontinuities. *Nature*, 378, 492–496.

Smeulders, A. et al. (2000). Content-based image retrieval at the end of the early years. *IEEE Transaction on Pattern Analysis And Machine Intelligence*, 22, 1349–1380.

Smith, J.R. & Chang, S.F. (1996). Tools and techniques for colour image retrieval. In I.K. Sethi & R.C. Jain (Eds.), *Proceedings SPIE Storage and Retrieval for Still Image and Video Databases IV*, 2670, 426–437.

Squire, D.M. & Pun, T. (1997). A comparison of human and machine assessments of image similarity for the organization of image databases. In M. Frydrych, J. Parkkinen & A. Visa (Eds.), *The 10th Scandinavian Conference on Image Analysis*,Lappeenranta, Finland, 51–58.

Stricker, M.A. & Orengo, M. (1995). Similarity of colour images. *Proceedings Storage and Retrieval for Image and Video Databases III*, 381–392.

Stricker, M.A. & Dimai, A. (1996). Color indexing with weak spatial constraints. *Proceedings SPIE. Storage Retrieval Still Image Video Databases IV*, 2670, 29–40.

Sutter, A. & Graham, N. (1995). Investigating simple and complex mechanisms in texture segregation using the spped-accuracy tradeoff method. *Vision Research*, 35, 2825–2843.

Swain, M.J. & Ballard, D.H. (1991). Colour indexing. *International Journal of Computer Vision*, 7(1), 11–32.

Szummer, M. & Picard, R.W. (1998). Indoor-outdoor image classification. *Proceedings of the IEEE Workshop on Content-based access of image and video databases (CAICVD'98)*, Bombay, India, 42–52.

Tanase, M. (2005). *Shape decomposition and retrieval.* Dissertation. Utrecht University, Utrecht, The Netherlands.

Tamura, H., Mori, S. & Yamawaki, T. (1978). Texture features corresponding to visual perception. *IEEE Trans. on Systems, Man and Cybernetics*, 8, 460–473.

Thoden, U. (1978). Neurophysiologische Terminologie. In G. Baumgartner, et al. (Eds.), *Sehen* (427–470). München: Urban & Schwarzenberg.

Thorpe, S.J., Fize, D. & Marlot, C. (1996). Speed of processing in the human visual system. *Nature*, 381, 520–522.

Thorpe, S.J., Gegenfurtner, K.R., Fabre-Thorpe, M. & Bülthoff, H.H. (2001). Detection of anamals in natural images using far peripheral vision. *European Journal of Neuroscience*, 14, 869–876.

Treisman, A.M. (1993). The perception of features and objects. In A. Baddaley & L. Weiskrantz (Eds.), *Attention: Selection, awareness and control* (5–35). Oxford: Clarendon.

Treisman, A.M. & Gelade, G. (1980). A feature-integration theory of attention. *Cognitive Psychology*, 12, 97–136.

Turner, M.R. (1986). Texture Discrimination by Gabor Functions. *Biological Cybernetics*, 55, 71–82.

Tversky, A. (1977). Features of Similarity. *Psychological Review*, 84, 327–352.

Tversky, A. & Gati, I. (1982). Similarity, separability, and the triangle inequality. *Psychological Review*, 89, 123–154.

Vailaya, A., Jain, A. & Zhang, H.J. (1998). On image classification: City images vs. landscapes. *Pattern Recognition*, 31, 1921–1935.

De Valois, R.L., Albrecht, D.G. & Thorell, L.G. (1982). Spatial-frequency selectivity of cells in macaque visual cortex. *Vision Research*, 22, 545–559.

Veltkamp, R.C. & Tanase, M. (2000). Content-based image retrieval systems: A survey. *Technical Report UU-CS-2000-34, October 2000*.

Veltkamp R.C. & Hagedoorn M. (2001). State-of-the-art in shape matching. In M.S. Lew (Ed.), *Principles of Visual Information Retrieval* (87–119). Berlin: Springer.

Venters, C.C., Eakins, J.P. & Hartley, R.J. (1997). The user interface and content-based image retrieval systems. *Proceedings of the 19th BCS-IRSG Research Colloqium*, Aberdeen.

Voorhees, H. & Poggio, T. (1988). Computing texture boundaries in images. *Nature*, 333, 364–367.

Walter, J. & Ritter, H. (2002). On interactive visualization of high dimensional data using the hyperbolic plane. In *IEEE Int. Conf. Data Mining*, 355–362.

Walter, J. (2004) *Datamining: Methoden integrativer Datenpräsentation*. Göttingen: Cuvillier Verlag.

Walter, J., Wessling, D., Essig, K. & Ritter, H. (2006). Interactive hyperbolic image browsing - towards an integrated multimedia navigator. *ACM MDM/KDD Multimedia Data Mining and Conf Knowledge Discovery and Data Mining*.

Wang, J.Z. (2001). *Integrated Region-Based Image Retrieval*. Dortrecht: Kluwer Academic Publishers.

Ware, C. & Mikaelian, H. (1987). An evaluation of an eye tracker as a device for computer input. *Proceedings of SIGCHI+GI'87, Human Factors in Computer Systems*, ACM Press, 183–188.

Wichmann, F.A., Sharpe, L.T. & Gegenfurtner, K.R. (2002). The contributions of color to recognition memory for natural scenes. *J. Exp. Psychol. Learn. Mem. Cogn.*, 28, 509–520.

Wooding, D.S. (2002). Eye Movements of large populations: II. Deriving regions of interest, coverage, and similarity using fixation maps. *Behavior Research Methods, Instruments & Computers*, 34, 518–528.

Wolfe, J., Cave, K. & Franzel, S. (1989). Guided search: An alternative to the feature integration model for visual search. *Journal of Experimental Psychology: Human Perception and Performance*, 15, 419–433.

Yamada, M. & Fukuda, T. (1986). Quantitive Evaluation of Eye Movements as Judged by Sight-Line Displacement. *SMPTE Journal*, 1230–1241.

Yamato, M., Monden, A., Matsumoto, K., Inoue, K. & Torii, K. (2000). Button selection for general GUIs using eye and hand together. *Proceedings 5th International Working Conference on Advanced Visual Interfaces (AVI2000)*, ACM Press, 270–273.

Yarbus, A.L. (1967). *Eye movements and vision*. New York: Plenum Press.

Yeshurun, Y. & Carrasco, M. (2000). The locus of attentional effects in texture segmentation. *Nature Neuroscience*, 3, 622–627.

Young, L.R. (1971). Pursuit eye tracking movements. In P. Bach, Y. Rita, C. Collins & J.E. Hyde (Eds.), *Control of Eye Movements* (429-443). New York: Academic Press.

Zeki, S. (1993). *A vision of the brain*. London: Blackwell.

[1] EyeVisionBot: http://diebner.de/installations/EyeVisionBot.html

[2] MPEG 7 HomePage: http://www.chiariglione.org/mpeg/

[3] Annotated groundtruth database, Department of Computer Science and Engeneering, University of Washington, 1999, http://www.cs.washington.edu/research/imagedatabase/groundtruth

[4] Hugh's Home: http://www.skidmore.edu/~hfoley/images/Retina.jpg

[5] Text Retrieval Conference: http://trec.nist.gov

[6] Color Vision: http://webvision.med.utah.edu/Color.html

[7] Clip Art: http://www.novadevelopment.com/Products/Clipart.aspx

[8] Schmeil-Fitschen: http://www.deutschesfachbuch.de/info/detail.php?isbn=3494013683

[10] Visual Path: http://brisray.com/optill/vpath1a.jpg

[11] Vector Quantization: http://www.geocities.com/mohamedqasem/vectorquantization/vq.html

[12] Blobworld: http://elib.cs.berkeley.edu/blobworld/

[13] EyeVisionBot: http://www.medienkunstnetz.de/werke/eye-vision-bot/

[14] Image Gallery Vision and Eye: http://www.phys.ufl.edu/~avery/course/3400/vision/eye_human2.jpg

[15] Nervous System: http://www.pennhealth.com/health_info/body_guide/reftext/images/cranial_nerves.jpg

[16] Krauzlis Lab: http://www.snl-k.salk.edu/images/project%201.gif

[17] Color Vision: http://webvision.med.utah.edu/imageswv/cortex.jpeg

[18] Group of zebras: http://images.inmagine.com/168nwm/fstop/fs068/fs068021.jpg

[19] Theorie der visuellen Aufmerksamkeit: http://www.informatik.uni-ulm.de/ni/Lehre/SS04/HSSH/pdfs/trittel.pdf

[20] MySQL: http://www.mysql.com

[21] Java: http://java.sun.com

[22] IPP: http://www.intel.com/cd/software/products/asmo-na/eng/perflib/ipp/302910.htm

[23] Wikipedia: http://en.wikipedia.org/wiki/Perceptron

[24] Fourward Technologies: http://www.fourward.com/_mgxroot/page_10786.html

Appendix A

A.1 Query Images

(a) image0063

(b) image0626

(c) image0342

(d) image0715

(e) image0380

(f) image1431

(g) image1569

(h) image1600

Figure A.1: The eight query images which were randomly selected from the flower database.

A.2 Attention Values for Query Images

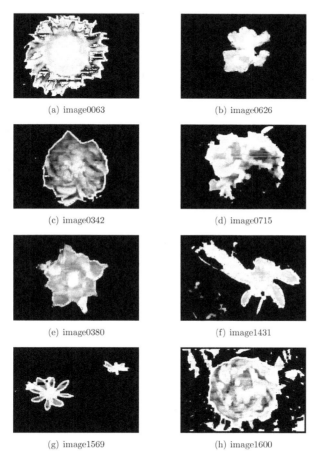

Figure A.2: Attention images of the eight query images.

A.3 Set 1

(a) image0063

(b) image0054   (c) image0610   (d) image0540

(e) image1918   (f) image1018   (g) image1221

Figure A.3: Start Configuration 1.

A.4 Set 2

(a) image0626

(b) image1891   (c) image0909   (d) image0024

(e) image0427   (f) image0161   (g) image0338

Figure A.4: Start Configuration 2.

A.5 Set 3

(a) image0342

(b) image1052   (c) image0290   (d) image1738

(e) image1971   (f) image0162   (g) image1107

Figure A.5: Start Configuration 3.

A.6 Set 4

(a) image0715

(b) image0778   (c) image1317   (d) image0075

(e) image1962   (f) image0211   (g) image1471

Figure A.6: Start Configuration 4.

A.7 Set 5

(a) image0380

(b) image0429   (c) image0353   (d) image1457

(e) image0650   (f) image0069   (g) image1133

Figure A.7: Start Configuration 5.

A.8   Set 6

(a) image1431

(b) image0879   (c) image1463   (d) image1225

(e) image0356   (f) image0243   (g) image1965

Figure A.8: Start Configuration 6.

A.9 Set 7

(a) image1569

(b) image1352

(c) image1930

(d) image1764

(e) image1582

(f) image0018

(g) image0759

Figure A.9: Start Configuration 7.

A.10 Set 8

(a) image1600

(b) image1660   (c) image0917   (d) image0772

(e) image0518   (f) image1672   (g) image0031

Figure A.10: Start Configuration 8.

www.ingramcontent.com/pod-product-compliance
Lightning Source LLC
La Vergne TN
LVHW022307060326
832902LV00020B/3319